Mindful and Relational Approaches to Social Justice, Equity, and Diversity in Teacher Education

MINDFULNESS IN EDUCATION

Series Editors: Karen Ragoonaden, The University of British Columbia, and Sabre Cherkowski, The University of British Columbia

This interdisciplinary series examines the theoretical and the practical applications of Mindfulness in Education (MIE). Coming from a range of academic disciplines, an increasing number of studies on mindfulness and related contemplative practices underscore the relevance of MIE. Prompted by the robust scientific findings of mindfulness as a tool to support physical, emotional and mental health in adult populations, several initiatives have emerged devoted to applying and evaluating mindfulness in K–12 and in higher education. Teachers are enrolling in mindfulness programs, administrators are introducing mindfulness to their schools, and researchers are devising ways to evaluate the effects of mindfulness in cohorts of students and teachers. In particular, the collected volumes of this series explore the impact of universal practices of mindfulness (being aware, paying attention, noticing, being in the present moment, being nonjudgmental) and the attributes that cultivate and support well-being in pedagogical contexts.

Titles in the Series:

Mindful Alignment: Foundations of Educator Flourishing, by Sabre Cherkowski, Kelly Hanson, and Keith Walker

A Mindful Teaching Community: Possibilities for Teacher Professional Learning, edited by Kelly Hanson

Mindful and Relational Approaches to Social Justice, Equity, and Diversity in Teacher Education, edited by Julian Kitchen and Karen Ragoonaden

Mindful and Relational Approaches to Social Justice, Equity, and Diversity in Teacher Education

Julian Kitchen
and Karen Ragoonaden

LEXINGTON BOOKS
Lanham • Boulder • New York • London

Published by Lexington Books
An imprint of The Rowman & Littlefield Publishing Group, Inc.
4501 Forbes Boulevard, Suite 200, Lanham, Maryland 20706
www.rowman.com

6 Tinworth Street, London SE11 5AL

Copyright © 2020 by The Rowman & Littlefield Publishing Group, Inc.

All rights reserved. No part of this book may be reproduced in any form or by any electronic or mechanical means, including information storage and retrieval systems, without written permission from the publisher, except by a reviewer who may quote passages in a review.

British Library Cataloguing in Publication Information Available

Library of Congress Cataloging-in-Publication Data

ISBN 9781498598910 (cloth)
ISBN 9781498598934 (pbk)
ISBN 9781498598927 (electronic)

Contents

Series Editors' Foreword · vii

Introduction · 1
Julian Kitchen

1 A Relational Approach to Social Justice in Teacher Education · 13
    Julian Kitchen

2 Contemplating Mindfulness and Social Justice in Diversity Classrooms · 31
    Karen Ragoonaden

3 Mindfulness and Relational Knowing: An International Novice Teacher Educator's Approach to Teaching Social Justice · 43
    Yumei Li

4 What Should Preservice Teachers Know about Race and Diversity? Exploring a Mindful and Critical Knowledge-Base · 61
    Benedicta Egbo

5 Transformative Frameworks for Promoting Social Justice: Mindful and Relational Teacher Education · 79
    Awneet Sivia

6 Embedding Lived Indigenous Perspectives in Teacher Education: Co-constructing Mindful Pathways for Truth, Reconciliation, and Social Justice · 101
    Terry-Lee Beaudry, Kevin Kaiser, and Karen Ragoonaden

7 A Relational Approach to Collaborative Research and Practice
   among Teacher Educators in Urban Contexts   115
   *Jane McIntosh Cooper, Leslie M. Gauna, Christine E. Beaudry,
   and Gayle A. Curtis*

8 Responding to Cries of Pain through Literature: A Mindful
   Approach to Preparing to Teach Children of War   131
   Barbara McNeil

Conclusion   153
   Karen Ragoonaden

Index   159

About the Contributors   167

Series Editors' Foreword

This interdisciplinary series examines the theoretical and practical applications of Mindfulness in Education (MIE). In particular, the collected volumes of this series explore the impact of universal practices of mindfulness (being aware, paying attention, noticing, in the present moment, nonjudgmentally) and the attributes that cultivate and support well-being in pedagogical contexts. This volume, *Mindful and Relational Approaches to Social Justice, Equity, and Diversity in Teacher Education*, engages in collective reflections about critical, transformative pedagogies as constructs supporting professional learning in teacher education.

Karen Ragoonaden, PhD
The University of British Columbia

Sabre Cherkowski, PhD
The University of British Columbia

Introduction

Julian Kitchen

Mindfulness is "the awareness that emerges through paying attention on purpose, in the present moment, and non-judgmentally to the unfolding of experience moment by moment" (Kabat-Zinn, 1990, p. 4). Jon Kabat-Zinn (2018), who developed the Mindfulness-Based Stress Reduction program, regards mindfulness as "a wise and potentially healing way of being in relationship to what befalls us in life" (p. ix). Such awareness is wise because it taps into a long and rich tradition of contemplation and meditation across secular, religious, and spiritual traditions. It is healing because it employs a range of contemplative practices to expose "unexamined habits of mind" (p. x) and develop an inward stance of "coming to terms with things as they are" (p. ix). Acceptance opens us up to how we "might redefine and thereby transform our relationship with what is actually so" (p. x). While Kabat-Zinn's work involves patients responding to illness and pain, mindfulness has caught on with many others seeking to live thoughtfully and meaningfully in the world. Mindfulness has resonated with many educators seeking both to improve their practice and enhance student learning and well-being (Lantieri, 2008; Oberle & Schonert-Reichel, 2016; Palmer 1998; Roeser, Skinner, Beers, & Jennings, 2012). The Mindfulness in Education series, to which this volume belongs, began with Ragoonaden's (2015) *Mindful Teaching and Learning: Developing a Pedagogy of Well-Being*. Subsequent volumes delved more deeply into mindful teacher education practices (Ragoonaden & Bullock, 2016) and mindful practices within a school community (Hanson, 2017). This volume, *Mindful and Relational Approaches to Social Justice, Equity, and Diversity in Teacher Education*, focuses specifically on how relational and mindful approaches might contribute to preparing teachers to be more equitable, respectful of diversity, and committed to social justice.

I was first introduced to mindfulness in 2015 when I attended an American Educational Research Association session in which Karen Ragoonaden and Shawn Bullock discussed the concept in relation to their critical friendship. In the chapter that resulted from the presentation, Ragoonaden and Bullock (2016) wrote of their "progression from the lure of technique towards the dynamic complexity of practical wisdom" (p. 14) in teaching and the importance of mindfulness and the "relational" (p. 29) domain in their collaborative professional development. Bullock remarked that my work on relational teacher education (Kitchen, 2005a; 2005b; 2016) involved being mindful of oneself, supportive of students, and attentive to student learning needs through relational pedagogy. Subsequent reflection helped me see my personal and professional practices as essentially mindful. Mindfulness, as Bullock (2016) notes, is ultimately about attention: attention to oneself, to the moment, and to others. Relational knowing (Hollingsworth, Dybdahl, & Minarik, 1993) is similarly about "knowing through relationship to self and others" (p. 8) in order to better serve learners. My own work on relational teacher education is informed by Carl Rogers (1961), who wrote "This book is about me, as I sit there with that client, facing him, participating in that struggle as deeply and sensitively as I am able" (p. 4). "Floating with the complex stream of experiencing," Rogers came to regard experience as the highest authority and discovered that "what is most personal is most general" (1961, pp. 26–27). Underlying such relationships is respect for teachers as curriculum makers (Clandinin & Connelly, 1992) who draw upon their personal practical knowledge to inform their classroom practice.

At the same time, I was developing a new teacher education course focused on social justice issues. As I observed the heated discussion of equity issues then—and particularly now, in the era of Trump and ultra-nationalists—I was struck by the lack of light shed or enlightenment developed through these divisive public arguments. In teaching this course over the next two years, I sought to be invitational and relational in my approach and encouraged aspiring teachers to reflect on their own identities and experiences, as well as attend to the stories and learning needs of minoritized and marginalized students. When I shared a self-study of my experience at an American Educational Research Association session in 2017, I felt validated by positive comments by others in attendance and by social justice teacher educators in other sessions who adopted similar approaches. This led me to pitch this book to Karen Ragoonaden, as series editor, and together, formally approaching the authors and Lexington Books.

MINDFULNESS: A RICH TRADITION

The term mindfulness, as used in this volume, is a contemporary reframing of principles articulated in Indigenous, Eastern, and Western intellectual and spiritual traditions.

The English word "mindfulness" originally meant to be "heedful" or "aware of context." In the nineteenth century, mindfulness was adopted as the English translation of *sati* in Buddhism, *smrti* in Hinduism and similar concepts (Young, 2016). Buddhism identifies the self as connected with all things and promotes inner peace through meditation and acceptance of the gifts and travails of life. The "self is seen as a dynamic process occuring in individuals, but not an entity or substance," according to Faikhamta (2016), who adds, "The self can be changed . . . a person can change . . . to lead to new experiences of themselves" (p. 141).

Indigenous peoples have long felt a strong connection to the land and to all living things. Nature is viewed as sacred, all life is interconnected, and learning involves understanding these connections through the body, mind, and spirit (Cajete, 1994). Indigenous Elders who carry on these traditions take time each day to acknowledge the interrelated and dynamic core of nature and give thanks for the gifts they receive.

Mysticism, an important strand in Christianity, also esteems contemplative wisdom. Thomas Merton (1959, as cited in Miller, 1996), for example, identifies contemplation as the "highest and most essential spiritual activity" (p. 37), one that ultimately calls one "to be put to work in the service of love" (p. 37). Mindfulness in the Western tradition, however, primarily focuses on attentiveness as a means to alleviate pain (Kabat-Zinn, 1990), acquire self-knowledge (Brown & Ryan, 2003), or develop a spirit of service (Palmer, 1998) through systematic cultivation. Thus, it is useful to think of mindfulness as one or more of (1) *awareness*, (2) *practices* that improve awareness, and (3) broader *application* strategies for increasing awareness (Young, 2016).

While nature may be interrelated and dynamic, "the human world since the industrial revolution has stressed compartmentalization and standardization . . . [resulting in] the fragmentation of life" (Miller, 1996, p. 1): economic fragmentation, social fragmentation, fragmentation within ourselves, and loss of a shared reverence for life. Miller also observes that education is fragmented into subjects, units, and lessons. As Bateson and Bateson (1987) note:

> The truth that the aborigine and the peasant share is the truth of integration. By contrast, we must be concerned today because although we can persuade our children to learn a long list of facts about the world, they don't seem to have

the capacity to put them together in a single, unified understanding—here is no "pattern that connects." (p. 196)

Although materialism and technical-rationalism are in ascendency, there have always been countervailing movements of resistance. John Dewey's progressive education, which emphasizes the "organic connection between education and personal experience" (1938, p. 25) as necessary to recover "equilibrium" and "unison" with "the march of surrounding things" (1934, p. 14) continues to inform educational debates. Since the 1980's, the holistic education movement (Miller, 1996) has attempted to return "spirituality, or a sense of the sacred" (Miller, 1996, p. 3) to education by emphasizing balance, inclusion, and connection. Miller's (1993) *The Holistic Teacher*, for example, articulates a coherent philosophy of education, describes a range of mindful practices for personal mastery by teachers, and offers a range of holistic teaching strategies. Whereas the contemporary movement focuses on attentiveness, holistic education is equally concerned with curriculum. In *Holistic Learning: A Teacher's Guide to Integrated Studies*, Miller, Cassie and Drake (1990), offer teachers practical strategies for, and concrete examples of, curriculum designed for balance, inclusion and connection.

Parker J. Palmer's (1998) *The Courage to Teach* also resonates with educators seeking spiritual meaning in their work. Palmer writes:

> Knowing of any sort is relational, animated by a desire to come into deeper community with what we know . . . Knowing is a human way to seek relationship and, in the process, to have encounters and exchanges that will inevitably alter us. At its deepest reaches, knowing is communal. (p. 54)

Palmer recognizes that teaching is an embodied experience that involves a moral commitment to building a better world. Authentic teaching, Palmer (1998) writes, comes "from the depths of my own truth—and the truth that is within my students has a chance to respond in kind (p. 33) Palmer (2003) developed a two-year Courage to Teach program of eight weekend retreats "to provide public school educators with a space that is safe for their souls to show up and make a claim on the work that they do" (p. 380). These workshops focus on renewing the inner lives of teachers and their engagement with learners. Palmer's work echoes Hollingsworth, Dybdahl, and Minarik's (1993) relational knowing and Rogers (1961) relational approach to psychotherapy.

The practice of mindfulness is becoming more common within primary, secondary, and tertiary education as a means of renewing teachers and calming students. As Young (2016) observes, "there is nothing intrinsic in mindfulness that directly conflicts with . . . faith-based approaches" (p. 43). As Murphy (2019) suggests, "it is crucial that mindfulness practices [in public schools] are presented in ways that are secular" (p. 18); this entails avoiding terms like *spirit* and religious props. Framing contemplative approaches as mindfulness avoids church-state tensions in secular schools. Also, unlike holistic education, which more explicitly challenges Western materialism, mindfulness is "compatible with most commonly held worldviews" (Young, 2016, p. 43). Rather than directly challenging conventional pedagogies or curriculum, this secular framing of mindfulness can live alongside technical-rational schooling. Indeed, it may even improve performance within such schools by calming students in class and helping teachers cope more effectively with the stresses of their careers. By bypassing controversy, however, mindfulness education risks becoming viewed as a quick-fix that aids the individual in the moment while ignoring the social impact of materialism and injustice (Bai, Morgan, Scott & Cohen, 2016). A longer term challenge for mindfulness education is how to both expand mindfulness from a practice that increases attention and engagement in conventional classrooms to a vision that informs pedagogy and curriculum (Choudhury & Moses, 2016; Ragoonaden, 2015).

RELATIONAL TEACHING AS MINDFUL AWARENESS

The rich tradition of mindfulness in education described above arises from spiritual traditions. Even secular approaches, such as Mindfulness-Based Stress Reduction, involve the use of meditation and related practices to raise awareness. While relational approaches to education do not involve meditation or other contemplative practices, they too foster heightened teacher awareness of learners, the self and the educational context. As they too involve "paying attention on purpose, in the present moment, and non-judgmentally to the unfolding of experience moment by moment" (Kabat-Zinn, 1990, p. 4), they are consistent with a broad definition of mindfulness.

While education has always been concerned with the emotional and mental development of the child, contemporary schooling often focusses too much on the cognitive domain. A body of scholarship serves to remind us of the importance of caring and relationship in student learning. Carl Rogers (1961) writes, "[S]ignificant learning may take place if the teacher can accept the student as he is, and can understand the feelings he possesses" (p. 287). Noddings (1992) writes:

> To care and be cared for are fundamental human needs . . . caring cannot be achieved by formula. It requires address and response; it requires different behaviours from situation to situation and person to person. . . . Schools, I will argue, pay too little attention to the need for continuity of place, people, purpose and curriculum. (pp. xi–xii)

Rogers emphasizes the importance of caring in helping relationships. Rogers (1961), speaking "as a person, from a context of personal experience and personal learnings" (p. 1), regards experience as "more trustworthy than my intellect" (p. 17). Drawing on his background as a psychologist, Rogers advocates professional relationships of nonjudgmental acceptance through *empathic understanding* and *unconditional positive regard*. Rogers (1969) observes that meaningful learning in schools possesses the "quality of personal involvement" and is "self-initiated," "pervasive," "evaluated by the learner" and has as its essence "meaning to the learner" (p. 5). The model teacher that Rogers (1983) describes at the beginning of *Freedom to Learn for the 1980's* had students working individually and in groups on a range of activities. This teacher's "liking for the kids was obvious" and, to Rogers's amazement, every child stopped their activities immediately when he spoke up to give an instruction. Rogers wrote, "It could only have been out of respect for and loyalty to him" (p. 9). Such authentic and caring relationships between teacher and students, proposes Rogers (1969), are more educative than ones reliant on authority.

Hollingsworth, Dybdahl, and Minarik (1993) identify *relational knowing* as crucial to meaningful interactions between teachers and students. Relational knowing involves "knowing through relationship to self and others [as] central to teaching the child" (p. 8); they also employ the term to include collaboration and personal conversations among teachers that have the potential to increase teacher passion and commitment in the classroom. Similarly, *relational teacher development* (Kitchen, 2009) is a conception of professional development grounded in authentic relationships between teachers in the milieus in which each lives and works. It is a reciprocal approach to enabling teacher growth that builds from the realization that we know in relationship. *Relational teacher education* (Kitchen, 2005a; 2005b) applies relational principles to the preparation of teachers.

Relational approaches to education illustrate attentiveness and caring in action. In turn, mindfulness activities such as meditation have much to offer the relational practitioner.

THE PROMISE OF MINDFULNESS FOR SOCIAL JUSTICE TEACHER EDUCATION

We live in interesting and exciting times. On the positive side, we have largely overcome famine, plague, and war (Harari, 2015). We also live in prosperous societies in which there is increased diversity, greater equity of opportunity and tremendous opportunities to communicate with others. On the other hand, the limits of growth threaten the ecology of our planet, wealth distribution remains uneven, and illiberal forces threaten progress toward social inclusion. We live in close proximity in densely populated urban centers, yet feel isolated from our neighbors. We are interconnected through technology, yet our lives are often fragmented. Our societies are more diverse than ever, yet teacher educators experience considerable resistance to social justice advocacy. Social justice education is challenging work for both teacher candidates and the teacher educators who prepare them to work in a diverse and changing world. Social justice has been a perennial challenge for many years and it is generally recognized that courses and programs have had limited success in reaching predominantly white, middle class teacher candidates (Banks et al., 2005). Preaching the good word does not seem sufficient. As Loughran (2006) states, effective pedagogy extends beyond "merely the action of teaching" to the "relationship between teaching and learning" "as together they lead to growth" through "personal relationship between teachers and students" (p. 2).

Mindfulness is a promising practice in social justice education because it may increase attentiveness and receptivity in both instructors and learners. Teacher educators potentially benefit from being self-aware, calm, and attentive to relational knowing of themselves, teacher candidates, and colleagues. Teacher candidates, in addition to benefitting from the modelling and attention of mindful and relational teacher educators, may also learn strategies for thoughtfully reflecting on challenging issues in their university classes along with ways of being more attentive to their diverse classrooms. Finally, through daily mindfulness practices, elementary and secondary students and learn to meet each moment in the school day (and beyond) "with greater awareness, attention, and resilience" (Murphy, 2019, p. 7). Murphy (2019) suggests that mindfulness "can contribute to an understanding of our interconnectedness and to positive social change" (p. 16).

This collection by educators on the front lines of social justice teacher education in North America is both topical and timeless. These accounts by practitioners convey the pressing need to address social justice issues thoughtfully during a difficult time in which teacher educators encounter resistance—both silent and vocal—to equity, diversity, inclusion, and social justice. The authors adopt relational and mindful approaches to help educators open themselves to being agents of change in the world.

Julian Kitchen, in "A Relational Approach to Social Justice in Teacher Education," presents relational teacher education (RTE). After identifying the seven characteristics of RTE, I discuss how I have lived out RTE as a means of living and teaching alongside teacher candidates over twenty years of practice. I then discuss the lessons learned from a self-study over the course of teachers teaching a social justice related course, with a focus on how living authentically alongside teacher candidates lead to growth for me and them. Central to the chapter are the tensions inherent in being a relational social justice teacher educator who is respectful of the lived experiences of teacher candidates.

In "Contemplating Mindfulness and Social Justice in Diversity Classrooms," Karen Ragoonaden considers how mindfulness can inform discussions of inclusion and diversity in teacher education. Viewing mindfulness practices as transformative pedagogies that contribute to "a more just, compassionate and inclusive society," Ragoonaden suggests that contemplative approaches both enable consideration of equitable ways of being teachers and support the holism and well-being. This chapter offers mindfulness practices, strategies for applying in teacher education for social justice, and principles for addressing sensitive issues that may arise.

This is followed by the narrative of a doctoral student from China teaching a social justice course in the USA. Yumei Li, in "Mindfulness and Relational Knowing: An International Novice Teacher Educator's Approach to Teaching Social Justice," frames her experiences around three characteristics of RTE. This chapter conveys the tensions faced by international scholars working alongside American teacher candidates in this most challenging of topics. Li's approach to these classes suggests that mindfulness and knowing in relationship can bring together teacher educators and teacher candidates to build a bridge to more equitable and diverse schools.

"What Should Preservice Teachers Know about Race and Diversity? Exploring a Mindful and Critical Knowledge-Base" by Benedicta Egbo explores the need for teacher candidates to engage with knowledge about race and diversity by examining their worldviews and belief systems while being open to critical perspectives that may challenge their assumptions about power and privilege. Egbo—who writes with considerable attentiveness to the needs of students, teachers, and communities that have experienced discrimination—advocates for transformative frameworks for teaching about race and diversity.

"Transformative Frameworks for Promoting Social Justice: Mindful and Relational Teacher Education" by Awneet Sivia considers how teacher education can be reframed through mindful and relational practices. She argues that teacher educators need to serve as critical agents who expose social inequity and advocate for meaningful reforms. Building on the work of Benedicta Egbo on transformative frameworks (see chapter 4), Sivia employs diversity pedagogy, critical pedagogy, and peace education to frame the learning of her predominantly white, middle class teacher candidates. Expanding on previous research on the tensions and challenges of teaching using Egbo's (2009) textbook *Teaching for Diversity in Canadian Schools*, her self-study considers the impacts of transformative frameworks on her professional identity and conceptions of social justice. In particular, she proposes that teaching in this way is "by nature relational and mindful as it involves learning about self and others, learning about the world and learning for transformation through a contemplative and 'critical' curriculum."

Relational teacher development (Kitchen, 2009) is a powerful approach to professional development relationships among educators. "A Relational Approach to Collaborative Research and Practice among Teacher Educators in Urban Contexts" is an account of how Jane McIntosh Cooper, Leslie M. Gauna, Christine E. Beaudry, and Gayle A. Curtis have engaged in collaborative support and research on their practice as social justice teacher educators for eight years. In this chapter, the self-described Chicas Críticas, use relational teacher development as a lens for examining the characteristics that make this group a powerful support to their personal and professional survival and growth in this challenging work. They recount stories that characterize the group's effectiveness. They offer Chicas Críticas as a model for professional development that offers insights into productive relationship building.

An important social justice issue in many former colonies is the treatment of the people who lived on the land. In Canada, the Truth and Reconciliation Commission was established to report on the intergenerational effects of the Indian Residential School (IRS) system on the First Nation, Inuit and Métis Peoples of Canada. Between 1886 and 1996, Indigenous children were forcibly removed from their families, forbidden to speak their respective languages and learn about their respective traditional customs. While the intergenerational IRS trauma continues to impact the Indigenous population, the recent release of a report by the Truth and Reconciliation Commision (2015) provides pathways and directions to redress the legacy of residential schools and advance the process of Canadian reconciliation through ninety-four calls to action. "Embedding Lived Indigenous Perspectives in Teacher Education: Co-constructing Mindful Pathways for Truth, Reconciliation, and Social Justice" by Terry-Lee Beaudry, Kevin Kaiser, and Karen Ragoonaden documents a two-year journey toward indigenizing a redesigned teacher education program at the Okanagan School of Education in order to help teacher candidates become more responsive to the needs of Indigenous learners and communities. Land-based learning, localized teachings of culture and language, and engaging teacher candidates with community "in ceremony" serve as foundational pillars to reveal the beauty of Indigenous intelligences while unveiling the truths of colonization and past social injustices. Holistic ways of knowing and Indigenous pedagogy are employed to make heart-mind connections and inspire "a new way of being" for beginning educators. This initiative is notable for its effort to attend to mindfulness at the program and institutional levels.

While mindful and relational pedagogy is relevant to everyone, it seems particularly helpful to students who have experienced trauma. In "Responding to Cries of Pain through Literature: A Mindful Approach to Preparing to

Teach Children of War," Barbara McNeil considers how mindful and relational engagement affects children of war. Her personal engagement with memoirs by children of war models deep empathy and engagement in the struggles of others. Mindfulness and empathy, however, are combined with a rich understanding of social justice that stirs in McNeil and her readers a call to action. Drawing on her research with refugees who have experienced the trauma of war and dislocation, as well her experience as an educator, McNeil offers six considerations to teachers open to teaching about and to children of war. These considerations, which are both hopeful and realistic, can be adapted by mindful and relational teachers to a range of school curriculum.

"The most powerful mindfulness strategy in your classroom is your own practice," writes Murphy (2019, p. 17). All the chapters in this volume involve teacher educators "paying attention on purpose, in the present moment, and non-judgmentally to the unfolding of experience moment by moment" (Kabat-Zinn, 1990, p. 4) in order to address issues of diversity, equity, and social justice in their classrooms. The stories of these dedicated educators offer a diverse range of ways in which mindfulness and relational teaching can improve teacher preparation and make schools more responsive to the diverse students they serve in our rapidly changing world.

REFERENCES

Bai, H., Morgan, P., Scott, C., & Cohen, A. (2016). Holistic-contemplative pedagogy for twenty-first century teacher education: Education as healing. In J. P. Miller, K. Nigh, M. J. Binder, B. Novak, and S. Crowell (Eds.), *International handbook of holistic education* (pp. 108–117). New York: Routledge.

Banks, J., Cochran-Smith, M., Moll, L., Richert, A., Zeichner, K., LePage, P., Darling-Hammond, L., & Duffy, H. (2005). Teaching diverse learners. In L. Darling-Hammond & J. Bransford (Eds.), *Preparing teachers for a changing world: What teachers should learn and be able to do* (pp. 1–39). San Francisco: Jossey-Bass.

Bateson, G. & Bateson, M. C. (1987). *Angels fear: Towards an epistemology of the sacred.* New York: Macmillan.

Brown, K. W. & Ryan, R. M. (2003). The benefits of being present: Mindfulness and its role in psychological well-being. *Journal of Personality and Social Psychology, 84*(4), 822–848.

Cajete, G. (1994). *Look to the mountain: An ecology of Indigenous education.* Durango, CO: Kivaki Press.

Choudhury, S. & Moses, J. M. (2016). Mindful interventions: Youth, poverty, and the developing brain. *Theory & Psychology, 26*(5): 591–606. doi:10.1177/0959354316669025.

Clandinin, D. J. & Connelly, F. M. (1992). Teacher as curriculum maker. In Philip Jackson (Ed.), *Handbook of research in curriculum*, pp. 363–401. New York: MacMillan.

Dewey, J. (1938). *Experience and education.* New York: Collier Books.

Faikhamta, C. (2016). Self-study preparing science teachers: Capturing the complexity of pedagogical content in teaching science in Thailand. In J. Kitchen, D. Tidwell, and L. Fitzgerald (Eds.), *Self-study and diversity II: Inclusive teacher education in a diverse world* (pp. 137–149). Rotterdam, The Netherlands: Sense.

Hanson, K. (Ed.). (2017). *A mindful teaching community: Possibilities for teacher professional learning.* Lanham, MD: Lexington Books.

Harari, Y. N. (2015). *Homo deus: A brief history of tomorrow.* Toronto, ON, Canada: Signal.

Hollingsworth, S., Dybdahl M., & Minarik, L. T. (1993). By chart and chance and passion: The importance of relational knowing in learning to teach. *Curriculum Inquiry*, *23*(1), 5–35.

Kabat-Zinn, J. (1990). *Full catastrophe living: Using the wisdom of your body and mind to face stress, pain and illness.* New York: Dell.

Kabat-Zinn, J. (2018). *The healing power of mindfulness: A new way of being.* New York: Hachette.

Kitchen, J. (2005a). Looking backwards, moving forward: Understanding my narrative as a teacher educator. *Studying Teacher Education,* *1*(1), 17–30.

Kitchen, J. (2005b). Conveying respect and empathy: Becoming a relational teacher educator. *Studying Teacher Education,* *1*(2), pp. 195–207.

Kitchen, J. (2009). Relational teacher development: Growing collaboratively in a hoping relationship. *Teacher Education Quarterly*, *36*(2), 45–62.

Kitchen, J. (2016). Looking back on 15 years of relational teacher education: A narrative self-study. In J. Williams and M. Hayler (Eds.), *Professional learning through transitions and transformations: Teacher educators' journeys of becoming* (pp. 167–182). Singapore: Springer.

Lantieri, L. (2008). *Building emotional intelligence: Techniques for cultivating inner strength in children.* Boulder, CO: Sounds True.

Loughran, J. (2006). *Developing a pedagogy of teacher education: understanding teaching and learning about teaching.* London & New York: Routledge.

Miller, J. P. (1993). *The holistic teacher.* Toronto, ON, Canada: OISE Press.

Miller, J. P. (1996). *The holistic curriculum, revised and expanded edition.* Toronto, ON, Canada: OISE Press.

Miller, J. P., Cassie, J. R., & Drake, S. M. (1990). *Holistic learning: A teacher's guide to integrated studies.* Toronto, ON, Canada: OISE Press.

Murphy, S. (2019). *Fostering mindfulness: Building skills that students need to manage their attention, emotions, and behavior in classrooms and beyond.* Markham, ON: Pembroke.

Noddings, N. (1992). *The challenge to care in schools: An alternative approach to education.* New York: Teachers College Press.

Oberle, E., & Schonert-Reichl, K. A. (2016). Stress contagion in the classroom? The link between classroom teacher burnout and morning cortisol in elementary school students. *Social Science & Medicine, 159*, 30–37.

Palmer, P. (2003). Teaching with heart and soul: Reflections on spirituality in teacher education. *Journal of Teacher Education 54*(5), 376–385.

Palmer, P. J. (1998). *The courage to teach: Exploring the inner landscape of a teacher's life.* San Francisco: Jossey-Bass.

Ragoonaden, K. (Ed.). (2015). *Mindful teaching and learning: Developing a pedagogy of well-being.* Lanham, MD: Lexington Books.

Ragoonaden, K. & Bullock, S. M. (Eds.). (2016). *Mindfulness and critical friendship: A new perspective on professional development for educators.* Lanham, MD: Lexington Books.

Roeser, R. W., Skinner, E., Beers, J. & Jennings, P. A. (2012). Mindfulness training and teachers' professional development: An emerging area of research and practice. *Child Development Perspectives*, 6: 167–173. doi: 10.1111/j.1750-8606.2012.00238.x.

Rogers, C. (1961). *On becoming a person.* Boston: Houghton Mifflin.

Rogers, C. (1969). *Freedom to learn.* Columbus: Charles E. Merrill.

Rogers, C. (1983). *Freedom to learn for the 80's.* Columbus: Beck & Howe.

Truth and Reconciliation Canada. (2015). *Honouring the truth, reconciling for the future: Summary of the final report of the Truth and Reconciliation Commission of Canada.* Winnipeg: Truth and Reconciliation Commission of Canada.

Young, S. (2016). What is mindfulness? A contemplative perspective. In K. A. Schoner-Reichl and R. W. Roeser (Eds.). *The handbook of mindfulness in education* (pp. 29–45). New York: Springer.

Chapter One

A Relational Approach to Social Justice in Teacher Education

Julian Kitchen

"The arc of the moral universe is long, but it bends toward justice," proclaimed President Barack Obama in a eulogy for one of the victims of a mass shooting at Emanuel African Methodist Episcopal Church in Charleston, South Carolina (Kakutani, 2015). These words, first expressed in a sermon by Theodore Parker in the 1850s and made famous by Martin Luther King Jr. in the 1960s, offered hope in a difficult time. We continue to live in a challenging time in which darkness threatens human rights and risks bending the arc of history away from justice. When Martin Luther King called on us to fight for justice, he warned that the ongoing battle can only be won through light and love: "Returning hate for hate multiplies hate, adding deeper darkness to a night already devoid of stars. Darkness cannot drive out darkness; only light can do that. Hate cannot drive out hate, only love can do that" (King, 1963/1981, p. 49). In order to help bend the arc toward social justice in a changing world, teacher educators have a responsibility to celebrate diversity, promote equity, and teach inclusive classroom practices. Mindful and relational approaches to teacher education offer guidance as we constructively engage teacher candidates in social justice.

Multicultural teacher education is guided by the lofty goal of developing "inclusive practices that embrace and value difference" (Ragoonaden, 2015c, p. 83). Sleeter (2001) begins with a vision of successful, equitable education for all, while Banks (2007) focuses on ways of enacting multicultural education. Practitioner-researchers who employ such frameworks have identified the importance of connecting knowledge to teacher identity, increasing cultural knowledge (Hollins, 2008), identifying power and inequality in schooling (Zeichner & Liston, 1990), and building institutional support for diversity

(Darling-Hammond, 1995). Progressive academics, including teacher educators, often stand bravely on the vanguard of resistance to hatred and are quick to call out inappropriate words and deeds by allies and foes alike. While I share their concerns, I caution against labelling teacher candidates who do not share our views, as this limits our ability to connect knowledge of diversity to their identities and experiences. I fear that characterizing their families, places of worship, and communities as prejudiced reinforces their "tribal" loyalties rather than opening them up to greater cultural knowledge. I worry that asserting our authority to advocate for social justice prompts resistance, often silent, and the perception that we use our power unfairly. I am concerned that this does little to build institutional support for diversity, especially in areas that are conservative. As a mindful and relational teacher educator, I have deep respect for teacher candidates as decent people motivated by love of learning and commitment to making a better world. This gives me the strength to love rather than judge them or the communities from which they come, even as I encounter resistance to equity and diversity. My instincts as a relational teacher educator are to shed light by sharing knowledge and by conveying respect and empathy as I help them become more effective, caring, and inclusive teachers.

As a Canadian teacher educator developing and teaching a new School and Society course from 2016 to 2018, I was mindful of cultural tensions and a backlash against social justice in the United States and other countries. In my reflections on practice (Schön, 1987), I puzzled over ways in which I could help teacher candidates make sense of these issues and their implications for teaching:

> In my planning of the course, I focused on building a climate of safety and trust. This was based on my experiences as a teacher educator. At the heart of my conception is relational teacher education, particularly a belief that conveying empathy and respect is central to engaging teacher candidates in facing problems of practice and building their capacity as educators. Few topics are more sensitive than diversity and social justice, so even more explicit attention is needed to the safe conditions necessary for trust in oneself, one's classmates and one's instructor. This, I have learned through critical incidents in my teacher education experiences. (Journal, September 8, 2016)

I drew on relational teacher education as a framework for designing and delivering the course in a manner that was respectful of teacher candidates and fair to people and communities whose voices are often unheard or silenced.

In 2005, I wrote a self-study in which I presented relational teacher education (RTE) as an approach to preparing teachers (Kitchen, 2005a; 2005b). Underlying this work was an understanding that "education is development from within" (Dewey, 1938, p. 17) and a belief that teacher educators play a crucial role in fostering "experiences that lead to growth" (Dewey, 1938, p. 40) for preservice teachers. In these articles, I identified seven characteristics as important to RTE:

1. Understanding one's own personal practical knowledge
2. Improving one's practice in teacher education
3. Understanding the landscape of teacher education
4. Respecting and empathizing with teacher candidates
5. Conveying respect and empathy
6. Helping preservice teachers face problems
7. Receptivity to growing in relationship

RTE as a means of living and teaching alongside teacher candidates has guided my practice for twenty years (e.g., Kitchen, 2016b). I continue to be active in teacher education and have published extensively on my efforts to live authentically alongside preservice teachers in relationships that lead to growth (e.g., Kitchen, 2010, Kitchen & Bellini, 2012). In this chapter, I revisit RTE as a mindful approach to attending to social justice issues in initial teacher education. I share my experiences teaching a new School and Society course in the Trump era from 2016 to 2018 and how mindfulness and RTE have informed my practice and the social justice experiences of teacher candidates. The authority of lived experience guides my teaching practices and research methods. After reviewing relevant literature on mindfulness, RTE, and social justice, I outline the research methods that guide this study. I then frame my experiences around the seven characteristics of RTE, using evidence collected along the way to chronicle my experiences and those teacher candidates as they grappled with social justice. I consider the tensions inherent in being a relational social justice teacher educator while recognizing that "truth is found neither in the thesis nor the antithesis, but in an emergent synthesis that reconciles the two," according to Martin Luther King Jr. (1963/1981, p. 1).

GUIDED BY THE AUTHORITY OF EXPERIENCE

"There is a tension in the teaching profession between teachers' development, understanding, and use of practical knowledge, and the generally acceptable understanding that knowledge is propositional, according to Munby, Russell and Martin (2001, p. 900). While propositional knowledge concerning equity, diversity, and social justice is important, so too are the *authority of experience* (Munby & Russell, 1994) and the *craft knowledge* of educators. Teacher educators "know that there is much more to their knowledge than knowing the subject matter to be taught" (Munby, Russell, & Martin,

2001, p. 900). Martin and Russell (2019) write that "learning from the experience of classroom practice is more difficult than is suggested by the familiar assumption that theory is first learned and then applied." Thus, we need to better understand ourselves, and effective practices in order to improve the quality of social justice learning in the teacher education programs. Mindfulness can guide educators to inner wisdom and attentiveness, while relational teacher education offers a path toward social justice teacher education that respects them, their authority of experience, and the contexts in which they work.

Mindfulness

Mindfulness as a way of being in the world arises from contemplative practices across cultures. Kabat-Zinn (1990) describes it as "the awareness that emerges through paying attention on purpose, in the present moment, and non-judgmentally to the unfolding of experience moment by moment" (p. 4). As Ragoonaden (2015a) writes, "contemporary practice includes paying attention and being aware of one's everyday activities" (p. 17) in order to become more kind, compassionate, attentive, authentic, and intentional. Buddhist and other Eastern conceptions of mindfulness focus attention on self, others, and the environment without judgment, whereas secular mindfulness training (e.g., Langer, 1997) promotes mindfulness as a means of thoughtfully and intentionally engaging in the world. Kabat-Zinn (2018) describes mindfulness as a "radical openness" to experience one's deepest intuition. Mindfulness education, similarly, is concerned with both attending to the inner lives of teachers and students, and developing pedagogies that cultivate attentiveness and resilience (Lantieri, 2008). Teacher educators and classroom teachers who embrace mindfulness (e.g., Ragoonaden, 2015b; Ragoonaden & Bullock, 2016; Hanson, 2017) "purposefully [position it] as a reflective exercise for novice practitioners which can also be integrated as professional and personal development" (Ragoonaden, 2015a, p. 20).

Relational Teacher Education as a Mindful Practice

"Good teachers are centrally concerned with the creation of authentic relationships and a classroom environment in which students can make connections between the curriculum of the classroom and the central concerns of their own lives," writes Beattie (2001, p. 3). A body of scholarship has emerged that emphasizes the importance of caring and relationship in student learning. Noddings (1992) writes, "To care and be cared for are fundamental human needs" (p. xi), while Hollingsworth, Dybdahl, and Minarik (1993) identify *relational knowing* as crucial to meaningful interactions between teachers and students. Relational knowing resonated for me in my doctoral inquiry into the professional development of a struggling teacher (Kitchen, 2005a; 2005b; 2009). I was also drawn to the work of humanist psychologist Carl Rogers: "This book is about me, as I sit there with that client, facing him, participating in that struggle as deeply and sensitively as I am able" (1961, p. 4). I became increasingly aware that I often acted as an expert employing external criteria rather than as a "helper" (Rogers, 1961), celebrating experience and seeking to help teachers discover order in the flowing, changing process of life. "Floating with the complex stream of experiencing," Rogers (1961) came to regard experience as the highest authority and discovered that "what is most personal is most general" (pp. 26–27). His mindful and relational qualities, such as *empathic understanding* and *unconditional positive regard*, resonated with my experiences. *Relational teacher development* (Kitchen, 2005c; 2008b; 2009), my conception of professional development grounded in purposeful engagement and authentic relationships between teachers, has informed my practice as a university instructor over the past twenty years. The seven characteristics of relational teacher education offer guidance to teacher educators seeking to explicitly focus on understanding themselves to help preservice teachers become adaptive experts within teacher education classrooms that model relational knowing and community. Examples from my practice over twenty years (e.g., Kitchen, 2008a; 2010; Kitchen & Bellini, 2012) illustrate what RTE might look like and what it means to be a relational teacher educator. While RTE is not a formula, as the most important element is a commitment to relationally knowing one's teacher candidates, its seven characteristics highlight how to intentionally and explicitly address in one's professional practice.

At the heart of RTE is attention. While attentiveness requires no specialized skills, it is difficult to achieve because the teacher educator needs to take the time and effort to listen to each teacher candidates' stories in order to help them address professional challenges in ways that are meaningful to them. This is achieved not through the application of a formula or well-meaning sentiments, but through in-depth efforts to understand one's own personal practical knowledge and direct efforts to engage preservice teachers so that they appreciate the efforts made on their behalf. While professional knowledge—a solid repertoire of teaching skills and understandings of students, curriculum and context—matters, most important is empathetic understanding and commitment to facing problems. After understanding one's own personal professional knowledge and identifying the needs of the individual teacher candidates, the teacher educator needs to draw on this deep professional aptitude to select appropriate strategies and teach them to preservice teachers. Crucial to my engagement has been receptivity to growing in relationship. By studying my practice, I constantly work to improve my teaching so that I may become a better teacher educator. Also, by doing this, I contribute to the academic discourse on teacher education and become part of a community of practitioners committed to enhancing the pedagogy of teacher education (e.g., Russell & Loughran, 2007).

Parker Palmer (1998) writes:

> Authority comes as I reclaim my identity and integrity, remembering my selfhood and my sense of vocation. Then teaching can come from the depths of my own truth—and the truth that is within my students has a chance to respond in kind. (p. 33)

Relational teacher education is a mindful approach to becoming a teacher educator whose identity and integrity makes a positive difference in the lives of teacher candidates and the students they teach.

Attending to Social Justice

"Relationships of trust are fundamental to teaching and learning," wrote Lesley Coia (2016, p. 311), particularly in "courses that aim to be transformative: courses where students are engaged in thinking deeply about themselves, schools and schooling as they move towards a vision of a more equitable and just society" (p. 311). Teacher educators committed to social justice can use relational teacher education to create "a secure environment where all voices are heard and everyone freely asks questions based on respect and caring" (Lee, 2011, p. 7). By respecting teacher candidates' experiences, while inviting them to attend to the voices and experiences of others, a relational approach to social justice may open minds that are closed to more didactic approaches.

As a teacher educator, my deep commitment to presenting a strong equity, diversity, and social justice cases based on critical discourses (McNeil, 2011) sits in tension with my respect for teacher candidates' personal experiences and my commitment to relational teacher education. Therefore, I have tended toward a moderate approach aimed at effectively engaging my teacher candidates where they are positioned (predominately white, middle class, and rural/suburban). A recognition that teacher "identities are produced through participation in discourse" (Danielewicz, 2001, p. 11) has led me to frame the course in a manner that recognizes, addresses, and competes with the alternative discourses that may already exist in their heads through their families, communities, and the media.

In this chapter, I draw on my experiences as a relational teacher educator of a social justice course to illustrate the potential of a relational approach. By respecting and empathizing with teacher candidates, as well as conveying respect and helping them face problems/challenges in their constructions of identity and inclusion, I seek to assist them in growing into teachers who celebrate diversity and promote equity. *Embodied care*, which Trout (2017) introduced to teacher education, conveys my sense of caring as a way of living thoughtfully alongside teacher candidates. Like Trout, I wrestle critically and reflectively with teacher candidate concerns, while attempting to embody the caring I urge them to apply to their students.

METHODS

I study my practice as a School and Society professor in order to improve my future practice (LaBoskey, 2004). I have engaged in the self-study of teacher education practices (S-STEP or self-study) for many years because this is an inquiry approach that encourages teacher educators to focus on their teaching practices while engaging in scholarly endeavors (Loughran, 2002). As Ragoonaden (2015a) observes, self-study offers "a natural pathway toward integrating and interconnecting principles and concepts of mindfulness and well-being into educational practice" (p. 21). Data collected in 2016–2017 (2 classes—55 participants) and 2017–2018 (3 classes—66 participants). To ensure trustworthiness (LaBoskey, 2004), several data sources were collected.

Maintaining a teacher education journal is a means to making sense of one's experiences as a teacher educator, while maintaining ongoing records of practice and reflection through which one can gain insight into *personal practical knowledge* and the threads of one's story (Connelly & Clandinin, 1988). In journal entries written at least once a week, I reflected on the classes and the written responses of teacher candidates.

Recognizing the importance of listening to the voice of the other, as well as the self, I solicited feedback from teacher candidates through exit cars, especially during the first few lessons. As Patka, Wallin-Ruschman, Wallace, and Robbins (2016) note, use of exit cards is a strategy that has been demonstrated to be effective for engendering dialogue with teacher candidates, especially conveying concerns and offering opportunities to adapt instruction. By being responsive, instructors build rapport with teacher candidates. In order to assess the effectiveness of the lessons/activities, I asked participants to provide feedback on their experience through a series of questions or prompts (Luaer, 2006) at the end of most classes.

Teacher candidates wrote and submitted two reflections on experiences as learners or teachers as formative tasks during the first weeks; these proved important in identifying issues and concerns during the course. At the end of the course, longer portfolios were collected as summative evaluation. They also wrote response journals on the weekly readings. These responses were both critical and reflective in nature. Like the exit cards and reflections, they revealed how teacher candidates were responding as the course progressed, as did feedback contained in course evaluations. These data sources provided me with insights into their experiences.

Critical friendship (Mishler, 1990) serves as an important means of demonstrating credibility through interaction. I engaged a critical friend as an external collaborator with whom I could correspond concerning my experiences and the challenges of teaching such a course to predominantly mainstream teacher candidates. She also read and commented on drafts of this chapter. Manu Sharma, an assistant professor at University of Wisconsin (River Falls), is a South Asian woman with a rich history of studying and enacting social justice as an elementary teacher, graduate student, and teacher educator in Canada (including courses in my university). Her identity contrasts nicely with mine as a white male who has grown up in relative privilege and faced little discrimination as an openly gay teacher educator. Manu brings different perspectives and experiences along with an understanding of my context (as she has taught in my university and other universities in Canada).

ATTENDING TO SOCIAL JUSTICE THROUGH RELATIONAL TEACHER EDUCATION

In this section, I organize my experiences around the seven characteristics of relational teacher education in order to illustrate how I attempted to apply relational principles to teaching for social justice. In "Attending to the Concerns of Teacher Candidates: A Self-Study of a Teacher Educator" (Kitchen, 2019b), based on the same research, I consider the experiences of teacher candidates and four themes that emerged from their responses.

Understanding One's Own Personal Practical Knowledge

Educators need to reflect on their experiences because, as Connelly and Clandinin (1988) suggest, "if you understand what makes up the curriculum of the person most important to you, namely yourself, you will better understand the difficulties, whys, and wherefores of the curriculum of your students" (p. 31). "Inquiry into my experiences as a preservice teacher has helped me recognize many of the limitations of traditional teacher education" (Kitchen, 2005a, p. 22) and understand that my pedagogy of teacher education arises from the authority of my experience and the craft knowledge I have developed through critical reflection. Early in my career, "reflection motivated me to develop curriculum and establish classroom environments that foster collaboration and reflection on personal experiences in order to address the challenges of classroom teaching" (Kitchen, 2005a, p. 23).

A commitment to social justice in my work has led me to reflect on how my experiences as a gay man and a middle class, white male inform my identity and performative self. In "Inside Out: My Identity as a Queer Teacher Educator," I examined my experiences, drawing "on narrative inquiry and queer theory to identify key tensions for me as a teacher educator and for heteronormativity" (Kitchen, 2016a, p. 18). Recalling the "turmoil" I experienced in "coming out and living out in a heteronormative culture" helped me appreciate the "reality for many queer youth grappling with identity formation" (pp. 18–19). The tension "between needing to be accepted as gay (and accept myself) and wishing to be recognized as a complex, multi-faceted individual" (p. 19) helped me better appreciate similar tensions and the intersectional identities of others who face greater challenges. While openly identifying as queer categorizes me as belonging to a *subordinate masculinity*, I have often benefitted from norms of *hegemonic masculinity* (Connell, 2005), "the cultural ideal of masculinity that legitimizes patriarchy and the collective, institutional power of men in institutions" (Kitchen, 2017, p. 88).

While consciousness of my privilege helps me understand the perspectives of mainstream teacher candidates, I must be careful not to be too accommodating to their resistance. When I expressed sympathy for teacher candidates who were troubled by the term privilege, critical friend Manu Sharma reminded me of my "ethical responsibility as an educator" (Letter, January 25, 2018) to be an ally. Manu's experiences as a visible minority afford her cultural understandings of the predominantly white, middle class teacher candidates that are sometimes overlooked by a cultural insider like myself.

By acknowledging and problematizing my privileged and marginalized identities, I am better able to help teacher candidates reflect on their intersectionalities.

Improving One's Practice in Teacher Education

While understanding personal practical knowledge in relation to social justice is important, so too is the development of pedagogy that imparts knowledge, encourages reflection, and prompts action. As an experienced teacher educator, I possess a wide repertoire of classroom strategies and, in particular, an ability to create safe spaces in which teacher candidates could explore controversial issues in class and through written reflection. I had collected and developed a number of activities specifically designed to open them up to alternative perspectives and engage as they explored sensitive issues. A workshop on gender identity and sexual orientation by Kitchen and Bellini (2012) illustrated this. I also continued to explore strategies to address specific themes, such as poverty and race.

By collecting data on student perceptions, particularly through the collection and analysis of exit cards and writings during the first weeks, permitted me to factor their input into lesson planning and develop relationships of respect and empathy with teacher candidates (Kitchen, 2005b). While I have always planned my lessons with care, I spent considerable time finding resources and developing a range of materials and activities. At the conclusion of each year, I solicited detailed feedback and adapted my pedagogy accordingly.

Understanding the Landscape of Teacher Education

Understanding one's personal practical knowledge and improving practice, while crucial to RTE, need to be combined with an understanding of the teacher education context. As a novice teacher educator, I noticed a significant disconnect between education colleges and schools and perceived a gap between theory and practice (Kitchen, 2005a). Today, after surveying teacher education locally and internationally (Kitchen, 2019a; Kitchen & Petrarca, 2016; Petrarca & Kitchen, 2017), I am keenly aware of the need for integrated programs that connect theory to practice, offer depth in curriculum, prompt deep reflection by teacher candidates, and make connections across courses. Such integration is notably lacking in the area of social justice, which is often decontextualized from practice and personal experience. In my School and Society course, I attempt to connect social justice principles to experience and practice.

At the same time, it is important to be attuned to the wider socio-cultural landscape. The election of President Trump, along with the rise of ethnic nationalism world-wide, highlights the deep disconnect between liberal intellectual elites—who have largely embraced the rhetoric of social inclusion, even as they benefit from inequity—and less educated white citizens. Tomasky (2017), for example, argues that liberal elites "haven't made their peace with middle America," people who may value religion, are unselfconsciously patriotic, respect the police, possess guns, and are not attentive to identity issues (such as gay rights or migrant rights). In universities, conservative religious students who do not share the prevailing ethos of the academy often feel silenced or are in fact silenced (Kristof, 2016). Being aware of the discourses that affect teacher candidates enables me to respond to these concerns in class. For example, in the first year, expressions of concern about political correctness led to a mini-lesson on the history of the term and how it has been manipulated to shift sympathy toward dominant groups (Journal, September 12, 2016). More generally, awareness of the charged and polarized political environment motivated me to create a safe space in which teacher candidates could learn and reflect.

Respecting and Empathizing with Teacher Candidates

Relational teacher education is based on respect for adult learners and a belief that each prospective teacher must construct her or his own meaning as a curriculum maker. I have made respect for participants a core ethical principle in my practice (Kitchen, 2005b) and research (Kitchen, 2019c); I focus on points that are constructive and cast participants in a positive light. For example, in a self-study on workshops on queer issues, we treated resistance with respect during the sessions and wrote thoughtfully about the willingness of teacher candidates to move outside their comfort zone (Kitchen & Bellini, 2012).

Respect and empathy informed how I introduced the course and approached the concept of privilege. A Step into the Circle activity, in which teacher candidates moved based on a list of fourteen statements about privilege, was used to unsettle thinking. On an exit card, one wrote, "I enjoy[ed] this activity because it helped reveal my privilege and create a positive and safe space, while getting to know each other." A follow-up worksheet activity helped individuals consider how their identities involve range of elements (e.g., race, gender, class) and intersectionalities. This was reinforced in the first reader response as they grappled with McIntosh on privilege and the demands of Gay's culturally responsive teaching. Throughout the course, I offered up challenging critical perspectives to consider while acknowledging that they could not embrace it all. I did, however, ask them to listen to other voices and called on them to address equity and diversity within their comfort zones as new teachers. Their candid reflections revealed genuine engagement with these issues and a willingness to engage as they were able. Reading discussion groups (facilitated by a group member) also proved useful as a means of exploring their own ideas. According to exit card feedback, this "increased knowledge, foster[ed] deep discussion," offered "other people's interesting perspectives." Also, the seminars and inclusive curriculum development assignment permit them to develop lessons relevant to their subject and interests. Overall, respecting their values and commitment, through correspondence and discussion in class contributes to personal professional growth.

Conveying Respect and Empathy

As a relational teacher educator, I convey respect and empathy "by listening attentively, responding mindfully, praising individual contributions to class, following up on concerns by email, and [by] providing extensive commentaries on their written narratives and critical reflections" (Kitchen, 2005b, p. 204). In School and Society, I was particularly mindful of the potential struggles teacher candidates might face as their implicit and unexamined worldviews were challenged. As the previous section illustrates, I challenged them to join me on a journey, while also providing scaffolding and respecting their individual journeys of discovery.

Guided by the axiom "Be the change you wish to see in the world," attributed to Gandhi, I attempted to model respect and empathy. I noted the complexities of equity discourse and acknowledged that many good people might not be able to fully embrace a progressive agenda. I adopted an invitational approach, offering experiences from communities that are often not heard or understood and invited them to be open to these stories. For example, according to my journal in January 2018, I began the third lesson by noting "that their feedback indicate[s] high degrees of empathy and openness along with a certain level of anxiety about being judged for lack of knowledge or improper use of language." I urged them not to be anxious: "anxiety does little good . . . doesn't improve practice and has the effect of 'othering' students from diverse backgrounds; this makes the sources of danger rather than people to be welcomed and come to know." Instead, in the spirit of mindfulness, I proposed being "grateful for what they had, that gratitude was the beginning of seeing other people empathetically." I encouraged cognitive empathy—"seeing the world through the eyes of others and reflecting as a means to understanding where they might be coming from"—and the resilience develops through self-compassion and the willingness to take considered risks for the sake of others. In turn, I made explicit my own vulnerability and decision making as a teacher educator (Loughran, 2006).

I also conveyed respect and empathy through one-on-one communication. For example, I wrote:

> I have interesting conversations with some of the students who are less progressive. Rather than shutting them down, I try to be supportive and build them up. For example, Paul in a previous journal talked about being shut down by fellow art students for his views, to which I responded that that was simply unfair and unkind. In Paul's current journal he makes a claim for "strong family structures which include fathers" and "enforcing importance of families in school," I responded that it was good to celebrate the family but it might be wise to do so in ways that do not undercut single-parent families who are doing their best. (Journal, March 17, 2018)

Paul later "walked back" his heated words and thanked me for engaging him respectfully. Feedback overall suggests that I was successful in putting teacher candidates at ease and helping them feel cared for. Overall, teacher candidates liked the straightforward presentation, factual information provided. Caring also entails a balance between professionalism and "relations intimate enough for personal understanding" (Noddings, 1992, p. 101).

Helping Preservice Teachers Face Problems

As a relational teacher educator, I commit to help teacher candidates, collectively and individually, "face problems and reconcile theory with practice" (2005b, p. 205). As Dewey (1938) writes in *Experience and Education*, "Teachers discriminate between experiences that are worthwhile educationally and those that are not" (p. 33), in order to promote growth. In a letter to my critical friend, I wrote, "I try not to dismiss their worldviews as I do not think that I can inform their thinking unless I strive [to] demonstrate respectfulness. I work to balance safety with risk, respect with challenge" (Letter, January 15, 2018).

This commitment to helping teacher candidates face problems is evident in another interaction with Paul. On an exit, he wrote:

> In many cases of social justice I do not agree with the dominant points of view expressed by school boards and leading figures in the field. I'm learning to what he said I must go along with these ideas and the degree to which I can express my own opinions without it being a deterrent to my career

I responded:

> I read your query on the ticket out with interest. I would suggest taking some time to talk [before class]. I am happy to listen without judgement to your concerns about what can be said and not in a school, as well as where professionalism obliges you to follow along regardless of your own opinions. I am also confident that there are many ways in which you can make positive contributions to inclusiveness without going against your own principles. I am pleased that you feel comfortable raising this with me.

In my feedback to a teacher candidate grappling with tensions between two concepts, I suggested that both sides on these issues may have positives and negatives: "I find it useful to hold both at the same time, and tack right and left as I steer a course that is respectful, constructive, inclusive and oriented to social justice." To another, I wrote, "The reason they offer no surefire remedies is because there are none!" I have also learned that trying to force people to change simply does not work.

By helping teacher candidates frame and understand problems, my goal is to create an environment in which they can wrestle with complex and important ideas. As I wrote to one teacher candidate, "I can only invite consideration and trust you to do your best."

Receptivity to Growing in Relationship

The examples above have hopefully demonstrated both a commitment to helping teacher candidates grow in their understanding of and engagement in equity, diversity, inclusion, and social justice. I also hope that the examples also convey my receptivity to learning alongside them.

After each class, I wrote an extensive journal account in which I described and reflected on the lesson. I also read the exit cards and reflected on the patterns of response. In planning the next lesson, I both responded to issues that arose and adapted in response to suggestions. I also made explicit the pedagogical choices I made. When some feedback was critical of the racism lesson for being too focused on African American history, I explained my choice and acknowledged that the choice to delve into one example in depth reduced breadth. I also made a point to incorporate more Canadian examples as we addressed subsequent themes. When they asked for more concrete strategies, I provided more along with additional resources, while also stressing the importance of foundational understandings and the ability to enact in context.

By explicitly studying my practice, I was mindful to their learning needs and by role as a facilitator of learning. By struggling with how to be more effective, and sharing these struggles with teacher candidates, I demonstrated my receptivity to growing in relationship.

CONCLUSION

> I wanted to take the time to write you this quick note of thank you for how you ran and managed the School and Society course. . . .
>
> While I think that you and I may differ on issues, even fundamentally, as may have been evident in the write-ups of mine that you read, I don't think that I have ever encountered a professor as genuinely interested in creating a welcoming and engaging environment. Despite the seriousness of the issues discussed (or perhaps because of this), you never took to seeing your position as a professor as a soapbox. You offered your perspectives in eminently fair and level-headed ways, always with humility and grace. You offered strong positions on both sides of arguments, and had a mastery of the topics on which you offered your opinion. This demonstrates not only a profound respect for the profession of teaching, but a likewise profound respect for the search for truth and unity.
>
> . . . Suffice it to say that your approach to teaching difficult subjects is a model that I hope to be able to follow, and should be a model for all professors.
>
> Email from Bashir (Teacher Candidate), August 13, 2018

Bashir's feedback four months after the course are validating because his experience of the course reflects my intentions in designing the course and working alongside teacher candidates. Although more eloquent, it is also reflective of course evaluation feedback. Bashir's intelligence and outspokenness presented challenges, but I enjoyed his engagement with issues and maintained a respectful and empathetic stance as I encouraged him to consider other perspectives. Also, I was relieved that he and others with diverse and intersectional identities found my approach respectful to their experiences, even though the composition of the class was mainly white.

Attention to social justice in education and attentiveness to the personal and professional growth of teachers go hand-in-hand. As morality cannot be legislated, it is "only through an inner spiritual transformation" that we as teacher educators can "gain the strength to fight vigorously the evils of the world" (King, 1963/1981, p. 18). Mindfulness helps us engage in social justice work with "a humble and loving spirit" (King, 1963/1981, p. 18) that has the potential to be received in kind. Relational teacher education is an approach to entering into helping relationships that are respectful of the aspiring teacher's capacity for caring and growth. While humble in delivery, applying the seven characteristics of RTE requires intentionality, adaptive expertise, and commitment from teacher educators who are idealistic yet realistic.

REFERENCES

Banks, J. (2007). *Educating citizens in a multicultural society* (2nd Edition). New York: Teachers College Press.
Beattie, M. (2001). *The art of learning to teach: preservice teacher narratives*. Upper Saddle River, NJ: Merrill Prentice Hall.
Bullough, R. V. & Pinnegar, S. (2001). Guidelines for quality in autobiographical forms of self-study research. *Educational Researcher, 30*(3), 13–21.
Clandinin, D. J., & Connelly, F. M. (1992). Teacher as curriculum maker. In P. Jackson (Ed.). *Handbook of curriculum* (pp. 363–461). New York: Macmillan.
Coia, L. (2016). Trust in diversity: An autobiographic self-study. In D. Garbett and A. Ovens (Eds.), *Enacting self-study as methodology for professional inquiry* (pp. 311–316).
Connell, R. W. (2005). *Masculinities* (2nd. Ed.). Berkeley, CA: University of California Press.
Connelly F. M., & Clandinin, D. J. (1988). *Teachers as curriculum planners: Narratives of experience*. Toronto: OISE Press.
Danielewicz, J. (2001). *Teaching selves: Identity, pedagogy, and teacher education*. Albany, NY: State University of New York Press.
Darling-Hammond, L. (1995). Inequality and access to knowledge. In J. Banks and C. Banks (Eds.), *Handbook of research on multicultural education* (pp. 465–483).
Dewey, J. (1938). *Experience and education*. New York: Collier Books.
Hanson, K. (Ed.). (2017). *A mindful teaching community: Possibilities for teacher professional learning*. Lanham, MD: Lexington Books.
Hollingsworth, S., Dybdahl, M., & Minarik, L. T. (1993). By chart and chance and passion: The importance of relational knowing in learning to teach. *Curriculum Inquiry, 23*(1), 5–35.
Hollins, E. (2008). *Culture in school learning: Revealing the deep meaning* (2nd edition). Mahwah, NJ: Lawrence Erlbaum.
Kabat-Zinn, J. (1990). *Full catastrophe living: Using the wisdom of your body and mind to face stress, pain and illness*. New York: Dell.
Kabat-Zinn, J. (2018). *The healing power of mindfulness: A new way of being*. New York: Hachette.
Kakutani, M. (2015). Obama's eulogy, which found its place in history. *New York Times*, July 3, 2015. https://www.nytimes.com/2015/07/04/arts/obamas-eulogy-which-found-its-place-in-history.html.
King, M. L. (1963; 1981). *A gift of love: Sermons from strength to love and other preachings*. Boston: Beacon.
Kitchen, J. (2005a). Looking backwards, moving forward: Understanding my narrative as a teacher educator. *Studying Teacher Education, 1*(1), 17–30.
Kitchen, J. (2005b). Conveying respect and empathy: Becoming a relational teacher educator. *Studying Teacher Education, 1*(2), pp. 195–207.

Kitchen, J. (2005c). Relational teacher development: A quest for meaning in the garden of teacher experience. Unpublished doctoral dissertation, Ontario Institute for Studies in Education of the University of Toronto, Toronto.

Kitchen, J. (2008a). The feedback loop in reflective practice: A teacher educator responds to reflective writing by preservice teachers. *Excelsior, 2*(2), 37–46.

Kitchen, J. (2008b). *Relational teacher development: A quest for meaning in the garden of teacher experience.* Cologne, Germany: Lambert Academic Publishing.

Kitchen, J. (2009). Relational teacher development: Growing collaboratively in a hoping relationship. *Teacher Education Quarterly, 36*(2), 45–62.

Kitchen, J. (2010). Making education law meaningful to beginning teachers: A narrative inquiry. *In Education, 16*(2). http://ineducation.ca/.

Kitchen, J. (2016a). Inside out: My identity as a queer teacher educator. In J. Kitchen, D. Tidwell, and L. Fitzgerald (Eds.), *Self-study and diversity II* (pp. 11–26). Rotterdam, The Netherlands: Sense.

Kitchen, J. (2016b). Looking back on 15 years of relational teacher education: A narrative self-study. In J. Williams and M. Hayler (Eds.), *Professional learning through transitions and transformations: Teacher educators' journeys of becoming* (pp. 167–182). Singapore: Springer.

Kitchen, J. (2017). Critically reflecting on masculinity in teacher education through narrative self-study. In R. Brandenburg, K. Glasswell, M. Jones, & J. Ryan (Eds.), *Reflective theory and practice in teacher education* (pp. 85–101). Singapore: Springer Nature.

Kitchen, J. (2019a). Ethical issues in reporting on teacher candidate perspectives in a cultural diversity course: Increasing trustworthiness, improving practice, and protecting participants. In R. Brandenburg & S. McDonough (Eds.), *Ethics, self-study research, methodology and teacher education.* Singapore: Springer Nature. (pp. 97–115).

Kitchen, J. (2019b in press). Attending to the concerns of teacher candidates in a social justice course: A self-study of a teacher educator. *Studying Teacher Education.*

Kitchen, J. (2019c in press). Pedagogy of teacher education in exemplary programs. In J. Kitchen, A. Berry, S. Bullock, A. Crowe, M. Taylor, H. Guojonsdottir, & L. Thomas (Eds.), *2nd international handbook of self-study of teaching and teacher education practices.* Rotterdam, The Netherlands: Springer.

Kitchen, J. & Bellini, C. (2012). Making it better for lesbian, gay, bisexual and transgender students through teacher education: A self-study. *Studying Teacher Education, 8*(3), 209–226.

Kitchen, J. & Petrarca, D. (2016). Approaches to teacher education. In J. Loughran and M. L. Hamilton (Eds.), *International handbook of teacher education research: Initial teacher education* (pp. 137–186). Rotterdam, The Netherlands: Springer.

Kristof, N. (2016). A confession of liberal intolerance. *New York Times,* May 7, 2016.

LaBoskey, V. (2004). Moving the study of self-study research and practice forward: Challenges and opportunities. In J. Loughran, M. L. Hamilton, V. LaBoskey, & T. Russell (Eds.), *International handbook of self-study of teaching and teacher education practices* (pp. 817–869). Dodrecht: Kluwer.

Langer, E. (1997). *The power of mindful learning.* Reading MA: Addison-Wesley.

Lantieri, L. (2008). *Building emotional intelligence: Techniques for cultivating inner strength in children.* Boulder, CO: Sounds True.

Lee, A. (2011). Self-study of cross-cultural supervision of teacher candidates for social justice. *Studying Teacher Education, 7*(1), 3–19.

Loughran, J. (2002). Understanding self-study of teacher education practices. In J. Loughran & T. Russell (Eds.), *Improving teacher education practices through self-study* (pp. 239–248). London: Routledge Falmer.

Loughran, J. (2006). *Developing a pedagogy of teacher education: understanding teaching and learning about teaching.* London & New York: Routledge.

Luaer, P. (2006). *An education research primer: How to understand, evaluate, and use it.* San Francisco: Jossey-Bass.

Martin, A. & Russell, T. (2019 in press). In J. Kitchen, A. Berry, S. Bullock, A. Crowe, M. Taylor, H. Guojonsdottir, & L. Thomas (Eds.), *2nd international handbook of self-study of teaching and teacher education practices*. Rotterdam, The Netherlands: Springer.

McNeil, B. (2011). Charting a way forward: Intersections of race and space in establishing identity as an African-Canadian teacher educator. *Studying Teacher Education, 7*(2), 133–145.

Mishler, E. (1990). Validation in inquiry-guided research: The role of exemplars in narrative studies. *Harvard Education/Review, 60*, 415–442.

Munby, H. & Russell, T. (1994). The authority of learning to teach: Messages from a physics methods class. *Journal of Teacher Education, 45*, 86–95.

Munby, H., Russell, T., & Martin, A. K. (2001). Teachers' knowledge and how it works. In V. Richardson (Ed.), *Handbook of research on teaching*, fourth edition (pp. 877–904). Washington, DC: American Educational Research Association.

Noddings, N. (1992). *The challenge to care in schools: An alternative approach to education.* New York: Teachers College Press.

Palmer, P. J. (1998). *The courage to teach.* San Francisco: Jossey-Bass.

Patka, M., Wallin-Ruuschman, J., Wallace, T., & Robbins, C. (2016). Exit cards: Creating a dialogue for continuous evaluation. T*eaching in Higher Education, 21*(6), 659–668. DOI: 10.1080/13562517.2016.1167033.

Petrarca, D. & Kitchen, J. (Eds.). (2017). *Initial teacher education in Ontario: The first year of four-semester teacher education programs.* Ottawa: Canadian Association for Teacher Education.

Pinnegar, S. & Hamilton, M. L. (2009). *Self-study of practice as a genre of qualitative research: Theory, methodology and practice.* Dordrecht, Netherlands: Springer.

Ragoonaden, K. (2015a). Mindful education and well-being. In K. Ragoonaden (Ed.), *Mindful teaching and learning: Developing a pedagogy of well-being* (pp. 17–31). Lanham, MD: Lexington Books.

Ragoonaden, K. (Ed.). (2015b). *Mindful teaching and learning: Developing a pedagogy of well-being.* Lanham, MD: Lexington Books.

Ragoonaden, K. (2015c). Self-study of teacher education practices and self-study: The fifth moment in a teacher educator's journey. *Studying Teacher Education, 11*(1), 81–95.

Ragoonaden, K. & Bullock, S. M. (Eds.). (2016). *Mindfulness and critical friendship: A new perspective on professional development for educators.* Lanham, MD: Lexington Books.

Rogers, C. (1961). *On becoming a person.* Boston: Houghton Mifflin.

Russell, T. & Loughran, J. (Eds.). (2007). *Enacting a pedagogy of teacher education: Values, relationships and practices* (pp. 182–191). Abingdon, UK: Routledge.

Schön, D. (1987). *Educating the reflective practitioner.* San Francisco: Jossey-Bass.

Sleeter, C. (2001). Preparing teachers for culturally diverse school: Research and the overwhelming presence of whiteness. *Journal of Teacher Education, 52*(2), 94–106.

Tomasky, M. (2017). Elitism is liberalism's biggest problem. *New Republic*, May 30, 2017.

Trout, M. (2017). Embodying care: Igniting a critical turn in a teacher educator's relational practice. *Studying Teacher Education, 14*(1), 39–55.

Weiner, L. (1993). *Preparing teachers for urban schools: Lessons from 30 years of school reform.* New York: Teachers College Press.

Chapter Two

Contemplating Mindfulness and Social Justice in Diversity Classrooms

Karen Ragoonaden

Tagore (1929) stated that the highest education is that which does not merely give us information but makes our life in harmony with all existence. In seeking to maintain this equilibrium, this chapter discusses why and how the integration of secular versions of mindfulness can address issues relating to inclusion and diversity in teacher education. By reconceptualizing mindfulness practices as transformative pedagogies that seek to reenvision higher education for a more just, compassionate, and inclusive society, contemplative approaches can provide the time and space to consider democratic and equitable ways of being and ways of doing. Further, as a pathway to creating awareness of the self and society at large, the cultivation of mindfulness practices can support the holistic, harmonious balance of the physical, emotional, mental, and spiritual dimensions of the individual. The impact of self-awareness and awareness of community can be essential ingredients in the progression toward equitable change ensuring success for all. In teacher education, informal and formal mindfulness practices can support students as they reflect on how their identity locations shape their reactions to mandated curricula choices and assessment applications. Within this context, taking the time to be present and to consider long held beliefs and assumptions can nurture and support students as they reflect and potentially unlearn the effects of systemic inequity, marginalization and oppressive practices relating to gender, class, and race. Students can then learn to recognize, understand, and be accountable for their responses. The chapter also recognizes that when mindfulness practices are introduced, a myriad of responses emerge, particularly from students whose voices have been historically marginalized according to race, gender, and class. Appreciating that the focus on self-reflection, prevalent in contemplative practices, can unintentionally trigger intense reactions, the chapter concludes with useful principles to help faculty address potentially sensitive issues that may arise during the formal and informal practices (Germer, 2005).

MINDFULNESS PRACTICES IN HIGHER EDUCATION

The emergence of formal and informal contemplative practices, like mindfulness, in North American tertiary education has provided opportunities for a new generation of students and faculty to cultivate presence and self-reflection. Owen-Smith (2018), recognizing the multiplicity of definitions regarding contemplative education, introduces contemplative practices as specific pedagogical exercises that can be integrated into university coursework. Defined as metacognitive modes and first-person investigations that nurture inner awareness, concentration, insight, and compassion, these practices include silence, reflection, listening, dialoguing, journaling, breath awareness, mindful movement, and mindful inquiry into one's field of awareness. Within this context, the integrative nature of learning, combined with the ability to critically reflect on self and society, teaches students to respond to challenging course content with an open and nonjudgmental mind (Berila, 2014). For teacher education students, this critical first-person reflection and inquiry is essential when discussing diversity course content relating to race, gender, and class. Diversity pedagogy is an approach that recognizes the privileged and non-privileged ways in which individuals participate in established socio-economic systems (Kanpol, 1999; Kincheloe, 2004; Sheets, 2005). This type of *conscientization* (Freire, 2013) can provide foundational directions for implementing inclusive pedagogical approaches. By cultivating the tools for recognizing, observing, and understanding internal and external reactions to diverse realities, students can come to a deeper reflection and an insightful realization of either their privileged or their marginalized roles in societal systems. Understanding the intense discussions emerging from both privileged perspectives and non-privileged perspectives, the nurturing of critical self-inquiry where students are able to recognize, to understand, and to be accountable for their own reactions can provide a medium for culturally safe, authentic discussions relating to race, gender, and class (Ladson-Billings, 1995; 2000).

Aware that the subject matter in diversity courses often summon a variety of intense emotions and, in some cases, heated discussions, it is important to acknowledge the creation of culturally safe spaces where all voices are relevant, respected, and reciprocated (Ragoonaden, 2010). This becomes increasingly important when leading mindfulness practices. Experienced educators in diversity pedagogy grasp that students whose identities have been systematically marginalized by societal systems may feel frustration, anger, sadness, or powerlessness. For these students, quotidian acts of micro-aggressions that accumulate over time often result in oppression-based trauma (Berila, 2014; Williams, 2013). Internalized oppression can also occur when individuals' identities are shaped by the biases, assumptions, and stereotypes pervading mainstream culture. The traditional guidance from mindfulness facilitators *"to be present, to be aware and to accept without judgment"* can be overwhelmingly difficult, if not impossible, for participants living in less than inclusive societies. In these contexts, it is important to note that students' reactions can present as deeply embedded coping mechanisms reflective of previously or presently endured trauma (Germer, 2005). While contemplative pedagogy can provide compassionate ways of sitting with and potentially healing, an active awareness of how these self-reflective practices can induce long-held memories of difficult and in some cases traumatic experiences, cannot be ignored (Berila, 2014).

Alternatively, students who are characterized as members of mainstream contexts may also feel frustration, anger, or resistance to the idea that they have privilege in a society, especially if they do not feel that they have benefited much in their lifetimes. Rather than characterizing their reactions as resistance to equity-based discussions, Berila (2014) argues that these reactions are precisely the complex terrain that must be explored if we are truly to learn the self-reflection that is critical to unlearning the effects of oppression. She suggests that it would be much more productive to offer the students ways to learn to meet and process their reactions as *inevitable by-products of systems of oppression* (p. 62). Author bell hooks (1994) refers to this ability as an "engaged pedagogy" that emphasizes well-being through integrated, holistic, and progressive education (p. 14). Within the confines of a culturally safe place led by a well-trained educator, the informal and formal mindfulness practices can serve as platforms for invaluable teaching moments where the student has the opportunity to frame his or her emotions and reactions, to learn to sit with them, and to develop sustained responses to otherness

Similar to Berila's (2014) discourse on the complexity of mindfulness practices in diversity education, Burack (2014) discusses several challenges associated with the introduction of contemplative practices in higher education. These include:

1. when and how to introduce contemplations;
2. how to integrate contemplations with more conventional pedagogies;
3. how to maintain safety;
4. how much instructor experience, knowledge, and skill are needed;
5. how to maintain separation of church and state.

Burack (2014) incorporates the following contemplative practices in his courses: breath meditation, body scan, mindfulness of sound, mindfulness of thoughts, mindfulness of feelings, mindfulness of sensations, mindful inquiry into one's field of awareness, and visualizations, The practices often evoke non-ordinary experiences, so the students gain a holistic understanding of the subject matter.

WHEN AND HOW TO INTRODUCE MINDFULNESS PRACTICES

In his experience, Burack (2014) suggests introducing a reflective practice in the very first course meeting. After reviewing the syllabus, he invites students to silently reflect on what drew them to the subject area, and to reflect on their learning intentions for the course. By establishing the value of silence and contemplation right at the beginning of class, a potentially deeper sense of collective connection to the self and to the other, including a shared educational journey, may arise. Interestingly, an implicit message is also conveyed: the value in connecting deeply with personal thoughts, feelings, and perceptions before sharing with others.

HOW TO INTEGRATE MINDFULNESS WITH MORE CONVENTIONAL PEDAGOGIES

Throughout his career, Burack (1999) has integrated contemplative practices into more conventional pedagogies such as lecture, discussion, debate, oral presentation, and creative exploration. By beginning with a more didactic approach, students are given the option to contemplate one of the concepts, issues, or ideas that were discussed with a minute or two of silent freewriting or freedrawing to record their experiences. Optional sharing in pairs, small groups, and with the full class, is available. He suggests that this movement from inner experience and silent expression to various levels of interpersonal and intrapersonal communication mirrors and reinforces the dialogical processes of teaching and learning. The discursive process of dialogue in dyad and the integrative interpersonal and intrapersonal attunement anchors them to the everyday experience of themselves and the world (Hanson & Mendius, 2009; Siegel, 2007).

In more mainstream courses, Burack (2014) uses contemplative practices to support intersections and connections to course concepts, theories, methods, and findings as they relate to individualized experiences. By inviting students to contemplate an experience that reflects the topic under consideration, like social attributions, prejudice, or stereotypes, a critical reflective period begins. This contemplation can be their own personal experience, their observation of others' experiences, or their observation of broader societal phenomena. For example, in a unit on prejudice, students are invited to observe their prejudices and to notice the subtle ways in which their beliefs and biases enter into their perceptions and behavior. This type of critical inquiry can develop a more mindful awareness about the attitudes and judgments they form of others and, in some cases, to be more respectful toward individuals and groups who do not share their views and values.

Burack (2014) also utilizes contemplative exercises to decipher students' initial holistic understanding of the course subject matter. This exercise produces a brief survey of the spectrum of perspectives present in the room, as well as a baseline from which to examine the subsequent impact of the course material on that range of perspectives. For example, in a diversity course, students would reflect on their understanding of diversity in contemporary society. A second contemplation would evoke their understanding of their own inherent diversity or diversities. At the end of the course, the two contemplations are repeated, and students have a chance to discuss how their understandings of these concepts have evolved.

HOW TO MAINTAIN SAFETY AND INSTRUCTOR EXPERIENCE, KNOWLEDGE, AND SKILL

An important consideration of Burack's (2014) practice is the creation and maintenance of places which respect the safety and well-being of students. It is important to recognize that contemplative practices are powerful and must be thoughtfully, sensitively, and skillfully introduced. Many mindfulness practitioners recognized that while brief, simple contemplations of ideas, texts, questions, or images can be effectively conducted by many educators, the extensive use of contemplation in educational contexts should be reserved for skilled practitioners with a background in Western counseling approaches (Berila, 2014; Cullen, 2011; Germer, 2005; Ragoonaden, 2017). If contemplative practices are mishandled, trauma induced memories can emerge suddenly and swiftly providing little or no recourse for the teacher or the student (Germer, 2005; Wilber, 1997). Disturbing reactions can be triggered when students have loose psychological boundaries or insufficient ego strength, or when the contemplations are too deep and prolonged or focus too intensively on students' unconscious material. While this is not often discussed in the literature, an unexperienced instructor can unintentionally thwart the perceived positive impact of the practices. The damage done can be minor or major, temporary or permanent.

In anticipation of potential issues, at the beginning of each course, Burack (2014) explains that all contemplations are voluntary. None of the informal or formal practices are required components:

> As always, this practice is completely voluntary. Only participate if you feel comfortable and prepared to do so; there is no problem at all with not participating. (p. 43).

In cases where students experience difficulties, he insists:

> Stop doing the contemplation if you experience discomfort or agitation that you feel you cannot handle—and immediately open your eyes. (p. 44).

Students who are having an especially difficult time are invited to inform the professor immediately. In this situation, they are encouraged to do some freewriting or to do whatever silent reflection they find beneficial.

Lastly, Burack (2014) advises limiting the frequency, length, and type of contemplation introduced into coursework. He emphasizes the importance of balancing mindful practices with other pedagogical practices and discourages the former to dominate classroom time. Generally, his contemplative practices are between two to ten minutes in duration with the typical contemplation ranges of around five minutes.

HOW TO MAINTAIN THE SEPARATION OF CHURCH AND STATE

Burack (2014) recognizes the controversial nature of introducing contemplative practices in higher education. Acknowledging that contemplative practices arose out of long held spiritual practices in the East, the West, including Indigenous epistemologies, resistance to mindfulness initiatives in educational contexts can be traced to the historical tenets originating in Eastern contemplative traditions, specifically Buddhist philosophic and spiritual traditions. In this contemporary age with a focus on secular mindfulness, he emphasizes the importance of knowing the history and the discourse of the philosophical, religious, medical, and psychological mindfulness practices (McCown, Reibel, & Mecozzi, 2010).

STRESS MANAGEMENT AND RESILIENCY TECHNIQUES (SMARTEDUCATION)

Respecting the West's focus on the separation of Church and State, a number of secular-based mindfulness programs have emerged. On a purely secular level, mindfulness has entered into contemporary consciousness through the work of Jon Kabat-Zinn (PhD) who adapted his own Buddhist meditation practice and yoga practice for his clinical patients. Named Mindfulness-Based Stress Reduction (MBSR), this clinical intervention was designed for cancer patients dealing with intense pain and suffering. Forty years of research on MBSR has demonstrated that this course of action provides benefits in a number of areas like anxiety, depression, chronic pain, immune system function, heart disease, substance abuse, eating disorders, and improving attention skills (Davidson et al., 2003; Greeson, 2009; Ludwig & Kabat-Zinn, 2008). More recently research has offered compelling evidence to support the use of mindfulness practices in a variety of professional and educational contexts. Scientific, peer-reviewed studies have shown that mindfulness training develops one's concentration, attention, executive function (planning, decision making, and impulse control), emotional balance, pro-social behavior, compassionate action, and promotes mental well-being (Mackenzie, 2015). This new wave of research has had many implications for the field of education, specifically as it relates to sustainable and holistic approaches to well-being for educators and their students.

SMARTEDUCATION

The evidence-based nature of regular practice of mindfulness-based initiatives has demonstrated the potential to revitalize purpose, improve achievement, and to foster positive interpersonal and intrapersonal attunement, communication and relationships (Ragoonaden, 2015; 2017). Following forty years of research, an adaptation of MBSR was conceptualized, developed and operationalized by the University of British Columbia (UBC) in 2013 (Ragoonaden, 2017). Based on MBSR, smartEducation (Stress Management and Resiliency Techniques) is a mindfulness-based professional learning initiative positioned in a teacher education program at UBC's Okanagan campus. Following similar evidence-based initiatives of mindfulness in education, the secular smartEducation curriculum is comprised of nine sessions introducing awareness, movement, visualizations, and meditations. This renewal program supports the development of self-care techniques to cultivate personal and professional resilience through a greater understanding and control of breath, movement, and the physiology of emotions. The twenty-hour program consists of eight two-hour sessions and a four-hour silent retreat. The mindfulness-based initiative that is smartEducation shows promising results, suggesting that this enterprise may be effective as professional learning supporting preservice teacher candidates as they confront some of the stresses inherent in the teaching profession. While also supporting teacher well-being, the mindfulness skills developed in a professional learning oriented course like smartEducation can act as an important component of the prosocial classroom, ensuring the emergence of a culture of learning for all students. Emerging research exploring the bidirectional relationship between classroom improvement and student improvement emphasizes how teacher social-emotional competence relates to both classroom climate and student outcomes (Jennings et al., 2011; Benn et al., 2012; Roeser et al., 2012).

As a smartEducation facilitator, while leading some of the mindfulness practices, I was able to observe participants' willingness, unwillingness, and in some cases, inability, to come to a self-reflective state. Being present with one's thoughts, emotions, and sensations, is often challenging. In most cases, I would begin the course with a purposeful embodied practice, using mindful movement to prepare the mind, heart, and body for the practices. In particular, the concept of observing one's self in a nonjudgmental way seemed to be beneficial. I did notice that there was no one way in which participants came to this state. As the course progressed, participants found their own way to become present and settling into their space.

In contexts where the professor is leading diversity-related discussions, skills acquired through informal and formal mindfulness practices can increase teachers' sense of well-being and teaching self-efficacy, as well as their ability to manage classroom behavior and establish and maintain supportive relationships with students. By engaging in this type of critical self-inquiry, professors can invite students to more fully integrate, rather than compartmentalize, their experiences. In this way, students can become more present and aware of diverse perspectives and experiences. Ultimately, integrating these practices in thoughtful and intentional ways into university classrooms, particularly those that address topics of diversity and oppression, can allow for a deeper, more embodied, and transformative learning process. As Berila (2014) states, courses that deal with oppression and diversity can greatly benefit from contemplative practices, because they can help us unlearn the conditioned responses that uphold or result from systems of oppression.

RELATIONAL MINDFULNESS

Regarding educational contexts, Fulton (2005) proposes that mindfulness can build relational competence among educators and students when it is practised implicitly as part of one's professional way of being. Called relational mindfulness, Safran and Reading (2005) suggest that this is an approach inviting us to listen in depth to ourselves, to the other, and to the relational field between the self and the other. Within this context, relational mindfulness can be described as a deepening awareness of the present relational experience, with acceptance, where connection is described as the core of psychological well-being and is the essential quality of growth, fostering and healing relationships (Surrey, 2005). Coming back to the psychotherapeutic origins of secular mindfulness, the integration of mindfulness practices has the potential to assist educators to maintain equanimity in intense pedagogical environments, to support teachers' sense of well-being and teaching self-efficacy, as well as their ability to manage, establish, and maintain supportive and safe environments for students.

While research has demonstrated that mindfulness practices can support the development of environments where students learn how to respond calmly to unsettling and provocative discussions and to not escalate these behaviors by their own reactions (Burrows, 2011; Day, 2004; Jennings & Greenberg, 2009), a high degree of social and emotional competence is required in order to successfully negotiate the challenges of teaching diversity courses (Burrows, 2011; Jennings et al. 2011).

PEDAGOGIES OF SENSATION

It is of note that teaching and learning does not often focus on the mind-body connection, known as embodied learning. Mindfulness practices can become a valuable tool to help students more fully cultivate a sense of embodiment involving the intellectual, physical, and emotional facets of the self in the pedagogical experience. Embodied mindfulness practices can help students understand and regulate their own intellectual and emotional reactions. This critical reflection allows time and space to comprehend why their reactions might differ from others, a critical step toward relational learning. Ellsworth (2005) calls this "pedagogies of sensations." Since embodied learning is generative, students become cocreators of knowledge by recognizing the body as a dynamic epistemological site. Consequently, as the various intellectual, emotional, or physical reactions emerge during meditation or yoga, teachers can help students make sense of them in the context of oppressive systems that have helped produce them. We can begin to see the reactions as more than just the typical "wandering mind," but instead as inevitable byproducts of living a particular identity in an inequitable society. The combination of students with differently positioned identities and bodies in a safe, open, and honest classroom is a vibrant and dialectical opportunity for co-creation.

To conclude this chapter, I refer back to Berila (2014) who presents the informal and formal mindfulness practices as platforms for students to frame their emotions and reactions, to learn to sit with them, and to develop thoughtful responses to diversity pedagogy. Understanding the complexities of integrating mindfulness practices in higher education, Burack (2014) identifies the main challenges focusing on when and how to introduce practices alongside conventional pedagogies, instructor experience, and creating safety in the course, and the controversy surrounding the spiritual aspects of the practices. In keeping with the West's preoccupation of maintaining the separation of the Church and the State, a number of secular mindfulness programs, like smartEducation, have emerged. Stress management and resiliency techniques (smartEducation) incorporates informal and formal practices aimed at self-reflection and self-improvement. This serves as exemplars of practices which can easily be integrated into university curricula. Author bell hooks's (1994) *engaged pedagogy* and Ellsworth's (2005) *pedagogy of sensation* focus on embodied conceptions of teaching and learning involving the intellectual, emotional, and physical selves. By reconceptualizing mindfulness practices as transformative pedagogies that seek to reenvision higher education for a more just, compassionate, and inclusive society, contemplative approaches can provide the time and space to consider democratic and equitable ways of being and ways of doing. As a caution, educators need to be fully informed of the historical and spiritual tenets of contemporary mindfulness practices and when possible, develop their own sustained practices. A general knowledge of psychotherapy, including Western counseling skills, would also be an asset when leading mindfulness practices in higher education (Germer, 2005). There is a particular negotiation that is required to create culturally safe spaces where students can reflect and discuss identity and otherness. The creation and sustained effort it takes to cultivate this space is wholly dependent on the educator's relationship with students, self, and the other. To support this pathway, Berila (2014) provides seminal suggestions for intentionally integrating contemplative practices:

1. Assume that someone in the room has suffered from trauma
2. Prepare the students for these possible reactions beforehand
3. Offer the option of opting out
4. Provide support resources
5. Hold the space

Based on Berila (2014) and Burack's (2014) recommendations, mindfulness practices incorporated into diversity pedagogy can provide pathways toward creating awareness of the self and society at large. The impact of self-awareness and awareness of others are essential ingredients in the progression toward equitable change ensuring success for all voices. Reflecting on personal and professional identity positions students to question and interrogate privilege, marginalization, and otherness in contemporary society. Within this context, taking the time to be present and to consider long held beliefs and assumptions can nurture and support teacher education students as they reflect and, potentially, unlearn the effects of systemic inequity, marginalization, and oppressive practices relating to gender, class, and race.

REFERENCES

Benn, R., Akiva, T., Arel, S., & Roeser, R. (2012). Mindfulness training effects for parents and educators of children with special needs. *Developmental Psychology, 48*(5), 1476–1487. doi:10.1037/a0027537.

Berila, B. (2014). Contemplating the effects of oppression: Integrating mindfulness into diversity classrooms. *Journal of Contemplative Inquiry (1)*, 55–58.

Burack, C. (1999). "Returning meditation to education." *Tikkun 14*(5), 41–46.

Burack, C. (2014). Responding to the challenges of a contemplative curriculum. *Journal of Contemplative Inquiry (1)*, 35–53.

Burrows, L. (2011). Relational mindfulness in education. *ENCOUNTER. Education for meaning and social justice. 24*(4), 24–29.

Cullen, M. (2011). "Mindfulness-based interventions: An emerging phenomenon." *Mindfulness 2*(3), 186–193.

Davidson, R. J., Kabat-Zinn, J., Schumacher, J., Rosenkranz, M., Muller, D., Santorelli, S., et al. (2003). Alterations in brain and immune function produced by mindfulness meditation. *Psychosomatic Medicine 65*, 4, 564–570.

Day, C. (2004). *A passion for teaching*. UK. Routledge/Falmer.

Ellsworth, E. (2005). *Places of learning: Media, architecture, and pedagogy*. New York: Routledge.

Freire, P. (2013). *Education for critical consciousness*. New York: Bloomsbury Academic.

Fulton, P. 2005. Mindfulness as clinical training. In *Mindfulness and psychotherapy*, edited by C. Germer, R. Siegal, & P. Fulton. New York: Guildford Press.

Germer, C. K. (2005). Teaching mindfulness in therapy. In C. K. Germer, R. D. Siegel, & P. R. Fulton (Eds.), *Mindfulness and Psychotherapy* (pp. 113–129). New York: Guilford Press.

Greeson, J. M. (2009). Mindfulness research update 2008. *Complementary Health Practice Review, 14*(1), 10–18.

Hanson, R. & Mendius, R. (2009). *Buddha's brain: The practical neuroscience of happiness, love, and wisdom*. Oakland, CA: New Harbinger.

hooks, b. (1994). *Teaching to transgress: Education as the practice of freedom*. New York: Routledge.

Jennings, P. A., & Greenberg, M. 2009. The prosocial classroom: Teacher social and emotional competence in relation to child and classroom outcomes. *Review of Educational Research 79*: 37–46.

Jennings, P., Snowberg, K., Coccia, M., & Greenberg, M. 2011. Improving classroom learning environments by cultivating awareness and resilience in education (CARE): Results of two pilot studies. *Journal of Classroom Interaction 46*(1): 37–46.

Kanpol, B. (1999). *Critical pedagogy: An introduction*. (2nd ed.). Westport, CT: Bergin & Garvey.

Kincheloe, J. (2004). *Critical pedagogy: Primer*. New York: Peter Lang Publishing.

Ladson-Billings, G. (1995). But that's just good teaching! The case for culturally relevant pedagogy. *Theory Into Practice, 34*(3), 159–165.

Ladson-Billings, G. (2000). Racialized discourses and ethnic epistemologies. N. Denzin and Y. Lincoln (Eds.). *Handbook of Qualitative Research*. (2nd ed.). Thousand Oaks, CA: Sage.

Ludwig, D. S., & Kabat-Zinn, J. (2008). Mindfulness in medicine. *Journal of the American Medical Association, 300*(11), 1350–1352.

Mackenzie, E. (2015). Mindfulness training. A transdisciplinary approach to assessing efficacy in education. In K. Ragoonaden (Ed.), *Mindful teaching and learning: Developing a pedagogy of well-being*. Lanham, MD: Lexington Books. An Imprint of Rowman Littlefield.

McCown, D., Reibel, D., & Micozzi, M. (2010). *Teaching mindfulness. A practical guide for clinicians and educators*. Philadelphia: Springer.

Owen-Smith, P. (2018). *The Contemplative mind in the scholarship of teaching and learning*. Bloomington, IN: Indiana University Press.

Ragoonaden, K. (2010). "Creating identity and culture in the great white north." *Citizenship, Social and Economic Education, 9*(1), 14–22.

Ragoonaden, K. (Ed.). (2015). *Mindful teaching and learning: Developing a pedagogy of well-being.* Lanham, MD: Lexington Books: A Division of Rowman & Littlefield.

Ragoonaden, K. (2017). "smartEducation: Developing stress management and resiliency techniques." *LEARNning Landscapes 10*(2), 241–255. http://www.learninglandscapes.ca/index.php/learnland/article/view/813.

Roeser, R. W., Skinner, E., Beers, J., & Jennings, P. A. (2012). Mindfulness training and teachers' professional development: An emerging area of research and practice. *Child Development Perspectives, 6*(2), 167–173.

Safran, J., & Reading, R. (2005). Mindfulness, metacommunication and affect regulation in psychoanalytic treatment. In *Mindfulness and psychotherapy,* edited by C. Germer., R. Siegal, and P. Fulton. New York: Guildford.

Sheets, R. H. (2005). *Diversity pedagogy: Examining the role of culture in the teaching-learning process.* Boston: Allyn & Bacon.

Siegel, D. (2007). *The brain in the mindful brain: Reflection and attunement in the cultivation of well-being.* New York: W. W. Norton and Co.

Surrey, J. (2005). Relational psychotherapy, relational mindfulness. In *Mindfulness and psychotherapy,* edited by C. Germer, R. Siegal, and P. Fulton. New York: Guildford.

Tagore, R. (1929). Ideals of Education. *The Visva-Bharati Quarterly* (April–July), 73–74.

Wilber, K. (1997). *The eye of spirit: An integral vision for a world gone slightly mad.* Boston: Shambhala.

Williams, M. T. (2013). Can racism cause PTSD? Implications for DSM-5. *Psychology Today.* Retrieved from http://www.psychologytoday.com/blog/culturally-speaking/201305/can-racism-cause-ptsd-implications-dsm-5.

Chapter Three

Mindfulness and Relational Knowing

An International Novice Teacher Educator's Approach to Teaching Social Justice

Yumei Li

Since the early twenty-first century, the demographics of the United States and the international world have changed tremendously with globalization (Shapiro, 2000). These changes and sociocultural developments require the infusion of multicultural education with a social justice orientation into teacher education curriculum, in terms of how best to prepare teachers for their complex work in increasingly global societies facing persistent inequities in educational success (e.g., Banks, 2015; Cochran-Smith, 2004; Gay, 2004; Pugachl, Gomez-Najarro, & Matewos, 2018).

The need for a multicultural curriculum and practice to prepare student teachers, also poses challenges to teacher educators, who are the central driving force of the ongoing process of learning, development, and change (Loughran, 2014). The challenges are particularly striking for novice teacher educators when they are in the middle of a professional transitioning and when the path to becoming a teacher educator is influenced by their prior identities and ability to construct a new professional identity as a developing teacher educator (Williams, Ritter, & Bullock, 2012). Therefore, it is important for novice teacher educators to first understand what constitutes their professional identity, social identity, and multiple other identities when beginning this process of becoming a teacher educator (Pugachl, Gomez-Najarro, & Matewos, 2018). They also need to think consciously about their role as teacher educators and engage in a critique of their own teaching practice with more conscious links to the programs in which they teach (Zeichner, 2005).

As a novice teacher educator and an international doctoral student, I have experienced the social and academic challenges faced by many international students in the United States (e.g., Le, LaCost, & Wismer, 2016; Mukminin & McMahon, 2013; Zhang, 2016), together with the pressure of becoming a teacher educator as a doctoral student due to the dual role and responsibilities (e.g., Abell, Rogers, Hanuscin, Lee, & Gagnon, 2009; Dinkelman, 2011; Feldman et al., 1998; Goodwin et. al, 2014). This chapter offers a personal narrative of how I navigated these challenges in teaching social justice in a teacher education program at the University of Houston in the past three years through a mindful and relational approach. This social education course is required for preservice teachers who will teach in early childhood and elementary schools in the United States. The chapter first shares my experiences and understanding of mindful and relational approaches to education from a cross cultural perspective. It then frames my experiences around three characters of relational teacher approaches proposed by Kitchen (2005a, 2005b), using evidence to exemplify how I approached the tensions in teaching social justice when both these preservice teachers and myself were grappling with these societal issues, and when I was experiencing the challenges as an international doctoral student in the United States. At the end of the chapter, I offer my understanding of teaching social justice through a mindful and relational approach, together with my thoughts about becoming an international teacher educator.

A PERSONAL NARRATIVE OF MINDFULNESS AND RELATIONAL KNOWING

My understanding of mindfulness and relational knowing is deeply rooted in traditional Chinese culture, which has developed into a united system of three streams of thought with Confucianism at the center supported by Daoism and Buddhism (Goossaert, 2005). Growing up in Confucian culture, I have been inculcated with the sense of moral responsibilities and the importance of reflective practices in becoming a whole person (Waley, 2012). Also, mindfulness plays a critical role in Chinese Buddhism, a religion that has existed in China for thousands of years and emphasized inner peace of a person (Jones-Smith, 2012; Kuan, 2008). As a temple visitor from an early age, I was greatly impressed by Buddhists' serenity meditation practices as a means to generate inner awakening for liberation (Kabat-Zinn, 2003). In addition, the search for inner peace and harmony between human and nature is the major theme in Chinese Daoism, explicated in *Tao Te Ching* (Hinton, 2015), a Chinese classic text written by the sixth-century BC sage Laozi. It also emphasizes naturalness, simplicity, and humility. This inner peace of an individual is relational in nature and could only be achieved through an integral harmonious relationship between individuals and their surrounding environment, and among humans in society.

From the pedagogical perspective, good teaching lies in good relations between the instructor and the student. In Confucianism, a good teacher is a helpful friend at the same time (良师益友). Having taught at universities in China and the United States for fourteen years, I am well aware of the importance of relating to my students in order to facilitate their learning in a more effective way. This reciprocal growth between students and instructor and the emphasis on humility are also articulated in *The Analects*. The Master said, "When I walk along with two others, they may serve me as my teachers. I will select their good qualities and follow them, their bad qualities and avoid them (三人行，必有我师焉；择其善者而从之，其不善者而改之)" (Waley, 2012).

My culturally-oriented understanding of mindfulness and relational pedagogies was deepened when I was exposed to interpretations offered by other scholars from a critical perspective (e.g., Dewey, 1933, 1938; Freire, 1993; Kitchen, 2005a; Langer, 1997; Ragoonaden, 2016; Stanley, 2012). This deepened understanding is based in interactive, attentive, and social justice-oriented praxis and inquiry. Mindfulness indicates retreats and meditation from some parts of society or interaction with others in order to potentially reevaluate it as we are redirecting our attention inwards to examine previous occurrences in the outer social world (Stanley, 2012). It is an engaged awareness by cultivating a critically distant stance toward the status quo of society and social values and encouraging the participant to experience control by shifting between these perspectives (Hanh, 2016). The knower is encouraged to step back and reflect on solutions and outcomes to determine deeper meaning within context (Langer, 1997). Mindfulness and relational approach are intertwined as mindfulness is a way of paying attention to whatever is happening in consciousness with a sharp discernment and focus. From a relational perspective, the practice of mindfulness is socially shared and contingent and only intelligible within on-going relationships of meaning-making, and it only makes sense within relational contexts, in the space between us and in our on-going activities and encounters with one another (Stanley, 2012).

Relational teacher education (Kitchen, 2005a; 2005b), a reciprocal approach to enabling teacher growth, also builds from the realization that we know in relationship to others and we grow together from the relationships. In order to relate, educators need to be mindful and create an internal self-reflection that enables a pause between our gut reactions and our external responses (Rendon, 2014). As an international novice teacher educator exposed to the interrelated Eastern and Western traditions, I employ self-reflection to examine my own positionality in society and my role in power systems (Schon, 1983; 1987; John Dewey, 1933). Self-reflection also allows me to relate to preservice teachers in exploring societal issues in education. This constant positioning and repositioning of myself in the course also presents me an organic and emergent frame to situate my professional development within (Ragoonaden, 2016).

METHODOLOGY

This chapter employs self-study methodology to provoke, challenge, and illuminate (Bullough & Pinnegar, 2001) my mindful and relational approach to teaching social justice in a teacher education program at a university in the mid-southern United States. Since self-study is founded upon the belief that teaching is partly an autobiographical act, I examine my self-knowledge of social education and reflect on my interaction with preservice teachers in order to seek an alternate rhetoric to improve practice (Samaras, Hicks, & Berger, 2004). This self-knowledge also provides me with an opportunity to have a big view of the educational landscape (Clandinin & Connelly, 2004) and understand that the individually important questions of practice is also related to the larger education community (Pinnegar & Russell, 1995). Through self-study approach, educators can examine self-knowing and professional identity formation in their practice and its impact on student learning. The holistic approach to personal and professional explorations offers me a natural pathway toward integrating and interconnecting principles of concepts of mindfulness and well-being into educational practice. An increasingly acute sense of my stance in the professional world and my critical dialogue and reflective practices with preservice teachers in the process of coming to know and understand (Pinnegar, Hamilton, & Fitzgerald, 2010) have laid the bedrock for this self-study research. The process of self-study research could present an opportunity for me to recognize different aspects of my shifting professional identity, my understanding of social justice in education, and its impact on preservice teachers' development (Allen, Rogers & Borowski, 2016).

The major sources of data for this chapter are my own narrative of entering teacher education, the teaching artifacts I collected concerning the course, and my personal journal documenting my experiences and thoughts assuming the role as an international teacher educator. Artifacts I have collected during my three teaching years include assignments, correspondence, class discussions and course evaluations from preservice teachers. My experiences and thoughts in assuming the role as a novice teacher educator were mainly documented in my eleven-entry journal in fall 2016, the semester I began my practice as a teacher educator. I started journaling from the second week and kept a journal almost every week to record some of the conversations and my thoughts. During subsequent semesters, I jotted down my thoughts infrequently and had seven journal entries in total. Through reading and rereading journal entries, along with critical conversations with mentors, I identified critical tensions in teaching social justice, especially teaching controversial issues like race and religion. Another theme that stood out was my own feelings in assuming the role, from initial anxiety and nervousness to gradual acculturation into this role with a deeper understanding of the cultural and educational context in the United States and a strong desire to teach social justice on an international landscape. Using these tensions and thoughts as the starting point, I searched supporting evidence from the teaching artifacts I collected. While this chapter is not focusing on preservice teachers' understanding of social justice, attention to preservice teachers' data sources is intended to inform questions about my own teaching practice.

I employ three of the seven characteristics of relational teacher education developed by Kitchen (2005a) as a framework for this chapter to exemplify how I approached those tensions in my teaching and my changing perspectives in teaching social justice as an international novice teacher educator. Relational teacher education "is a reciprocal approach to enabling teacher growth that builds from the realization that we know in relationship to others." The three characters of RTE used in this chapter are: understanding one's own personal practical knowledge; improving one's practice in teacher education; and receptivity to growing in relationship.

UNDERSTANDING MY PERSONAL PRACTICAL KNOWLEDGE

My journey as a teacher educator began in the fall semester of 2016 when I was assigned to teach a Social Education course to preservice teachers in the university's teacher education program. It was my third year of learning in a PhD program and staying in the United States.

Before I came to the United States for doctoral studies, I had perceived the United States as a nation of freedom, of rich resources and wealth for all its people. Although I have read about its history as one of invasion and exploitation, my exposure to movies and other media has convinced me that today's United States has moved beyond poverty or race. However, this perception of the United States as a country of wealth and equity for all was gradually challenged during my stay on this foreign land. Discussions with other fellow doctoral students on poverty, inequity, and other societal ills have opened my eyes to issues I was not aware of previously. The unequal educational resources allocated in different districts, homeless people wandering on the street and living under bridges, and media reports about the controversy between people of different backgrounds, all these presented different pictures of the United States to me.

I began my reflection when I was confronted with various perspectives about education and grappled to understand the societal problems permeating the increasingly diverse and challenging world. It was also my attempt to connect to my fellow doctoral students when I sometimes felt overwhelmed by the broad topics covered in our doctoral classes and fell far behind in the pace and tone of the discussion.

In "Rethinking Education through a Self-Study: An International Doctoral Student's Narrative" (Li, 2018), I described the culture shock I experienced during our early stage of staying in the United States. In order to connect and understand, I reexamined my story as a student from rural China and my experience as an international student in the United States. As an international doctoral student who stepped out of rural poverty in China, my reflection reminded me of the majority of rural children who were underserved in China's educational system. Advocating for individual hard efforts is one thing; it is equally, if not more, important to leverage the platform for children from disadvantaged backgrounds, taking the welfare for all into consideration. This examination of my own international background provided a platform to connect with other international doctoral students who were also trying to understand the different narratives of the society. It also offered me a venue to resonate with domestic doctoral students when they expressed their feeling of being marginalized and their desire to have their narrative heard by the society.

While gradually coming to understand these social issues in education, I considered it a great challenge to teach these issues to a group of preservice teachers, who were from diverse ethnic groups in the United States. My hesitation also came from my uncertainty of how these future preservice teachers would see me as their instructor. I did not share their educational or social backgrounds, and still need to understand where they came from.

I turned to my doctoral advisor, who introduced me to another professor. This professor has taught the course for several years and became my mentor throughout my teaching of this course. Every week, I would meet with her to discuss lesson plans for the class. I also shared my class dynamics and my thoughts with her and my advisor and received their feedback. During my teaching, I was constantly trying to position myself in the course and see how my role as an instructor could contribute to this conversation. I wrote down my concern considering the difference between me as an international doctoral student and my mentor as an experienced teacher educator in the United States, after she offered to co-instruct with me in my first class:

> Another concern I had was the difference I saw between my mentor and myself. As a doctoral student, I considered my own experience of learning to teach as apprenticeship, a journey I would embark on alongside my continuous learning from my mentors. My mentor has taught the course for several years.

> She is eloquent, compassionate, and she is a White American. These differences stood out when she kindly offered to help me in my first class, when she took over the conversations with these preservice teachers, developed their ideas, and resonated very well with them. I knew I had a lot to catch up. (Journal, August 31, 2016)

My desire to become a better teacher educator in social justice prompts me to do the same kind of reflection I asked preservice teachers to do in order to make sense of my own experiences (Zeichner, 2005). Being aware of the criticism of the disjuncture between the rhetoric and reality of social justice education (Dunn, 2016), I was in a constant search for my authentic voice and thoughts by revisiting my personal practical knowledge (Clandinin & Connelly, 1992), or tacit knowledge (Polanyi, 2015). Kitchen (2005a) has also highlighted the importance of looking back at one's own experience to gain self-understanding and establish authentic relationship to bridge classroom teaching practice and theory. The question that drove me into my inquiry is: How can I overcome my anxiety as an international novice teacher educator and invite the preservice teachers on the joint journey to uphold social justice commitments with genuine realization of inequity, acceptance of differences, and social action for change?

While taking a mindful stance to examine my own stories helped me connect to other fellow doctoral students, I utilize the same strategy as a teacher educator to relate to preservice teachers in my class.

IMPROVING MY PRACTICE AS A TEACHER EDUCATOR: MINDFUL OF CLASS DYNAMICS

The University of Houston where I studied and taught is located in the United States and has boasted great ethnic diversity among its students. According to its official report, students in the fall semester of 2018 at the university are Hispanics (31.8 percent), Whites (24.6 percent), Asian Americans (20.7 percent), African Americans (9.7 percent), and other ethnicities. My classes benefitted from this diversity and were always comprised of students from different ethnic groups. While exposure to differences has the potential to promote understanding, clash of opinions can occur as a result of our own different backgrounds and ways of knowing.

My stories of coming to understand as an international student helped me empathize with preservice teachers in my class when they expressed their sense of disconnection with people from other backgrounds. Our understanding of the world is dependent upon where we come from and who we are at the time. In order for the "background awareness" (Freire, 2000) to happen in my class, I used dialogue to explore our differences and commonalities. In addition, reflective writings were employed to continue the conversation.

Using Dialogic Inquiry to Locate Our Care Despite Differences

The value of dialogue in progressive education has long been recognized for its potential to be a transformative tool in the teaching of social justice through reciprocity and respect (Alexander, 2006; Burbules, 1993; Dewey, 1916; Freire, 2000). Through dialogic inquiry, ideas are shared by teachers and students on a reciprocal basis. As the goal of our Social Education course is to bring preservice teachers to an awareness of the inequity in society and develop an understanding and acceptance of differences between each other, dialogue is employed as one of the major instructional tools. In order for the dialogue to address real context issues, the course offers critical readings, videos, community investigations, and hands-on activities for preservice teachers to see the effects of these critical issues on a larger landscape of education. Being mindful of preservice teachers' feedback and engaging them in continuing dialogue was one of the strategies employed during my teaching practices to understand the mixed emotions and responses toward some critical issues in current society.

In order for preservice teachers to have effective discussion on religions, we first arranged for a class visit to a mosque. Knowing that very few preservice teachers in my class practice this religion, we chose a mosque with a purpose to understand differences and debunk the Islamophobia rampant in current society. This visit was led by a guide who went into details about what Islam is and their practices of the religion. After this visit, our class discussions were focused on the similarities and differences between religions by sharing preservice teachers' own religious beliefs and their thoughts about the visit. The majority agreed that despite all those differences in practices, all religions put an emphasis on love and caring for each other. Many also expressed their deeper understanding of a religion they have never taken the effort to explore. However, we also received some expressions of concern from the discussions. I put some of my surprising findings in the journal:

> When it came to religion, I was shocked when one student remarked that she was, and still is, scared that not believing in God would end her up in hell. This fear is something I have not really thought about. My school education in China has never seriously touched upon religions when the government is advocating for atheism. My understanding of Buddhism or Daoism does not have the concept of one God either. (Journal, September 30, 2016)

This also led me to think about the possible reasons why people are afraid of coming out of their confines. We are now living in a culture of fear exacerbated by the media in a fearmongering sociopolitical climate (Glassner, 2010). Having dialogue with people from different backgrounds can help us to locate the source of our fear and extend our care for each other.

Dialogue also brought us to an examination of where our conscious or unconscious bias came from. When preservice teachers were sharing their own religious beliefs with their peers, one of them stated that she found it unacceptable that women were less valued "by some specific religion." I questioned whether the expressions of devaluing women were present in many scripts of different religions and various social practices. She contemplated for a short while, and then went on to explain that although her religion (Catholicism) also had such expressions, it was written in old times and should be interpreted by its disciples in a new way (Class conversation, October 1, 2018). This led to our discussion of whether we could, or were willing to, extend our new interpretation for other religions, and realize many people tend to see the good virtues advocated for in their religion while defining people of other religions or cultures by the values considered deviant from their own.

In another class on religion, one preservice teacher explained that her religious belief has taught her values not consistent with those of the Lesbian, Gay, Bisexual, and Transgender community. Therefore, she found it hard to understand people from the community. While we were continuing the conversation, she mentioned that her uncle was gay, and she loved him and believed he was not defined by his gay identity (Class conversation, October 5, 2016). Her seemingly contradictory remarks reminded me of the complexities of human emotions and the possibility of extending "an ethic of care for the world" (Arendt, 1970). Our dialogue brought her to a further thought about her stance in treating people different from herself and the possibility of an alternative approach of acceptance.

Despite our individual or cultural differences, most cultures recommend civility, kindness to strangers, and honesty in interactions. However, we might embrace the differences of our very close family or friends, but we find it hard to accept differences from people we know nothing or little about, or strangers (Bateson, 2001). Dialogue brought preservice teachers and myself to an awareness of our differences in understanding our society and people from different backgrounds. They also serve as a tool for us to extend our care toward each other as equal human beings. However, while in-class dialogue can serve as an immediate approach to bring different perspectives together, the open confrontation risks shunning some preservice teachers from participation. When confronted with evidence of inequity that challenges our identities, we often respond with resistance in the form of silence, withdrawal, anger, or argumentation (Sensoy & DiAngelo, 2017). In this case, reflective journals extended our conversations when preservice teachers were reluctant to speak out for fear of encountering backlash.

Using Reflective Writing to Continue the Conversation

As an educator and an international doctoral student from a foreign country, I knew the feeling of being ignored and I experienced the fear of being rebuked for not being "on the same page" with others. While I expect every preservice teacher to be vocal participants in our discussion, I believe vocal can come both in oral and written forms. Reflective journals have proved to be another effective channel to communicate with my preservice teachers in order to continue the conversation unfinished in class, and to hear the words unsaid. A lot of times, preservice teachers will reexamine their thoughts and write down what they have failed to express in class or have not taken the time to consider.

When we examined the issue of white privilege, we used bell hooks's "Talking Race and Racism" (2003) as the reading material to start with and received very emotional feedback from the preservice teachers. I recorded the heated situation and resistance in my class:

> When it comes to race and white supremacy, bell hooks' article has got many white people on nerve. At least two have claimed that it was very hard for them to accept the "personal attack" as "this black woman was calling names and out of sense." Another preservice teacher just said it was interesting that this woman could connect everything to white supremacy when sometimes it has nothing to do with race. However, people of color loved her article and claimed that she has taken the words out of their mouth. Some students chose to remain silent throughout the discussion. How can I facilitate this conversation with people taking opposite sides and some keeping silent? (Journal, October 7, 2016)

In order to continue this conversation, I asked preservice teachers to reflect on their thoughts about personal biases based on their personal experiences and our class discussion. In their reflective writing, one white preservice teacher shared the reasons why she kept silent during the class debate on white privilege:

> These peers were so adamant about their feelings I felt I should not speak up and give my opinions. I seem to do this a lot in these types of situations. One thing about the topic of racism people feel so adamant about what they are saying that there is no point in fighting what they are saying because it is rare they will change their minds. (Student Reflection, October 18, 2016)

Another Hispanic preservice teacher also sensed the tension in our class discussion on white privilege and offered her understanding of the reasons of resistance and the importance of recognizing diversity:

> Our class was incredibly uncomfortable talking about racism as they felt like white people were being attacked for being born white. Although I can understand that it may be hard to hear, it is important that the realization that people of color feel attacked quite often should be more well-known. People are often stuck inside their own bubble of privilege and do not realize that there is a world of diversity outside. . . . However, I feel like people should be more open in order to get different viewpoints across to gain a better understanding of people not in your own community. (Student Reflection, October 20, 2016)

These comments offered me another venue to see the real thoughts of preservice teachers in my class and drew me to a constant questioning of my own role in bringing different voices together (Cowhey, 2006). Realizing we can never expect to address this big issue in one conversation, I would always summarize comments from different sides without identifying those contributors and pick up the topic over and over, by connecting it to other topics like poverty and inequity throughout the semester. The purpose was to further the discussion and see how these controversial topics are interrelated and having an impact in education. This frequent revisit of our thoughts also offered us an opportunity to examine the sources of our resistance and anger, and in a way, to connect our emotional response to the larger social and institutional context (Sensoy & DiAngelo, 2017).

As a result of this constant sharing and reexamination of perspectives, perception did change in the case of some preservice teachers. In the end of the semester, the same white preservice teacher who wrote down her reluctance to speak up reconsidered the whole class conversations and shared her thoughts:

> Yes, sometimes we would get a little heated or uncomfortable with one another but, these are things we feel strongly about and that is important. As we become teachers and are in schools with other teachers we will need to be able to understand that everyone has a right to their own opinion in any matter and we need to be respectful of that . . . I also learned how serious the topic of racism is and that it needs to be discussed in a sensitive way. (Student Reflection, December 13, 2016)

When I think back about these interactions, I realized when it comes to controversial issues, suppression of any voice might not be the solution. A mindful and relational approach is to offer different venues for dissent and reaching for a consensus for the common good, with the understanding that it is through our engaged awareness and shifting between different perspectives that we could develop a better understanding of each other and the status quo of our society (Hanh, 2016). These encounters, in turn, also enhanced our relationship with each other.

Receptivity to Growing in Relationship

Kitchen (2005b) demonstrated how his receptivity to the personal practical knowledge and to the distinct needs of each student has deepened his understanding and enriched his ability to assist others. For me as an international novice teacher educator, I perceive receptivity as a necessary approach to positioning myself in the Social Education course, to understanding others, and to making myself understood in our mutual growth as educators. I reflected on my personal growth in teaching the class:

> It is already Week Nine. It would be hard to imagine that time has gone by so fast from the moment I felt nervous about the teaching appointment. Looking back at my teaching, I have learnt a lot from the communication between students, who are expressive, talented and interesting.
>
> Topics we addressed in class always brought me back to my own understanding and my educational and social upbringing in China. The cultures of China's minority ethnic groups were never clear to me, except for one statement in the textbook that China has 56 ethnic groups. This number is for examinations. History was taught in a way that we had no idea of how the other political party contributed to our country and the society. We only learn the narratives from the winners.
>
> So, what have I learned so far? An understanding that we are always immersed in the narrative of the mainstream society, no matter where we are from. In the meanwhile, the personalization of American undergraduate students is very important to me as I only knew them through movies, a lot of which turns out to be far removed from the everyday reality of students' life. My nervousness has gone away. My thoughts were more about how I can facilitate the discussion, relate our themes to their daily experiences, and connect them to the international landscape of education. (Journal, October 20, 2016)

As a result of these authentic interaction with preservice teachers in my class, they have developed greater cultural awareness and better recognized inequities in the society. At the same time, my attempt to position myself in this course has also offered them an example to see the difficulty of becoming an educator for social justice. The openness of who I am and where my worries and concern came from invited their resonance and a rethinking of their own experiences and perspectives. They also provided their favorable feedback in their final evaluation on my performance as their instructor. One preservice teacher commented:

> I enjoyed hearing about you and your ideas about who we are as Americans. I am proud of you to have battled your fears of teaching in a different setting. I applaud you for that. (Student reflection, December 12, 2016)

Another preservice teacher expressed the similar sentiment:

> You were telling us about how you were kind of nervous about how you would do as a teacher, but I think you did very well. . . . I like that you are from another perspective because you bring a new opinion to the table. You weren't from this country, so you don't necessarily have the same mindset as us. (Student reflection, December 13, 2016)

My concerns about my differences also offered preservice teachers a starting point to think about their own differences. One preservice teacher expressed how they acted as an impetus for her to reexamine her own unique identity as a minority woman with ADHD:

> Your transparency with your own linguistic and cultural differences motivated me to embrace my cultural and cognitive uniqueness. (Student reflection, December 9, 2017)

The favorable feedback has underscored the importance of receptivity in teaching social justice in teacher education. Instead of pretending to be the person who always knows, I was honest with them about my stories of coming to know and to understand, and about my uncertainties and receptivity of their perspectives and feedback. The growth in relationship comes with our being true to ourselves and to others, addressing our concerns in a way that we acknowledge our differences while still treating each other with respect.

CONCLUDING THOUGHTS

Taking a mindful stance to examine my own evolving understanding of social justice and of my teaching practice, I have overcome my anxiety of becoming an international teacher educator in the United States. Adopting a relational teacher education approach, I improved my teacher education practice in teaching social justice through dialogic inquiry and reflective writings. I also gleaned from the connection and bonded with preservice teachers in my classes when they sincerely and honestly shared and examined their own experiences and thoughts. At the same time, I also share Kitchen's (2020) worry about silent resistance from preservice teachers who do not have the same backgrounds and thoughts. While I strived to create a safe space for preservice teachers to share, I was also cautious about the balance I need to keep in order to engage preservice teachers in an effective discussion without evading the important/controversial issues in society.

I was constantly reminded of the necessity of being mindful of dissent in my teaching practices as I recalled a comment from one preservice teacher in my class. She was on the conservative side and very vocal about her own opinions. She explained that she wanted others to see "conservatives are not bad people but people who stick more to traditional values" (Class conversation, October 2, 2017). When we visited the mosque, she conveyed to me her concerns and could not accept our way of wearing a scarf to show respect to the religion. Her behavior also drew different comments from her classmates. One progressive preservice teacher stated her opinion in her reflective journal:

> I noticed that there was one student in the class who did not feel comfortable wearing a scarf and it made me very upset and angry at first. I did not understand why someone would deliberately be disrespectful in someone else's house of worship. However, after reflection, I realized that she was not trying to be disrespectful to their religion, but she was trying to respect her own religion without missing out on an opportunity to be informed on Islam. While it still slightly upset me, I understood that I needed to respect her religion as well as the Islam. (Student journal, October 13, 2017)

I was inspired by how this preservice teacher has become mindful of her own reactions and learned to relate to other fellow preservice teachers from different backgrounds. I shared my thoughts regarding her understanding:

> Thank you for offering your changing interpretations of our classmate not wearing a scarf at the Mosque.... Education is not just about educating people who are on the same side, but also about offering people from other backgrounds a platform to understand and develop tolerance.

As an international novice teacher educator, I experienced the nervousness and anxiety of learning and teaching what I have yet to understand and went through the fear of encountering backlash in my class. The relational and mindful approach enabled me to remain true to myself and my own cultural and educational backgrounds. A recognition of my own personal practical knowledge (Clandinin & Connelly, 2004) and myself as a lifelong learner (Cowhey, 2006) motivated me to invite preservice teachers in this joint journey to explore social justice in society and to examine ourselves. Dialogue and reflection, with reciprocity and respect, brought different perspectives together and helped to build up a bond and growing relationship with each other. To address social justice in education, our mindful meaning-making process and the desire to connect with each other and to care about each other as fellow human beings transcend our differences in nationality, ethnicity, language, or culture.

ACKNOWLEDGMENTS

I would like to thank Cameron White and Dustine Thomas for their mentorship throughout my teaching of this social education course. My thanks also go to editors of this book, Julian Kitchen and Karen Ragoonaden, for their very detailed and constructive feedback for me to improve the manuscript. I would also like to thank those preservice teachers who shared with me their different perspectives, without which this chapter could never come into shape.

REFERENCES

Abell, S. K., Rogers, M. A. P., Hanuscin, D. L., Lee, M. H., & Gagnon, M. J. (2009). Preparing the next generation of science teacher educators: A model for developing PCK for teaching science teachers. *Journal of Science Teacher Education, 20*(1), 77–93.

Alexander, R. (2006). *Towards dialogic teaching*. 3rd ed. Thirsk: Dialogos.

Allen, J., Rogers, M. P., & Borowski, R. (2016). "I am out of my comfort zone": Self-study of the struggle of adapting to the professional identity of a teacher educator. *Studying Teacher Education, 12*(3), 320–332. DOI: 10.1080/17425964.2016.1228048.

Arendt, H. (1970). *Men in dark times*. Fort Washington, PA: Harvest Books.

Banks, J. A. (2015). *Cultural diversity and education*. New York: Routledge.

Bateson, M. C. (2001). *Full circles overlapping lives: Culture and generation in transition*. New York: Ballantine Books.

Bullough Jr, R. V., & Pinnegar, S. (2001). Guidelines for quality in autobiographical forms of self-study research. *Educational Researcher, 30*(3), 13–21.

Burbules, N. C. (1993). *Dialogue in teaching—Theory and practice*. New York: Teachers College Press.

Clandinin, D. J., & Connelly, F. M. (1992). Teacher as curriculum maker. In P. Jackson (Ed.), *Handbook of curriculum* (pp. 363–461). New York: Macmillan.

Clandinin, D. J. & Connelly, F. M. (2004). Knowledge, narrative and self-study. In J. J. Loughran, M. L. Hamilton, V. K. LaBoskeyey, & J. Russel (Eds.), *International handbook of self-study of teaching and teacher education practices* (pp. 575–600). New York: Springer.

Cochran-Smith, M. (2004). *Walking the road: Race, diversity, and social justice in teacher education*. New York: Teachers College Press.

Cowhey, M. (2006). *Black ants and buddhists: Thinking critically and teaching differently in the primary grades*. Portsmouth, NH: Stenhouse Publishers.

Dewey, J. (1916). *Democracy and education*. Toronto: Collier-Macmillan.

Dewey, J. (1933). *How we think: A restatement of the reflective thinking to the educative process*. New York: Houghton Mifflin Company.

Dewey, J. (1938). *Education and experience*. New York: Collier Books.

Dinkelman, T. (2011) Forming a teacher educator identity: Uncertain standards, practice and relationships. *Journal of Education for Teaching, 37*(3), 309–323. DOI: 10.1080/02607476.2011.588020.

Dunn, A. H. (2016). "It's dangerous to be a scholar-activist these days": Becoming a teacher educator amidst the hydra of teacher education. *Teacher Education Quarterly, 43*(4), 3.

Feldman, A., Alibrandi, M., Capifali, E., Floyd, D., Gabriel, J., Hitchens, F., & Lucey, J. (1998). Looking at ourselves look at ourselves: An action research self-study of doctoral students' roles in teacher education programs. *Teacher Education Quarterly, 25*(3), 5–28.

Freire, P. (2000). *Pedagogy of the oppressed*. New York: Continuum.

Gay, G. (2004). The importance of multicultural education. In D. J. Flinders & S. J. Thornton (Eds.), *The curriculum studies reader*, pp. 315–320. Psychology Press.

Glassner, B. (2010). *The culture of fear: Why Americans are afraid of the wrong things: Crime, drugs, minorities, teen moms, killer kids, muta*. New York: Basic Books.

Goodwin, A. L., Smith, L., Souto-Manning, M., Cheruvu, R., Tan, M. Y., Reed, R., & Taveras, L. (2014). What should teacher educators know and be able to do? Perspectives from practicing teacher educators. *Journal of Teacher Education, 65*(4), 284–302.

Goossaert, V. (2005). Chinese religion: Popular religion. 2nd ed. In L. Jones (Ed.), *Encyclopedia of religion*, Vol. 3, pp. 1613–1621. Detroit: Macmillan Reference USA.
Hanh, T. N. (2016). *The miracle of mindfulness: An introduction to the practice of meditation*. Boston: Beacon Press.
Hinton, D. (Trans.). (2015). *Tao Te Ching*. Berkeley, CA: Counterpoint.
hooks, b. (2003). *Teaching community: A pedagogy of hope*. New York: Routledge.
Jones-Smith, E. (2012). *Theories of counseling and psychotherapy: An integrative approach*. Thousand Oaks, CA: Sage.
Kabat-Zinn, J. (2003). Mindfulness-based interventions in context: Past, present, and future. *Clinical Psychology: Science and Practice, 10*(2), 144–156.
Kitchen, J. (2005a). Looking backwards, moving forward: Understanding my narrative as a teacher educator. *Studying Teacher Education, 1*(1), 17–30.
Kitchen, J. (2005b). Conveying respect and empathy: Becoming a relational teacher educator. *Studying Teacher Education, 1*(2), 195–207.
Kitchen, J. (2020). A relational approach to social justice in teacher education. In J. Kitchen & Ragoonaden, K. (Eds.) *Mindful and relational approaches to social justice, equity, and diversity in teacher education* (pp. 13–29). Lanham, MD: Lexington Books.
Kuan, T. (2008). *Mindfulness in early Buddhism: New approaches through psychology and textual analysis of Pali, Chinese and Sanskrit sources*. New York, NY: Routledge.
Langer, E. J. (1997). *The power of mindful learning*. Cambridge, MA: Da Capo Press, Perseus Books.
Le, A. T., LaCost, B. Y., & Wismer, M. (2016). International female graduate students' experience at a Midwestern university: Sense of belonging and identity development. *Journal of International Students, 6*(1), 128–152.
Li, Y. (2018). Rethinking education through self-study: An international doctoral student's narrative. *Reflective Practice, 19* (4), 530–542. doi: 10.1080/14623943.2018.1538946.
Loughran, J. J. (2004). A history and context of self-study of teaching and teacher education practices. In J. J. Loughran, M. L. Hamilton, V. K. LaBoskeyey, & J. Russel (Eds.), *International handbook of self-study of teaching and teacher education practices*, pp. 7–40. New York: Springer.
Loughran, J. (2014). Professionally developing as a teacher educator. *Journal of Teacher Education, 65*, 271–283.
Mukminin, A., & McMahon, B. J. (2013). International graduate students' cross-cultural academic engagement: Stories of Indonesian doctoral students on an American campus. *The Qualitative Report, 18*, 1–19.
Pinnegar, S., Hamilton, M. L., & Fitzgerald, L. (2010). Guidance in being and becoming self-study of practice researchers. In *The Eighth International Conference on Self-Study of Teacher Education Practices*, pp. 203–206. Provo, UT: Brigham Young University.
Pinnegar, S., & Russell, T. (1995). Introduction: Self-study and living educational theory. *Teacher Education Quarterly, 22*(3), 5–9. Retrieved from https://www.jstor.org/stable/23475828?seq=1#page_scan_tab_contents.
Polanyi, M. (2015). *Personal knowledge: Towards a post-critical philosophy*. Chicago: University of Chicago Press.
Pugach, M. C., Gomez-Najarro, J., & Matewos, A. M. (2018). A review of identity in research on social justice in teacher education: What role for intersectionality? *Journal of Teacher Education, 00*(0)1–13.
Ragoonaden, K. (2016). Introduction. In K. Ragoonaden & S. Bullock (Eds.), *Mindfulness and critical friendship: A new perspective on professional development for educators* (pp. vii–xiv). Lanham, MD: Lexington Books.
Rendón, L. I. (2014). *Sentipensante (sensing/thinking) pedagogy: Educating for wholeness, social justice and liberation*. Sterling, VA: Stylus Publishing, LLC.
Samaras, A. P., Hicks, M. A., & Berger, J. G. (2004). Self-study through personal history. In J. J. Loughran, M. L. Hamilton, V. K. LaBoskey, and T. Russell (Eds.), *International handbook of self-study of teaching and teacher education practices* (pp. 905–942). Netherland: Springer.

Schon, D. A. (1983). *The reflective practitioner: How professionals think in action* (Vol. 5126). New York: Basic books.

Sensoy, O., & DiAngelo, R. (2017). *Is everyone really equal? An introduction to key concepts in social justice education.* New York: Teachers College Press.

Shapiro, S. (2000). Empowerment. In D. A. Dabbard (Ed.), *Knowledge and power in the global economy: Politics and the rhetoric of school reform* (pp. 103–110). Mahwah, NJ: Erlbaum.

Stanley, S. (2012). Mindfulness: Towards a critical relational perspective. *Social and Personality Psychology Compass, 6*(9), 631–641.

Waley, A. (Trans.). (2012). *The analects of Confucius.* London, UK: Routledge.

Williams, J., Ritter, J., & Bullock, S. M. (2012). Understanding the complexity of becoming a teacher educator: Experience, belonging, and practice within a professional learning community. *Studying Teacher Education, 8*(3), 245–260.

Zeichner, K. (2005). Becoming a teacher educator: A personal perspective. *Teaching and Teacher Education, 21*(2), 117–124.

Zhang, Y. L. (2016). International students in transition: Voices of Chinese doctoral students in a US research university. *Journal of International Students, 6*(1), 175–194.

Chapter Four

What Should Preservice Teachers Know about Race and Diversity? Exploring a Mindful and Critical Knowledge-Base

Benedicta Egbo

EDITORS' NOTE

In this article, Benedicta Egbo makes a case for disrupting the delegitimization of the cultural capital and habitus of students from minoritized and racialized populations. We acknowledge that this article was reprinted from Journal of Contemporary Issues in Education, Volume 6 (2) *with the permission of the author, who retains copyright. Egbo's seminal textbook,* Teaching for Diversity in Canadian Schools, 2nd Edition *(2019), widely used in teacher education programs, addresses teaching and learning for diversity and equity. Within the frameworks of critical pedagogy and critical race theory, she underscores the importance of preservice teachers developing informed knowledge bases about race and diversity. She addresses teachers' discomfort about engaging in sensitive issues and decries the resounding discourses of silence adopted by many well-intentioned educators. We posit that mindful practices exploring the location of identity and the positionality of self in society can counter the effects of dysconscious racism and mitigate the strong feelings of guilt reported by mainstream students. The development of this critical consciousness supported by reflective practices, like mindful inquiry, may lead to paradigm shifts and powerful transformative practices examining power and privilege in contemporary society.*

INTRODUCTION

Nearly all stakeholders in education agree that diversity is, and will likely remain a stable feature of life in Canadian classrooms. This means that those who teach will have to learn ways of addressing the issue even before they become active practitioners in the profession. Such training is critical since research and anecdotal evidence suggest that while teachers often embrace ameliorative educational policies and programs in theory this support rarely manifests in practice (Solomon & Levine-Rasky, 1996). Paradoxically, many teachers will spend the bulk of their career in racially and culturally mixed educational environments (Egbo, 2019; Solomon et al., 2005; Sheets, 2005; Milner, 2003). While some teacher education curricula address diversity-related issues, there is little explicit discussion of race and how it is implicated in the outcomes of education for particular groups of students. Pollock (2001) has described this failure to seriously engage the issue of race in schooling as the suppression of the very question we most want to ask in education. Similarly, Lund and Carr (2010) have noted that "[r]acialized identities are problematic and highly contested notions, and the topic of racism is not usually addressed openly in polite company" (p. 231). Ironically, it seems logical to assume that given the unprecedented demographic shifts in wider society, deep understanding of the concepts of race and diversity, and the trajectories between both constructs and teaching and learning, should feature prominently in teacher education programs.

This chapter explores a salient but often neglected area that all teacher educators and programs should engage with—the typology of knowledge about race and diversity that preservice teachers, as aspiring and mindful educators, require for successful teaching in twenty-first-century Canadian classrooms. The chapter proceeds from the assumption that teachers' worldviews and belief systems have significant influence on their practice and subsequently, on their interactions with students. Indeed, this particular assumption foregrounds a common starting point in some foundation courses in teacher education programs—the identification of students' teaching/philosophy of education. The chapter also assumes that if the resilience of racism and the delegitimization of the cultural capital (Bourdieu, 1991) of students from some segments of society are to be disrupted, it is critical that as future frontline educators, preservice teachers develop a critical knowledge-base about race and diversity.

THEORETICAL FRAMEWORK

The discussion in this chapter is underpinned by critical race theory (henceforth CRT). Although CRT has its roots in critical legal studies, its application to education increased significantly following the publication of Gloria Ladson-Billings and William Tate's (1995) influential article *Toward a Critical Race Theory of Education*. As an emergent paradigm for conceptualizing the trajectories between race and education, CRT acknowledges the centrality of race and focuses on how elements of racism and prejudice are embedded in society and social institutions such as schools. According to two of its ardent advocates, Solórzano and Yosso (2001, as cited in Milner, 2007, p. 390), CRT "challenges the dominant discourse on race and racism as it relates to education by examining how educational theory and practice are used to subordinate certain racial and ethnic groups." With an emphasis on how race as a social construct is grossly under-theorized in analyses that purport to deconstruct the workings of society and social institutions (Omi & Winant, 1993), CRT is committed to social justice and to the elimination of all forms of inequalities, especially those that are racially motivated.

With regards to educational knowledge, adherents of CRT argue that while race is commonly used to sustain inequality in schools and society, its "intellectual salience . . . has not been systematically employed in the analysis of educational inequality" (Ladson-Billings & Tate, 1995, p. 50; see also Zamudio, Russell, Rios, & Bridgeman, 2011). One question that is often asked within the Canadian context is whether or not race *really* matters. Many educational practitioners, scholars, and researchers have engaged the issue arguing that the recognition of the salience of race is a *sine qua non* in any attempt at improving experiences and educational outcomes for racialized students in Canadian schools (see, for example, Lund, 2011; Lund & Carr, 2010; McNeil, 2011; Schick, 2011; Carr, 2008; Dei et al., 2000). As Ghosh (2008) warns us, "[w]hile race does not have scientific validity, we must not underestimate its power as a social construct to affect people's lived experiences, their daily lives as well as their futures. Race is a very real concept in our social consciousness, and it has real world consequences" (p. 27). Similarly, Fleras and Elliott (2003) argue that even though Canadians are ambivalent about the concept, it will continue to matter in everyday life and public policy, "not because it is real, but because people respond as if it were real. Race matters not because people are inherently different or unequal, but because perceived differences may be manipulated as a basis for sorting out privilege and power" (p. 52). This phenomenon is quite evident in the findings of a study on the determinants of the labor market outcomes for the children of immigrants in Canada and in the United States recently released by Statistics Canada (March, 2011), which show that while second generation immigrants may have discernible educational advantage, on average, black Canadians earn less in the labor market than their white peers.

Even more worrisome, racism can be so pervasive in society that according to Tatum (1997) (as cited in Nieto & Bode, 2008) it becomes a persistent "smog in the air" which people cannot help but breathe in. This pervasiveness is indeed the nexus of the claims by proponents of CRT such as Milner (2007) who argues that:

> Race and racism are so ingrained in the fabric . . . of society that they become normalized. Individuals from various racial and ethnic backgrounds may find it difficult to even recognize the salience, permanence, effects, and outcomes of racism because race and racism are so deeply rooted and embedded in our ways and systems of knowing and experiencing life. (p. 390)

The situation takes a somewhat more complicated turn in Canada where social attitude surveys tend to portray the image of a more racially inclusive society than for instance, the United States. This complexity according to Skerrett (2008) means that:

> [While] [t]he existence of racial and ethnocultural discrimination in Canada is most keenly perceived and experienced by visible minority groups and immigrant visible minorities, who make up one half of Canada's total immigrant population . . . census data that demonstrate inclusive social attitudes and practices in relation to diversity adds complexity to Canada's social landscape which ethnic minorities most strongly perceive as a vertical mosaic. (p. 266)

This illusion of inclusion may be one of the reasons why, despite increasing diversity among student populations in Canada, the teaching force remains predominantly homogeneous—white, middle class, and monolingual. As a consequence, teachers, and a significant number of their students, view the world through lenses that sustain intractable difficulties that can only be resolved when a serious scrutiny of the role of race in reifying social injustice through education becomes an integral part of the discourse on Canadian diversity (Egbo, 2019; 2001; Ghosh, 2008; Ghosh & Abdi, 2013; James, 2003; Dei et. al., 2000, 1997).

PRESERVICE TEACHERS, IDEOLOGY AND KNOWLEDGE-BASE

The reasons why teachers may be reluctant to embrace progressive policies and programs remains a matter of contention. However, most writers agree on at least two plausible reasons—teachers' ideological stance on issues that are related to race and diversity and, teachers' discomfort with engaging such "sensitive issues." Teachers' ideological stance includes the denial of racism in society and the belief that the individual is the sole determinant of his or her own school success even though this meritocratic ideology that fails to take into account how schools contribute to inequality in society has long been discounted on empirical and practical grounds. In the same vein, the reluctance or refusal to engage the issue of race and diversity may be the result of an uncritical acceptance of the status quo. King (1991) refers to this tendency among teachers (and prospective teachers), especially those who have had little or no experience with people who are different from themselves, as dysconscious racism—a form of racism that tacitly accepts the norms and privileges of the dominant group based on "an *impaired* [emphasis in the original] consciousness or distorted way of thinking about race as compared to, for example, critical consciousness" (p. 135).

For the growing number of scholars and practitioners who have joined the clarion call for progressive changes in teacher education programs (e.g., Cochran-Smith, 2000, 2005; Sheets, 2005; Milner, 2003, 2007; Solomon et al., 2005; McNeil, 2011), the rationale for such an appeal transcends the issue of increasing diversity among students although that is important in and of itself. However, no less fundamental and important a reason is the need to reconceptualize preservice teachers' knowledge-base since the ideological orientations of novice teachers can serve as barriers to adopting transformative practices. For example, research has shown that there is a tendency among preservice teachers toward interpreting cultural difference among students as a problem rather than a resource (Delpit, 2006). Moreover, cultural or racial differences are often grouped with other types of differences such as learning differences, intelligences, personality types, and so forth (Levine-Rasky, 1998; Battiste, 2013; Egbo, 2019). While one must not minimize the importance of other indices of difference as integral aspects of diversity, differences involving race, culture and ethnicity require a different kind of knowledge-base that should be learned in training (Gay, 2010; Nieto & Bode, 2008; Milner, 2003).

In addition to perceiving differences as problematic, teacher candidates do not often understand the language, culture, or the particular circumstances of their diverse students nor do they understand how some school-based problems and inequalities are historically, socially, and politically constructed. Without a critical knowledge-base about race and diversity, this orientation toward orthodoxy means that preservice teachers will be less positioned to support and empower students from racialized backgrounds and may, indeed, attribute student underachievement where that is the case, to exclusively individual variables as Levine-Rasky (1998) asserts:

> it is prevalent amongst prospective teachers to persist in interpreting social difference and inequality through the lens of meritocracy in which success is directly related to individual achievement and talent irrespective of environmental or broader social factors such as racial discrimination, poverty unequal treatment in public institutions language barriers and other patterns of oppression. (pp. 90, 91)

Other researchers share Levine-Rasky's assertions that prospective teacher candidates typically adhere to conservative ideologies (Carr & Klassen,

1997; Solomon et al., 2005). For example, a study by Solomon et al. (2005), which investigated teacher candidates' perceptions of, and understanding of "Whiteness" and white privilege in Canadian society, found that candidates from different racial and cultural backgrounds have different perceptions of oppression and white privilege. Through a discourse analysis of students' responses to Peggy McIntosh's (1990) well known piece, "White Privilege," which unmasks the privileges that accrue to members of the dominant group, the researchers found a general tendency toward the denial of such privileges by candidates from dominant group backgrounds. People do indeed see and interpret social phenomena through lenses that are tinted by their social positioning. However, a dysconscious acceptance of the status quo exposes a far greater problem—an ideological stance that is based on taken-for-granted assumptions about power relations in society as well as limited familiarity with the burgeoning literature that points to the role of privilege in educational success.

Beyond orthodoxy, the denial of the possession of privilege and the uncritical acceptance of the status quo may also be associated with feelings of guilt among preservice students vis-à-vis racism and discrimination. The following journal entry by an undergraduate student in an education course (quoted in King, 1991) exemplifies the kind of guilt that some white preservice students experience when the issue of race is discussed in class:

> With some class discussions, readings and other media, there have been times that I feel guilty for being White which really infuriates me because no one should feel guilty for the color of their skin or ethnic background. Perhaps my feelings are actually a discomfort for the fact that others have been discriminated against all of their life [sic] because of their color and I have not. (p. 136)

No one should, of course, be made to feel guilty about their own identity. However, this discomfort (ideological or psychological) may be a contributing factor to why the issue of race and diversity is not given the discursive space it warrants in teacher education programs, which, in turn, limits preservice teachers' future potential to challenge undesirable educational policies and practices.

TOWARD A TRANSFORMATIVE AND MINDFUL KNOWLEDGE-BASE

So what should teacher candidates know about race and diversity for successful teaching in diverse contexts? In her discussion of strategies for teacher development and educational reform, Cochran-Smith (2005) calls for a grounded theory of teacher education for social change that:

Has the potential to help all teachers prepare students to live productive and ethical lives in an increasingly diverse society, to work actively for equity and against racism, and to contribute to a more just society. . . . [A] theory of teacher education for social change that begins with the premise that teaching and teacher education are political and intellectual as well as practical activities that occur within complex historical, economic and social contexts. (pp. 247, 248)

Toward this objective, Cochran-Smith identifies four critical questions that should guide policy makers in enacting progressive teacher education programs. These include (1) questions related to the kind of knowledge and interpretive frameworks that inform the work of progressive novice and seasoned teachers; (2) the ideological and political underpinnings of the work of novice and veteran teachers; (3) the constituents of the pedagogy and practice of teachers who teach for social change; and (4) questions related to the characteristics of preservice and in-service teacher education programs and professional development, respectively. In Cochran-Smith's account, what is needed in teacher education is a critical theory that is mindful of the trajectories between the structural, macro, and micro level variables that impinge on educational success.

Like Cochran-Smith (2005), other writers (e.g., Nieto & Bode, 2008; Bennett, 2007; Sheets, 2005; Milner, 2003; Gay, 2010, hooks, 2003; Villegas & Lucas, 2002; Ladson-Billings, 2009) have, in different but coalescing ways, identified several diversity-oriented competency areas on which teacher education programs ought to focus. I broadly categorize these as follows: understanding the teaching-self, racial and cultural literacy, critical pedagogical practices, and competencies for conducting fair assessments. It should be noted here that I am not de-emphasizing the immense importance of the "regular" teacher education curriculum that is required for certification and licensure. Rather, I am advocating the broadening of the scope of the curriculum to include in deeply profound ways, the issue of race and diversity beyond a tokenistic platform. A starting point for an authentic diversity-cognizant teacher education program involves helping preservice teachers to understand who they are as educators.

Understanding the "Teaching Self"

Understanding the teaching self involves a process of autobiographical analysis that should enable teachers (new and experienced) to understand how their personal histories may intersect with their teaching practices. Such scrutiny is warranted by the very fact that we all grow up in cultural environments that promote the rationality and superiority of our own worldviews over those of others. It is therefore not unreasonable to expect that in order to empower others, educators must first understand who they are as well as the values and beliefs that inform their practices. Ladson-Billings (2009) summarizes the link between teachers' beliefs and their practices:

> Teachers who believe that society is fair and just believe that their students are participating on a level playing field and simply have to learn to be better competitors than other students. They also believe in a kind of social Darwinism that supports the survival of the fittest. . . . Teachers who . . . [are] *culturally relevant* assume that an asymmetrical (even antagonistic) relationship exists between poor students of color and society. Thus, their vision of their work is one of preparing students to combat inequity by being highly competent and critically conscious. (p. 30)

Unfortunately, while educators often ask questions regarding what to teach and how to teach it, they hardly ever inquire about who the "teaching self" is (Palmer, 1998; Irving, 2006). Seeing things through different lenses is a powerful precursor for developing new understandings and better ways of doing things in the classroom. Furthermore, an analysis of the teaching self helps teachers to understand that by virtue of their privileged position, they have considerable power over their students. A critical self-analysis should enable teachers to better understand the intersectionality of a complex amalgam of individual, social, and institutional variables that affect educational outcomes for many students, especially those from racialized backgrounds.

Cranton (1994) outlines the precursors of educator self-development and transformation as follows: "[t]he educator, in order to develop the meaning perspective of *being an educator* would: increase self-awareness through consciousness-raising activities, make his or her assumptions and beliefs about practice explicit, engage in critical reflection on those assumptions and beliefs, engage in dialogue with others and develop an informed theory of practice" (p. 214). Milner (2003, p. 205) suggests several critical questions that preservice teachers should ask themselves as they expand their knowledge of the link between the teaching-self and race:

- How will my race influence my work as a teacher with students of color?
- How do I, as a teacher, situate myself in the education of others, and how do I negotiate the power structure in my class to allow students to feel a sense of worth?
- How do I situate and negotiate students' knowledge, experiences, expertise, and race with my own?
- What are the most important issues for most of my students and myself? How will race impact on these issues?
- To what degree is my role as teacher and my experiences superior to the experiences and expertise of students?
- What knowledge can I learn from my students?

In effect, understanding the teaching-self involves becoming aware or developing critical consciousness, which should result in paradigm shifts. In addition to providing a foundational guide for critical self-analysis, Milner's questions highlight the need for infusing racial and cultural literacy across teacher education curricula.

Racial and Cultural Literacy

Also described as racial and cross-cultural competence (Banks, 2001), racial and cultural literacy should be a critical component of educating teachers in pluralistic societies like Canada. Anecdotal and empirical evidence, especially from the United States, has shown how teachers construct and interpret issues of race and diversity is linked to their perceptions and differential treatment of "other peoples' children" (Delpit, 2006; Howard, 2016; McLaren, 2015; Milner, 2003; hooks, 1994, 2003; Paley, 2000; Ladson-Billings, 2009). At the same time, the educational success of diverse students depends on teachers' willingness and ability to empower them which, in turn, rests on their perceptions of students and their communities (Cummins, 2000; Dei et al., 2000; Delpit, 2006). It therefore stands to reason as Milner (2003) points out, that successful teaching in pluralistic societies requires that teachers become racially and cross-culturally competent since these often provide particular challenges to those who teach students that are different from themselves. For Milner:

> [r]ace is such a significant dimension of all human beings' experiences, especially racially marginalized individuals' daily activities, that it seems inconceivable that teacher educators even consider preparing pre-service teachers to reflect without explicit dialogue . . . strategies, and techniques that address race. (p. 196)

This point is crucial since research evidence suggests that teachers often do not consider race and diversity-related issues priority areas even during their training (Solomon et al., 2005). Research also show that teachers' orientation to race, diversity, social justice, equity, and inclusion, more generally, can serve as powerful stimulus to the successful implementation of progressive and inclusive educational policies (Howard, 2016; Cochran-Smith, 2005). For example, teachers who are well versed in multicultural issues would be better positioned to respond positively to student diversity.

In her critically acclaimed book in which she analyzes the interplay between race, ethnicity, and teaching and learning, Lisa Delpit (2006) argues that teachers can positively transform the lives of racialized children if they dispensed with prejudice, stereotypes, and cultural assumptions that are in fact the consequence of miscommunications and miscues when primarily white educators teach children who are racially and culturally different from themselves. This is not only the practical thing to do she argues, it is the socially and morally just approach to educating all children. What Delpit is arguing for is both racial and cultural literacy which should, for all practical purposes, be non-negotiable components of progressive teacher education programs.

Racial and cultural literacy also involve learning critical discourse norms which, in this context, refers to the ability to use language critically (Banks, 2001). It is important for teachers to always remember that while it is easy to eliminate the most obvious biased language, sometimes the most offensive language and words are those that are ostensibly neutral and therefore, latent. Take for instance the innocuous phrase "these people" which is commonly used in wider society. In certain contexts, it serves as the manifest evidence of binary and dichotomizing thinking that creates a culture of "us" and "them" with the implicit suggestion of the superiority of the speaker. For instance, it is common practice in Canada to refer to First Nations Peoples, new immigrants, and other non-dominant group members as "these people" in ways that are oblivious to the implicit attitude of condescension the phrase embodies. Moreover, as Allgood (2001) points out, it is inappropriate to talk about any group of persons in ways that imply that they collectively have such shared characteristics.

Critical Pedagogical Practices

There are some who hold the view that teaching is a neutral activity. This is an illusory assumption since teaching is deeply intertwined with the existing political and social order as Seddon (as cited in Connell 1993) argues:

> Teachers' work which involves conscious and unconscious processes and effects, is both shaped within, and in turn shapes, relations of power. Teachers' practice in economic and cultural production creates asymmetries in individuals' and groups' capacities to define and realise their needs. Teachers' work is therefore also political action because, consciously or unconsciously, it serves to confirm or context the prevailing social order. (p. 70)

Villegas and Lucas (2002) provide two contrasting views of teachers and teaching that have direct bearing on how teachers approach their practices. According to the authors, at one end of the continuum is the view that sees teaching as an apolitical activity and teachers as technicians whose primary function is to "use accepted and proven means to impart knowledge and skills prescribed by the curriculum, which is designed by experts and selected administrators and policy makers, none of whom work in the classroom" (p. 55). Viewed from this perspective, it is quite logical to think of schools as socializing agencies that are charged with producing an uncritical citizenry. In contrast to the view of teaching as a neutral activity, Villegas and Lucas suggest that at the other end of the other continuum are beliefs that see teachers as agents of change whose practices are firmly grounded in transformative pedagogies. An example of such transformative framework, which preservice students should be taught to embrace, is critical pedagogy, which has to do with the critique, interrogation, and challenge of educational orthodoxies that privilege certain kinds of knowledge over others (Kincheloe, 2005). With an emphasis on how knowledge is constructed, situated, and contested within the context of power and marginality, critical pedagogists interrogate and challenge educational practices that privilege certain kinds of knowledge while devaluing others. This culture of knowledge devaluation is, however, not immutable (Egbo, 2019). Critical pedagogists believe that if schools subordinate some groups of students and their ways of knowing, they also hold the potential for change through just and inclusive practices that affirm all forms of diversity, including those that are race and culture-based, not the least of which are assessment practices.

Competencies for Fair Assessment Practices

Although not often perceived as such, assessment and diversity are interconnected in very important ways. First, assessment practices can promote or hinder social justice or anti-oppression education (Kelly & Brandes, 2008). Second, as constructivists have long argued, students learn and construct meaning differently; it seems logical that approaches to assessment and evaluation should be cognizant of student diversity. Third, cultural and linguistic factors have a significant impact on the outcomes of assessment and, not all assessment tools are reliable across the board for all students. Indeed, schools often ignore this fact—no assessment tool especially test-based traditional variants will achieve the same result across all ethnic or cultural groups (Corson, 2001).

As a consequence of this incongruence, certain kinds of assessments have been indicted as being favorably skewed toward students from dominant group backgrounds. Indeed, it is now a well established fact that standardized tests tend to be culturally biased, especially in demographically heterogeneous societies like Canada. A case in point—IQ tests which were once the gold standard for assessing intelligence are now deemed to be culturally biased because they only measure indices of intelligence that have been selectively identified from the point of view of the dominant culture. Another example: several Canadian studies have documented biases in placement tests among language minority students, especially by psychologists who lack the knowledge-base or cultural competence to assess such students (Corson, 2001).

Unfortunately, standardized and other school-based tests continue to be used as the basis for sorting and segregating students, especially students who come from racially, culturally, and linguistically diverse backgrounds (Sheets, 2005; Froese-Germain, 1999). Perhaps even more worrisome, some of the standardized assessment tools that teachers use are developed from the perspective of the "standard" student, which is codified language for students from dominant group background. It is important to remember as Froese-Germain (1999, p. 6) points out that while "tests may be standardized . . . students are not." One question that needs to be addressed is why unjust assessment practices persist in schools. Studies have explored and identified barriers that prevent teachers from adopting socially just approaches to student assessment. In one example that examined the link between teaching for social justice and classroom assessment practices (Kelly & Brandes, 2008), the researchers found that even teachers who desire to enact equitable assessment strategies are constrained by structural factors that include, "standardized tests . . . textbooks that perpetuate existing stereotypes and suppress discussion of conflicts; teachers' lack of pedagogical knowledge to challenge the official curriculum; *inadequate teacher education* [my emphasis]; and the power of parent groups with vested interests in maintaining the status quo" (p. 57). While arguably some of these constraints are beyond the scope of the mandate of teacher educators, some can, nevertheless, be addressed in particular and detailed ways in teacher apprenticeship programs. At the very least, preservice teachers must understand the need for adopting authentic approaches to assessment that have written, verbal and performance components in order to accommodate preferred learning styles, differential linguistic and communicative competence, as well as cultural backgrounds. That being said, it is important to bear in mind that using a variety of strategies to assess student learning in culturally diverse contexts, does not imply replacing cognitively challenging tasks with less rigorous ones.

Engaging the "Discourse" of Silence

As mentioned earlier, preservice students often experience discomfort when class discussions center on the discourse of race, racism, oppression, domination, marginalization, and colonialism (Solomon et al., 2005; Villegas & Lucas, 2002). Despite this discomfort, teacher education programs should engage in what Cochran-Smith (2005) refers to as "hard talk," which involves "a serious consideration of diversity, race and racism, and schooling from multiple, critical, personal and professional perspectives" (p. 270). Cochran-Smith further argues that the purpose of hard talk is not to arrive at a consensus but rather, to allow multiple voices and perspectives to challenge the status quo as well as to emphasize the need for social transformation through education. Some teacher educators address the issue head-on despite students' initial disinterest. For example, Milner (2006) provides a narrative of his successful effort (through a study of his own class) in getting students to engage with, as well as reflect on, the issue of race despite their initial resistance. According to Milner, the course expanded the students' knowledge and awareness of diversity so profoundly that it prompted comments such as the following from them:

> The articles [in the course] brought to my attention issues that I did not know existed. The hard part about the articles was trying to change the view I have had my entire life. I am trying to see diversity issues that obviously exist in my classroom that I am unaware of for the most part. (pp. 354–355)

> [The course] kind of opened my eyes. Some of the things we talked about kind of opened my eyes, and I started looking for things . . . looking for types of relationships between kids of different races or looking at how people treat each other and how people treat people of different races. (p. 355)

It is safe to argue that preservice students who are able to engage the issue of race will likely continue to do so as in-service teachers. Without proper training, even well-meaning teachers remain silent about race and diversity citing instead, "colour blindness" as the ultimate evidence of their aversion to racism and social injustices (Egbo, 2019; Henry & Tator, 2010; Ladson-Billings and Tate, 1995). As Nieto and Bode (2008) put it:

> Well-intentioned teachers are sometimes unintentionally discriminatory when they remain silent about race and racism. They may fear that talking about race will only exacerbate the problem of racism. As a consequence, most schools are characterized by a curious absence of talk about differences, particularly about race. Such silences about racism are sometimes thought to be appropriate because they demonstrate that teachers are "colour-blind," that is fair and impartial when it comes to judging people based on their race. (pp. 74–75)

Such teachers often make claims like "I love all my students"; "I do not see colour"; "I treat everyone equally" or "as far as I am concerned, everyone is the same" (Egbo, 2019, p. 13). While these claims are obviously well intentioned, they are practically unrealistic since race is often the first thing we tend to notice about people, especially in racialized societies. Moreover, it is literally impossible not to notice racial differences among students in the closed confines of a classroom. Indeed, such claims ought to be regarded as a negation of the identities of individual students. Even if for the sake of argument one concedes that some people are less prone to "noticing race" than others, the problem with testimonials asserting color-blindness is rather obvious. Even in culturally homogenous educational contexts, remaining oblivious to differences among students is clearly impossible and in some instances may be akin to bad teaching. It is therefore misleading to claim that every student can be treated equally since there are significant individual differences such as preferred learning styles (Gardner, 1999), abilities, disabilities, cultural differences, as well as personal circumstances that warrant differential treatment if teachers are to effectively meet the learning needs of all their students. The point I am making here is that teachers should not be oblivious to racial diversity among their students. However, preservice students should understand the importance of engaging such differences in ways that disrupt the culture of silence while simultaneously avoiding stereotyping, lowered expectations, and unfair treatment of particular groups of students.

CONCLUSION

The main thrust of the discussion in this chapter has been that there is a dire need for a corresponding change in teacher education programs relative to increasing diversity among Canada's student populations. While this concordance must be cognizant of the basic requirements for successful teaching, teacher candidates do, however, need deeper understandings of the intersectionality of race and diversity on the one hand, and schooling on the other through learned and expanded knowledge about both social constructs. Crucially, such understanding will, in all likelihood, precipitate consciousness-raising and subsequent interrogation of the existing social order. When teachers (including teacher candidates) begin to ask critical questions about social structures, social spaces, structural/educational forces and racial injustices, they become important advocates for their students as well as agents of change. As has been suggested throughout the chapter, teacher agency is a prerequisite condition for transcending everyday technical responsibilities in order to initiate critical transformative action. Finally, it is worth emphasizing that while teachers may have limited opportunities to influence macro-level policies, they can, however, create environments that foster positive educational outcomes for all students, especially those from racialized backgrounds. Empowering teachers to become agents of change should begin during their apprenticeship, which, within the scope of this edited volume, is a mindful and relational approach to promoting social justice and diversity in teacher education.

ACKNOWLEDGMENT

This chapter is reprinted from *Journal of Contemporary Issues in Education*, Volume 6 (22), Egbo, B, "What should preservice teachers know about race and diversity," p. 23–37, Copyright (2011). Please note that the author has made minor changes to reflect the themes of this book.

REFERENCES

Allgood, I. (2001). The role of the school in deterring prejudice. In Carlos Diaz (Ed.), *Multicultural education in the 21st century* (pp. 184–207). New York: Addison Wesley Longman.

Banks, C. A. M. (2001). Becoming a cross-cultural teacher. In C. F. Diaz (Ed.), *Multicultural education in the 21st century* (pp. 171–183). New York: Addison-Wesley Educational Publishers.

Battiste, M. (2013). *Decolonizing education: Nourishing the learning spirit*. Saskatoon, SK: Purich Publishing.

Bennett, C. I. (2007). *Comprehensive multicultural education: Theory and practice* (6th ed.), Boston: Allyn and Bacon.

Bourdieu, P. (1991). *Language and symbolic power*. Cambridge: Polity Press.

Battiste, M. (2013). *Decolonizing education: Nourishing the learning spirit*. Saskatoon, SK: Purich Publishing.

Carr, P. R. (2008). The "Equity Waltz" in Canada: Whiteness and the informal realities of racism in education. *Journal of Contemporary Issues in Education, 3*(2), pp. 4–23.

Carr, P., & Klassen, T. (1997). Different perceptions of race in education: Racial minority and White teachers. *Canadian Journal of Education, 22*, pp. 67–81.

Cochran-Smith, M. (2000). Blind vision: Unlearning racism in teacher education. *Harvard Educational Review, 70*, pp. 157–190.

Cochran-Smith, M. (2005). Teacher development and educational reform. In M. Fullan (Ed.), *Fundamental change: International handbook on educational change*. Dordrecht: Springer.

Connell, R. W. (1993). *Schools and social justice*. Philadelphia: Temple University Press.

Corson, D. (2001). *Language diversity and education*. Mahwah, NJ: Erlbaum Associates.

Cranton, P. (1994). *Understanding and promoting transformative learning: A guide for educators of adults*. San Francisco: Jossey–Bass.

Cummins, J. (2000). *Language, power and pedagogy: Bilingual children in the crossfire*. Clevedon (UK): Multilingual Matters.

Dei, G. J. S., James, I. M., Karumanchery, L. L., James-Wilson, S., & Zine, Jasmin. (2000). *Removing the margins: The challenges and possibilities of inclusive schooling*. Toronto: Canadian Scholars' Press.

Dei, G. J. S., Mazzuca, J., McIsaac, E., & Zine, J. (1997). *Reconstructing dropout: A critical ethnography of the dynamics of Black students' disengagement from school*. Toronto: University of Toronto Press.

Delpit, L. (2006). *Other people's children: Cultural conflict in the classroom*. New York: The New Press.

Egbo, B. (2001). Differential enunciation, mainstream language and the education of immigrant minority students: Implications for policy and practice. *Journal of Teaching and Learning, 1*(2), pp. 47–61.

Egbo, B. (2016). Making education count: Critical educational practice and the life chances of African Canadian children. In A. Ibrahim and A. Abdi (Eds.), *The education of African: Critical perspectives*. Montreal: McGill-Queen's University Press.

Egbo, B. (2019). *Teaching for diversity in Canadian schools* (2nd Edition). Toronto: Pearson Education.

Fleras, A., & Elliott, J. L. (2003). *Unequal relations: An introduction to race and ethnic dynamics in Canada* (4th Edition). Toronto, ON: Prentice-Hall.

Froese-Germain, B. (1999). *Standardized Testing: Undermining Equity in Education*. Ottawa, ON: Canadian Teachers' Federation.

Gardner, H. (1999). *Intelligence reframed: Multiple intelligences for the 21st century*. New York: Basic Books.

Gay, G. (2010). *Culturally responsive teaching: Theory, research, and practice* (2nd Edition). New York: Teachers College Press.

Ghosh, R. (2008). Racism: A hidden curriculum. *Education Canada, 48*(4), pp. 26–29.

Ghosh, R., & Abdi, A. A. (2013). *Education and the politics of difference: Select Canadian perspectives* (2nd Edition). Toronto: Canadian Scholars' Press.

Henry, F., & Tator, C. (2010). *The color of democracy: Racism in Canadian society* (4th Edition). Toronto: Nelson Thomson.

hooks, bell. (1994). *Teaching to transgress*. New York: Routledge.

hooks, bell. (2003). *Teaching community: A pedagogy of hope*. New York: Routledge.

Howard, G. R. (2016). *We can't teach what we don't know: White teachers, multiracial schools* (3rd Edition). New York: Teachers College Press.

Irving, M. (2006). Practicing what we teach: Experiences with reflective practice and critical engagement. In J. Landsman & C. W. Lewis (Eds.), *White teachers/diverse classrooms: A guide to building inclusive schools, promoting high expectations, and eliminating racism*. Sterling, VA: Stylus Publishing.

James, C. E. (2003). *Seeing ourselves: Exploring race, ethnicity and culture*. Toronto: Thompson Educational Publishing.

Kelly, D. M. & Brandes, G. M. (2008). Equitable classroom assessment: Promoting self-development and self-determination. *Interchange, 39*(1), pp. 49–76.

Kincheloe, J. L. (2005). *Critical pedagogy primer*. New York: Peter Lang Publishing.

King, J. E. (1991). Dysconscious racism: Ideology, identity, and the miseducation of teachers. *The Journal of Negro Education, 60*(2), pp. 133–146.

Ladson-Billings, G. (2009). *The Dreamkeepers: Successful Teachers of African American Children* (2nd Edition). San Francisco: Jossey-Bass.

Ladson-Billings, G. & Tate, W. (1995). Toward a critical race theory of education. *Teachers College Record, 97*(1), pp. 47–67.

Levine-Rasky, C. (1998). Pre-service teacher education and the negotiation of social difference. *British Journal of Sociology of Education, 9*(1), 89–112.

Lund, D. E. (2011). Examining shades of grey with Students: Social justice education in action, *Journal of Praxis in Multicultural Education, 6*(1), pp. 79–91. Retrieved from http://digitalcommons.library.unlv.edu/jpme/vol6/iss1/9.

Lund, D. E. & Carr, P. R. (2010). Exposing privilege and racism in *the great White north*: Tackling Whiteness and identity issues in Canadian education, *Multicultural Perspectives, 12*(40), pp. 229–234.

McIntosh, P. (1990). White privilege: Unpacking the invisible knapsack. *Independent School*, Winter, pp. 31–36.

McLaren, P. (2015). *Life in Schools: An introduction to critical pedagogy in the foundations of education* (6th Edition). New York: Taylor and Francis.

McNeil, B. (2011). Charting a way forward: Intersections of race and space in establishing identity as an African-Canadian teacher educator. *Studying Teacher Education, 7*(2), pp. 133–143.

Milner, H. (2003). Reflection, racial competence and critical pedagogy: How do we prepare pre-service teachers to pose tough questions? *Race, Ethnicity and Education, 6*(2), pp. 193–208.

Milner, H. (2006). Preservice teachers' learning about cultural and racial diversity: Implications for urban education. *Urban Education, 41*(4), pp. 343–375.

Milner, H. (2007). Race, narrative inquiry, and self-study in curriculum and teacher education. *Education and Urban Society, 39*(4), pp. 584–609.

Nieto, S. & Bode, P. (2008). *Affirming diversity: The sociopolitical context of multicultural education* (5th Edition). Boston: Pearson Education.

Omi, M., & Winant, H. (1993). On the theoretical concept of race. In C. McCarthy and W. Crichlow (Eds.), *Race identity and representation in education* (pp. 3–10). New York: Routledge.

Paley, V. G. (2000). *White teacher*. Cambridge: Harvard University Press.

Palmer, P. J. (1998). *The courage to teach: Exploring the inner landscape of a teacher's life*. San Francisco: Jossey-Bass Publishers.

Pollock, M. (2001). How the question we ask most about race in education is the very question we most suppress. *Educational Researcher, 30*(9), pp. 2–12.

Schick, C. (2011). Policy as performance: Tracing the rituals of racism, *Review of Education, Pedagogy, and Cultural Studies, 33*(5), pp. 465–483.

Sheets, R. H. (2005). *Diversity pedagogy: Examining the role of culture in the teaching-learning process*. Toronto: Pearson Education.

Skerrett, A. (2008). Racializing educational change: Melting pot and mosaic influences on educational policy. *Journal of Educational of Change, 9*, pp. 261–280.

Solomon, R. P., & Levine-Rasky, C. (1996). When principle meets practice: Teachers' contradictory responses to anti-racist education. *Alberta Journal of Educational Research, 42*(1), pp. 19–33.

Solomon, R. P., Portelli, J. P., Daniel, B. J. & Campbell, A. (2005). The Discourse of denial: How White teacher candidates construct race, racism, and "White privilege." *Race, Ethnicity and Education, 8*(2), pp. 147–169.

Statistics Canada. (2011). Seeking success in Canada and the United States: The determinants of labour market outcomes among the children of immigrants. Retrieved from http://www.statcan.gc.ca/pub/11f0019m/11f0019m2011331-eng.htm.

Villegas, A. M., & Lucas, T. 2002. *Educating culturally responsive teachers: A coherent approach*. Albany: State University of New York Press.

Zamudio, M., Russell, C., Rios, F., & Bridgeman, J. (2011). *Critical race theory matters: Education & ideology*. New York: Routledge.

Chapter Five

Transformative Frameworks for Promoting Social Justice

Mindful and Relational Teacher Education

Awneet Sivia

Preparing teachers for dynamic contexts and multiple diversities requires teacher educators to reimagine their visions and aims for teacher education. In a time when issues of social justice and diversity are being openly contested at the political and global level, the need for teachers to be prepared as culturally relevant, socially just pedagogues is even greater (Egbo, 2009, 2019; Gay, 2002; Ladson-Billings, 1995; Nieto, 2004; Lucas & Villegas, 2013; Sleeter, 2012). Teacher educators recognize teachers must be critical agents within education in order to address problems and reform approaches. Consequently, the challenge is for teacher education to expose social justice issues in education and educate teachers who can deliberate the tensions, challenges, and conditions of teaching for diversity (MacDonald, 2005; Ragoonaden, Sivia, & Baxan, 2015; Mogadime, 2011). The implications for teacher education programs are therefore significant: Teacher Candidates (TCs) are called to cultivate identities as culturally responsive pedagogues, develop a range of practices to contest dominant curricula, expose inequities in education, and hone capacities to facilitate transformative experiences for school-aged students. However, the barriers and challenges to such a robust vision are numerous. Gay (2002) reminds us that the predominantly white, middle class demographic in teacher education is in itself problematic. Montgomery (2013) claims that teacher education candidates are themselves complicit in the causes, conditions, and consequences of multiple racisms. Sleeter (2012) notes that increasing neoliberal pressures shaping teacher education into a business model further marginalizes culturally relevant curricula and pedagogies. Boutte (2012) and Darling-Hammond (2000) suggest that the dispositions of teacher educators themselves and programmatic policies and structures are impediments to enacting this vision of social justice in teacher education. Cochran-Smith (2004) posits a view of teaching as a problem, yet teacher education generally fails to address it as a problem. McKenzie and Scheurich (2004) identify "equity traps," such as white teachers who simply ignore racism, as one of the barriers that prevent teachers from adopting critical perspectives.

In an attempt to respond to these challenges, this chapter introduces diversity pedagogy, critical pedagogy, and peace education as "transformative frameworks" (Egbo, 2009) for promoting social justice in teacher education. Expanding on previous research on the tensions and challenges of teaching using Egbo's (2009) text *Teaching for Diversity in Canadian Schools* in a variety of teacher education contexts (Ragoonaden, Sivia, & Baxan, 2015; Baxan, Ragoonaden, & Sivia, 2016), this study presents my experiences of teaching transformative frameworks as part of a social justice course in a small western Canadian teacher education program. Using self-study research to reflect on my teaching, I explore the impacts of transformative frameworks on my teaching, identity, and conceptions of social justice. Several questions drive this research: How do transformative frameworks shape my teaching activities and content when working with TCs? What does teaching transformative frameworks reveal about my identity as a teacher educator? How do I conceptualize social justice education from this research? How does teaching for social justice relate to mindful and relational teaching? Through praxis-oriented research into my experiences, I present lessons learned from teaching for social justice. As an outcome of this research, I suggest that teaching for social justice is by nature relational and mindful: it involves learning about self and others, about the world, and for transformation through a contemplative and "critical" curriculum.

LITERATURE AND LINES OF THINKING

This work is grounded in critical race theory (CRT) and specifically draws on the following tenets: lived experiences and experiential knowledge are foundational for research, interdisciplinary perspectives across academic disciplines are applied to address research questions, and scholarship and engagement are centered upon racial and social justice (Solorzano 1997; Huber and Solorzano 2015). As a theoretical lens for exploring and analyzing questions about teaching for social justice, CRT allows me to perceive my lived experiences (Clandinin & Connelly, 1995; van Manen, 1997) as inherently contentious, problematic, and disruptive in ways that precipitate into rich and potentially informative insights about teaching and learning for social justice.

Researching my teaching also draws on the multidisciplinary nature of exploring experience, by drawing on multiple fields such as culturally responsive pedagogy, transformative teaching, and reflective practice (Schön, 1987) in order to analyze my teaching. Finally, I am reminded that the outcomes of this research must ultimately inform antiracist and social justice education.

This study also draws on the tenets of culturally relevant pedagogy (Ladson-Billings, 1995). Culturally relevant pedagogy (CRP) posits that the cultural capital and habitus of students ought to be considered in the design of learning and assessment approaches. CRP prompts teachers to develop a mindset that teaching is about improving the life chances of all students by seeing through their experiences of schooling (Delpit, 2006). Such teaching involves practices that reflect, integrate, and give space for the expression of the broad range of diversities found across society (Gay, 2002; Villegas & Lucas, 2002). Students—rather than curricular subjects and school structures—remain the focus. In schools, this requires teachers to develop comprehensive knowledge about their students, about the cultural capital they bring to the classroom, and to use this information in decisions about teaching and learning practices (Egbo, 2009; Jackson & Boutte, 2018).

One of the fundamental issues in teacher education is the manner in which a cultural focus is integrated. Gay (2002) suggests some specific measures to construct and deliver a curriculum that appeals to multiple epistemologies and cultural diversity in the classroom, stating, "in addition to acquiring a knowledge base about ethnic and cultural diversity, teachers need to learn how to convert it into culturally responsive curriculum designs and instructional strategies" (Gay, 2002, p. 108). Gay identifies three forms of curriculum: formal, symbolic, and societal. Formal curriculum consists of plans mandated by government policy and framed by standards. However, a culturally responsive teacher interprets and deciphers the "multicultural strengths" within mandated curriculum and explicitly addresses controversial issues of racism and historical experiences (Gay, 2002). The symbolic curriculum refers to symbols, images, statements, and other artifacts displayed in classrooms. The selection of these symbols can be culturally equitable to represent diverse ethnic groups, while remaining sensitive to images which provoke diverse perspectives. The societal curriculum is knowledge about cultures and ethnic groups that is portrayed through popular culture and media. Culturally responsive teachers create instructional activities to critically analyze how ethnic groups are stereotyped and how these misrepresentations can be counteracted through the education system (Ladson-Billings, 2005). The overall effect is to understand the conditions that teachers need to counteract when creating a culturally-sensitive and responsive curriculum and pedagogy (Gay, 2002; Villegas, 2007).

METHODOLOGICAL APPROACH

Drawing on these lines of thinking to inform my research, I turn to the self-study of teacher education practices (S-STEP) as a methodological approach for exploring my teaching experiences. S-STEP is a methodology for studying professional practice settings (Berry & Loughran, 2005) and can be described as "self-initiated and focused, improvement-aimed, interactive and using multiple, mainly qualitative methods with a validation process based in trustworthiness" (LaBoskey, 2004a, p. 817). This approach to research is committed to and primarily concerned with *what is* rather than epistemological questions about sources, structures, and justification of knowledge (MacKinnon & Bullock, 2016). Self-study is also informed by the "authority of experience" (Munby & Russell, 1994) which posits that researchers trust the learning that comes from *doing* (Loughran, 2007) teaching. Berry and Loughran (2005) remind us that self-study is an intentional and systematic inquiry into practice and is capable of surfacing complex, intricate, and tacit understandings of teacher education and teacher practice. Self-study research is centered on the belief that "for teaching to occur, there must be a *somehow* (italics in original), a way for an educator to know, recognize, explore, and act upon his or her practice" (Clarke & Erickson, 2004, p. 59). Finally, LaBoskey (2004b) encourages us to attend to and develop knowledge of the "self" in self-study research.

With these descriptions in mind, my research centers on specific experiences of teaching transformative frameworks. I reflect on these experiences by thinking back on particularly memorable moments in my teaching and by drawing on additional sources such as personal reflections, course syllabi, and feedback on student assignments. This process of internal meaning-making coupled with external sources is described as intimate scholarship (Hamilton, 1995), an approach that is fundamentally relational, "grounded in ontology, and developed from being in dialogue with ourselves and with research literature" (Pinnegar & Hamilton, 2014, p. 146) in order to generate knowledge. Intimate scholarship sees learning as emerging in the spaces between self and practice, activity and theorizing, explicit knowledge and implicit knowing, and belief and action (Pinnegar & Hamilton, 2009). In keeping with these tenets of intimate scholarship, *what is* (ontology) becomes a more appropriate view of the knowledge generated from this research, thus freeing me from the methodological constraints that can oftentimes encumber thinking and reflecting (Martin, 2018). Consequently, self-study through intimate scholarship invites "critical" research (Ragoonaden, 2015b) through praxis-oriented reflection in order to explore the nuances and intricacies of my teaching, and develop knowledge about my practice, identity, and conceptions of teaching for social justice.

Data for this inquiry was developed in two phases: by writing reflections on specific activities related to teaching transformative frameworks in my social justice classes; and by reviewing course outlines, emails, and responses to TCs' assignments. I was purposeful in the order in which I constructed the data sets. Writing the reflections before reviewing other data allowed for a "freshness" in describing the experiences and facilitated "in the moment" meaning-making of past episodes of teaching. I envisioned the reflections as opportunities to unpack and interact with my memories—in essence to exercise reflexivity in writing about teaching. After writing the reflections, I reviewed my course outlines. I focused on the introductions, which describe the theoretical and philosophic underpinnings guiding my teaching. My notes, course evaluations, and feedback on assignments further clarified how I envisioned teaching social justice education and what meaning I was attributing to the work TCs had done in the course. Following the constructing and gathering of data, I analyzed for themes and salient ideas by rereading each reflection and reviewing additional data sources.

DIVERSITY PEDAGOGY AS A TRANSFORMATIVE FRAMEWORK

Diversity pedagogy is based on the interconnection of culture, cognition, and schooling (Egbo, 2009). Effective teaching requires that all three are forefront in educational decisions regarding content in curriculum, pedagogical strategies, and forms of assessment. This leads to what Sheets (2005) refers to as a "union between classroom practice and theoretical scholarship explicating the role of culture in the cognitive development of children" (p. 19). Educators need to focus on students' diverse learning abilities, cultural ways of knowing, socioeconomic differences, and specialized learning needs. This means educators must create "a 'safe' classroom" that encourages language learning, uses inclusive resources, adapts instructional strategies to students' needs, and promotes ethnic identity development and social interaction (Sheets, 2005; Egbo, 2009). Diversity pedagogy is contingent on educators developing and embodying the capacities of culturally relevant pedagogues (Baxan, Ragoonaden, & Sivia, 2016).

Reflections on Teaching Diversity Pedagogy

"We teach who we are" (Palmer, 1998). When Parker Palmer wrote *The Courage to Teach*, he reminded educators that in the midst of becoming technically proficient, knowledgeable about content, and aware of children's development, we must not lose sight of the importance of teacher identity and integrity in learning to teach. While all of the tips and tricks of teacher development can be taught through methods courses and practice, cultivating the heart of a teacher (Palmer, 1998) and the integrity of aligning one's practices with well-articulated beliefs become the projects of teacher education. Egbo (2009) echoes this in her reminder that clarifying values and beliefs is foundational to demonstrating self-knowing and integrity in teaching.

Identity Bags

My actions as a teacher educator are guided by this idea that teaching teachers is about cultivating "selves" as the soul-work of teaching. We must know ourselves before we can begin to know others and in knowing others, we can teach in more integrated, wholistic, and focused ways. With this in mind, TCs in my social justice course start with an activity called "Identity Bags" where they are asked to bring three objects that represent their cultural identities, learner identities, and burgeoning teacher identities. After sharing in small groups, TCs write reflections on the activity from the lenses of teacher, student, and curriculum. Through debriefing the activity, it becomes apparent the power of this experience to foster self-knowledge and knowledge of others in the spirit of mutual connection. A response to one student's identity bag journal captured this for me:

> I appreciate the complexity of ideas that have emerged for each of you regarding identity, Canadian-*ness*, privilege, and the fluidity of culture, language and identity. What resonates for me are your concerns about "people first" language, the positioning of people as "other" by simple semantics and linguistic representations, and the place of First Nations Peoples as not fully included within the notion of *a* "Canadian identity." (Email, September 2017)

My comments reinforce how TCs use this activity to get at the deeper and "taken-for-granted" questions of identity and culture as they relate to their own emerging identities as future teachers.

Community Ethnographies

Following this lesson, TCs complete a Community Ethnography, where they explore schools through the lens of Gruenwald's (2003) dimensions of place. In groups, they visit schools and explore the geographical, ideological, sociocultural, political, and pedagogical aspects of the school to learn about the students, their lives in and outside of school, and how the school serves as a microcosm, or not, of the community in which it is located. In the activity handout, I reference Nodding's (2002) claim that standardized views of schools and students can promote a kind of generic education for "anywhere" and that such an education "might easily deteriorate to an education for 'nowhere'" (Noddings, 2002, p. 171). This seems to resonate for TCs as they reflect on their own "standardized" education that seemed to have very little to do with the dimensions of place surrounding their schools or their own lives as students. In the assignment, TCs make observations, develop inferences from "walk-abouts" in the community, take images from the vantage of students, and observe the ways in which students' academic, cultural, and social lives are reflected inside the school. The premise of this activity is to understand schools as complex systems where teachers, students, and community coalesce into an integrated and codependent set of relationships.

From the presentations of these community ethnographies, TCs begin to appreciate schools as infinitely more complex, intricately connected to community, informed by multiple perspectives and stakeholders, and filled with students with diverse backgrounds and learning needs. I am often struck by the power of this activity to inspire a more sophisticated and complex image of schools in TCs' minds. In one of my responses to TCs, the idea that teachers are active in constructing the culture of schools was highlighted:

> You have developed some powerful insights about the limitations of neutrality, based on Freire's notion that to remain neutral is to side with power, and used these to ask yourself deep questions. Will you be a "political" teacher? Absolutely! Will you be able to create the environment which will allow you to free yourself enough in order to open up spaces of learning? I have full faith you will! (Email, August 2018)

As a result, diversity transforms from an abstract concept and lofty ideal talked about in our course to an observable reality in teachers' lives. As TCs learn about the diversity of family constellations, cultural heritages, gender identities, languages, and socioeconomic status of students, they realize the enormity of being a teacher. Diversity pedagogy becomes paramount in the face of such realizations.

These activities are a critical piece in teaching diversity pedagogy as both an end and a means. As a teacher educator with a view of diversity pedagogy informed by Egbo's (2009) text, identity bags are designed to facilitate TCs developing a broader view of who they are as future teachers. Through this activity, it is my hope that they see their "whole" self as a teacher and find ways to express their authentic identities, even those aspects that they may not think are worth showing to their students. This activity reinforces the belief that authenticity and "being real" with students build relationship. The richness of this understanding becomes evident when TCs enter practicum where they observe authentic relationships and recognize the importance of teaching to the whole child. Identity work through activities like this also creates opportunities for greater self-knowledge and knowledge of others. As I noted in my response to one TC's identity bag reflection:

> It gives me great hope and pleasure to know that you will take this profound and deeply empathetic vision into schools and use your heightened awareness

of yourself to connect with all students. Your diversity IS your strength as you state so eloquently in your reflection. Your own experiences have fuelled your desire to ensure your students are not isolated, but connected, not marginalized but included and that you will connect them with the curriculum in meaningful ways. (Email, September 2017)

Through identity bags and community ethnographies, TCs are prompted to interrogate their own identities and examine the multidimensional aspects of schools as places of learning. Thus, diversity pedagogy facilitates a focus on identity development through TCs' growing understanding of the intersections of culture, cognition, and views of schooling. These approaches also contribute to a view that students' diversities, shaped by the communities surrounding the school as well as the internal learning environments, must inform curriculum planning and teaching.

CRITICAL PEDAGOGY AS A TRANSFORMATIVE FRAMEWORK

Critical pedagogy is fundamentally about power and centers on the discourses that have to do with the intricate and complex relationship between power and knowledge. The seminal work of scholars such as Freire (1970), Giroux (2011), McLaren (2015), and Apple (2004) brings to the fore the power of the dominant society over what counts as knowledge and how power mediates academic success in terms of schooling. Freire (1998) reminds us that pedagogies that are steeped in a conventional and hierarchical paradigm of education fundamentally disempower learners and position them as "oppressed" and lacking agency. Schools operate structurally and politically as sites that predetermine who has agency, who possesses the power, and who has voice in shaping decisions (Gay, 2003). Critical pedagogy positions educators as change agents who are called to mediate these concerns in schools. As Egbo (2009) suggests in her discussion of transformative frameworks, critical pedagogy requires educators advocate to change "undesirable education practices at the school level" (Egbo, 2009, p. 112). This perspective is predicated on viewing classrooms as sites for student empowerment through dialogic communication and problem-posing education (Freire, 1970; Shor, 1992). Such classrooms limit "teacher talk" and facilitate students' participation, co-constructed knowledge, and democratic practices (hooks, 1994; Villegas & Lucas, 2002; Cummins, 2000; Wolk, 1998).

Reflections on Teaching Critical Pedagogy

"Traditionally, schools are organized around hierarchical and monolithic models of instruction that de-emphasize values, learning styles, and worldviews of dominated groups . . . [and] through the hidden curriculum schools convey messages about who controls power in society, as well as whose voices matter," writes Egbo (Egbo, 2009, p. 16). I begin my course with this statement on the screen and ask TCs to talk about what this means to them. They complete a placement activity where they enter into the personal and social meaning-making that characterizes the constructivist approach in my teaching. Through these initial conversations, I become aware of the privilege and ease with which many of my TCs experienced schooling, further strengthening my commitment to teaching critical pedagogy as a framework for examining education.

Hidden Curriculum

Teaching this transformative framework means exposing the discriminatory practices and structures of institutions such as schools in which the TCs in my class generally found success. It is a double-edged sword. On one hand, the TCs represent the ways in which the hidden curriculum benefited them—the structures of their schooling, from awards to teaching styles, favored their habitus or cultural capital, particularly if they were from the dominant white majority. However, in teaching for critical awareness—exposing injustices and problematizing status quo practices of schooling—TCs are asked to interrogate the reasons for their own success and recognize they are somewhat complicit in institutional hegemony and systemic racism. Not all do this with ease and this creates tensions which I try to address through classroom meetings or "temperature checks."

As the hidden curriculum becomes visible, the aim of critical pedagogy is to raise consciousness and empower TCs to become "inequity hunters" who seek to create more inclusive and democratic policies and structures in schools. In order to do this, TCs must first understand what is hidden. They engage in a carousel activity where they are assigned one common school practice and asked to discuss how the practice is discriminatory and disempowering. For example, one of the carousel stations is on awards. Often, awards and student selection practices are based on assumptions about what constitutes success or effort. They then assess how the practice of student awards is inherently problematic, the assumptions underlying the practice, how it promotes hegemony, and how they would change the practice or policy so it becomes more inclusive and just. The point of the exercise is to have preservice teachers view taken-for-granted educational practices from multiple perspectives in order to expose their problematic nature. In asking them to revise the practice to make it more inclusive and socially just, they consider whose voices are being overlooked, who is not represented, and which learning preferences are excluded.

This activity often results in epiphanies about the ways in which schools enact discriminatory practices and operate with a hidden curriculum that favors the dominant majority. I notice that many TCs wrestle with the idea that what they thought were "good" practices in schools were actually harmful to certain groups of students. In my course outline, I remind students that "teaching is about uncovering unwelcome truths—this means we must question the status quo and the things that worked for 'us' as students" (Course Syllabus, 2017). This realization is part of the critical lens I hope they develop as future teachers in order to challenge mainstream curriculum, question practices that serve to marginalize, such as academic streaming or pull-out programs, and to "understand that issues of social justice cannot be separated from teaching and learning" (Egbo, 2009, p. 144).

Culturally Inclusive Curriculum

A follow up to this activity is the use of Egbo's "Checklist for the Analysis of Culturally Inclusive Instructional Material" (Egbo, 2009, p. 142) to rate a cross-section of children's fiction and nonfiction literature. TCs work in pairs using the checklist and rating sheet to rank the resources as most inclusive to least inclusive. They examine stereotypes in stories, lack of representations of diverse peoples, languages and cultures, one-dimensional character development, mainstream images, and assumptions of a Eurocentric worldview in the storyline. The checklist uses a 1–5 scale for rating how effectively, for example, illustrations reflect the realities of a culturally pluralistic society, or how historically accurate and authentic the content is that is presented through the resource. This activity creates what I referred to in earlier research as a "critical space" (Ragoonaden, Sivia, & Baxan, 2015), where bias in language, image, curriculum, and content is enunciated. I encourage TCs through conversations in this critical space to recognize their own agency as future teachers to change and challenge practices by selecting literature and resources that are more culturally relevant (Gay, 2002; Ladson-Billings, 2005).

Critical pedagogy enacted through such activities fosters a vision of dialogic communication and student-centered learning for TCs. They engage in activities where their own past experiences as school-aged students are deconstructed in order to reconstruct an image of inclusive and equitable teaching and learning. We deliberate these ideas as a classroom community in an effort to model this kind of dialogic, constructivist, and inclusive education. In my journal, I have written about this as the "mirrored journey" where the experiences that TCs live out in my class become the basis for constructing the pedagogy of hope and freedom espoused by Freire. "If the TCs feel this sense of freedom to 'become,' maybe they will transfer this and embody it into their ways of being as teachers with their own students" (Journal Entry, 2017).

The conversations we have serve to further our collective understanding of decentralizing the power in classroom learning (Villegas & Lucas, 2002; Freire, 1998; Wolk, 1998). As the instructor in this course, I pose questions such as "who is education for?," "who decides what is to be learned?" and "what assumptions do we have about the roles of teachers and students in schools?" to inspire TCs to reflect on these aspects of the education and construct their own meanings and understandings from experiencing a "critical" curriculum. Thus, critical pedagogy becomes a powerful framework for me, as the instructor, to engage TCs in constructing an image of teaching and learning that contests assumed roles, status quo identities, and inequitable power relations.

Peace Education as a Transformative Framework

The United Nations Universal Declaration of Human Rights states that peace education is "directed to the full development of the human personality and the strengthening of respect for human rights and fundamental freedom [that promotes] understanding, tolerance, and friendship among all nations, racial or religious groups" (United Nations, 1948, Article 26). In a time when global realities are impacted by migration and displacement of Peoples, war and human suffering, and lack of freedoms, education that teaches for peaceful coexistence is even more paramount. Iram (2006) correlates teaching about peace education and teaching peaceful ways of being with diversity education because peace is predicated on tolerance and acceptance. Peace education is fundamentally about creating proactive frameworks for preventing conflict, reducing prejudice, and advocating for diversity (Egbo, 2009). While these seem lofty ideals, they remind educators of the importance of constructing attitudes, beliefs, and dispositions as goals of education. Achieving peaceful solutions to conflict and living peacefully mean that one must *be* a peaceful and peace-loving individual.

Reflections on Teaching Peace Education

According to Bar-Tal (2002), peace education requires students develop peace-building behaviors and communication styles. This can be nurtured by involving students in projects or causes that teachers undertake because they are relevant to the school and surrounding communities. Part of this vision includes the importance to teaching about social injustices in the world through literature and media sources where the voices and lives of racialized and marginalized populations are introduced to young people. Students must also be exposed to the ways in which peace is threatened, both globally and locally, in order to understand the root causes of violence and discrimination. Yet another aspect of peace education is teaching a conception of peace as living with compassion and integrity, building intercultural respect, building solidarity, living in harmony with the Earth and cultivating inner peace (Toh & Cawagas, 2010). Such a conception can lead educators to consider peace education as a fundamental component of teaching for cross-cultural understanding and respect of human rights. At the core, peace education is aligned with creating empathy and understanding across differences in an effort to prevent violence and conflict.

Komagata Maru

In efforts to promote knowledge development about peace education, TCs in my course engage in activities to learn about historic injustices and global migration. The first activity is centered on the Komagata Maru Incident of 1914 when a ship of migrants from Punjab, India, were detained in the Vancouver harbor for several months and prevented from disembarking. The laws at the time discriminated against nonwhite foreigners resulting in this ship being turned back to India where the passengers faced persecution and violence on their return. The incident is particularly relevant given the large South Asian diaspora in the region and has been recognized formally as an injustice in Canadian history. The activity involves TCs reading and watching a video about the event and taking the perspectives of a passenger, lawmaker, politician, family member in waiting, and child on the ship. Through expert group jigsaw, they refine their ideas and organize into groups that include all five perspectives. They then share their response through a poem, a statement, a reflection, a story, or an image that represents the perspective of that individual.

It is a powerful experience for me as the teacher educator to witness TCs, some of whom are members of the South Asian diaspora, come to learn about this injustice that is so close to home. In debriefing the activity, TCs often express frustration that they did not know this history of their province as it was not in textbooks or in their lessons in schools. This prompted one of my TCs to delve into her own family's history as first generation South Asian immigrants. My response to her paper acknowledged the power of sharing stories of early settlers as a necessary component of peace education:

> I am so pleased you shared your family's story in class and I do hope you pursue submitting your family's pioneer story to the 100 Year Journey group. I especially appreciate that you have used this as a basis to explore the "gaps" in the curriculum and the injustices of misrepresenting or failing to represent the *actual* history of people in this province and region. You may not be able to change your experience but you can certainly change the status quo for future

learners and teach them about the "truths" that are absent from the textbooks they read. (Email, September 2018)

As I reflect on this particular activity, I realize that the curriculum that *I* was taught was also bereft of this kind of truth, among many others, and that my own education was completely narrow and devoid of real-world lessons. I wondered if I could *ever* teach social justice to prospective teachers effectively when my own education, both as a child and as an adult, was lacking this content. Despite this, I remain committed to destabilizing the canons of knowledge that prevented me, in the past, and TCs in this course from learning about truths.

Refugee Stories

This activity is designed to expose current global concerns of migration and displacement. Using a strategy of "snowball writing," TCs read award-winning stories written by adolescent refugee students now living in Canada. These stories detail the hardships, dangers, and resilience of these individuals and their families. The activity involves one student writing a response to a sentence stem such as "If I had to accompany this child in their journey, I would . . ." and then crumpling up the paper and throwing it into a bin and picking up a peer's "snowball." They read the first entry and highlight key phrases or words, and then write another reflection in response and with a new sentence stem such as, "If this individual was in my class, I would . . ." to create a set of reflections on the refugee story. By the end of "snowball writing," the student who started the thread of reflections retrieves their paper and reviews the writing and highlighting done by their peers. TCs are invited to read sections of their reflections. Many become emotional as they read of the experiences of these young refugee students and they are moved by the powerful writing and reflecting contributed by their peers. Two aspects of this activity stand out for me. TCs in my class begin to recognize their own peers (future colleagues) as part of a "community of compassionate change agents," and their regard for the profession becomes elevated knowing they are entering a profession with teachers who are so moved and inspired by the resilience and courage of young people. TCs also begin to consider the implications of having students in their practicum classes who have firsthand experiences as refugees. As I share the statistics of the number of Syrian families who have settled in the region, we discuss the implications of teaching students who have been displaced and experienced war and violence at young ages.

As the instructor, my thoughts return to the importance of peace education in the preparation of teachers because of the values, perspectives, and empathy such learning fosters in them. I am inspired by Ghandi's iconic message that we must "be the change we wish to see in the world" in teaching this particular framework. Peace education creates a space in my classroom to model a way of teaching that sees the world as our curriculum and for the lives of students to be the subjects we teach, rather than math or social studies. Pinar (2004) suggests educators enact an "autobiographical curriculum" that centers on the lives of the students who undergo it in order to combat the teaching of inert knowledge devoid of real-world content. I strive to do this through teaching transformative frameworks.

ASSERTIONS ABOUT TRANSFORMATIVE FRAMEWORKS FOR PROMOTING SOCIAL JUSTICE

As a self-study, this research was self-focused and improvement aimed (Berry, 2007). In grounding my inquiry in the spaces between activity and theorizing, explicit knowledge and implicit knowing, and belief and action (Hamilton & Pinnegar, 2015), I came to several assertions about my practices, identity, and conceptions about social justice as a teacher educator. By analyzing these experiences, ones that were symbolic of the ways in which I teach the transformative frameworks, I propose there are connections and synergies between teaching for social justice and mindful and relational teaching. The following sections discuss the "lessons learned" and present these as evidence to suggest the mindful and relational nature of teaching for social justice in teacher education.

Lessons Learned about Practice

My practices of teaching Egbo's (2009) transformative frameworks are characterized by discord and dissonance, as both means and ends in my vision for creating transformative experiences in my classes. In each activity, my efforts centered on disrupting canonical knowledge, prior assumptions, and challenging status quo ideologies. I refer to this as discord—the root meaning of which is "apart from the heart"—because of the importance of teaching *with heart*. Palmer (1998) reminds us that the heart of a teacher is developed through integrity, when the beliefs and actions of teachers are integrated and aligned. Introducing discordant experiences—examples where teachers' beliefs do not align with their actions—is intended to prompt TCs to reflect on their visions for teaching.

Similarly, dissonance is associated with conceptual change, a process that guides my teaching practices. In my doctoral research, I articulated teaching as a "cycle of dissonance," a framework to enhance TCs' learning. In this framework, content and strategies are purposefully designed to prompt conceptual shifts in understanding through a recurring process of disrupting previously held assumptions and confronting misconceptions. Egbo (2009) refers to this as TCs' conceptual realignment about teaching and learning.

When teaching involves dissonance as a constant feature, TCs are prompted to problematize, deconstruct, and reconstruct their images of teaching for diversity. My practice becomes grounded in challenging my TCs' images of schooling and facilitating, through transformative frameworks activities, the development of a compassionate, empathetic, and thoughtfully constructed view of themselves as social justice teachers.

Lessons Learned about Identity

Studying my experiences of teaching for social justice revealed several aspects of my identity as a teacher educator. I perceive my role as that of a change agent. I set out to engage TCs in an anti-racist and equity-centered curriculum to model how educators enact agency and confront educational practices that need to be changed. A key facet of change agency is recognizing my capacities to empower TCs to think differently, more sophisticatedly, and more compassionately about issues that affect the lives of students in their classrooms. I strive to model for TCs this kind of critical awareness, empathy, and reflection in my teaching.

Respecting others emerges as a cornerstone of my identity as a teacher educator, given the diverse and oftentimes opposing views that surface in teaching for social justice. I value their perspectives, even when I disagree with them. Teaching transformative frameworks requires that a culture of respect be established in my classroom where I am intentional about listening attentively and modeling respectful and nonjudgmental language. In doing so, I attend to a key premise of social justice education—*being* socially just as an educator is conditional to *enacting* a social justice pedagogy. For me, this is critical to model for TCs.

Lessons Learned about Conceptions of Social Justice

I have conceptualized social justice education as teaching a decentered curriculum that challenges canonical knowledge, includes multiple and traditionally marginalized perspectives, and reflects diversity of people and places. Further, teaching social justice involves an integrated vision of teaching about/for self, teaching about/for the other, teaching about/for change, and teaching about/for equity—an effective heuristic for designing lessons and developing curriculum as a teacher educator. I envision social justice as pervasive—a continuous thread in my courses regardless if I am teaching science methods or technology education courses. Teaching for social justice is also dual focused: it aims to build capacities of socially just teachers such as empathy and compassion, and inspires teachers to fundamentally reimagine mandated, generic curriculum as emergent, identity-centered, culturally relevant, and globally connected. These ideas are foundational to my teaching and support my vision to prepare teachers who *are* socially just and who *create* social justice-focused curriculum.

The lessons learned about my practices, identity, and conceptions of social justice from this self-study solidify for me the importance of teaching transformative frameworks for social justice. Not only do TCs experience a provocative, student-centered, and culturally relevant curriculum through teaching in this way, *my* growth as a teacher educator is implicated by teaching transformative frameworks in my course. Reflecting on this analysis, I return to the fourth question driving this inquiry: How does teaching for social justice relate to mindful and relational teaching?

RELATIONAL TEACHING

Relational teaching (Kitchen, 2005) involves the following principles: Understanding one's own personal practical knowledge; improving one's practice in teacher education; understanding the landscape of teacher education; respecting and empathizing with teacher candidates; conveying respect and empathy; helping TCs face problems; and, receptivity to growing in relationship. According to Kitchen (2005; 2006), these principles are based on the belief that teachers develop from within and cultivate beliefs about teaching through reflection on their experiences. Relationships are founded on these principles and informed by a deep sense of trust that those who choose to become teachers are loving, genuine, caring individuals who want to make the world a better place (Kitchen, 2009). Further, O'Connor (2016) and Sivia and MacMath (2016) in their research on field seminars, suggest that relationality enhances TCs' ability to build stronger connections between theory and practice. Reeves and LeMare (2017) assert that relational pedagogy "is manifest in teachers who are aware of and explicitly focus on the quality of their interactions with students to develop classroom communities that promote academic, social, and emotional growth" (p. 86). Placing value on relationships, developing empathy and respect through reflection on experiences, and fostering productive and healthy relationships are essential to teaching for social justice.

MINDFUL EDUCATION

Mindfulness is when master teachers are aware of themselves and attuned to their students (Schoeberlein & Sheth, 2009). As a practice, it supports knowing self and knowing and relating to others through contemplation, connection, and reflection. In a study of introducing mindful practices in a first-year access course, Ragoonaden (2015a) suggests that mindful practices aligned with a (w)holistic approach that draws on teachings of the Indigenous medicine wheel facilitate a culturally responsive pedagogy (Gay, 2002). Educators who use mindfulness-based practices enable their students to develop an increased sense of well-being and self-efficacy resulting in increased clarity and stability of attention (Cullen, 2011; Flook et al., 2013; Roeser et al., 2012). Of import are three concepts attributed to a mindful approach in education: intention, attention, and attitude (Schoeberlein & Sheth, 2009). Intention describes teaching that is well-thought out, focused, and designed to ensure success for all learners. Attention is the ability to observe and engage while suspending judgment. Attitude allows for the expression of kindness and compassion toward others. These components of mindful education represent a conception of mindful teaching as being focused on developing human capacities, knowledge of self and others, and caring relationships—a powerful framework that aligns well with teaching for social justice.

TRANSFORMATIVE FRAMEWORKS FOR SOCIAL JUSTICE: MINDFUL AND RELATIONAL TEACHING

Teaching transformative frameworks for promoting social justice in teacher education is by nature both mindful and relational. My experiences reveal that TCs who are taught about (and through) transformative frameworks become mindful—they contemplate their identities and practices in teaching for diversity and addressing inequities in education. This includes being attentive to curriculum—the content, the strategies to engage diverse learners, and inclusive and equitable classrooms. The concepts of mindful education (Schoeberlein and Sheth, 2009) also inform teaching practices. Intentional teaching means that TCs must set high expectations rather than promote deficit thinking, develop clear social justice aims, and set parameters to ensure the success of all learners. Attentive teaching cultivates open-mindedness and fosters a nonjudgmental attitude to promote inquiry and learning. Attitudes of kindness, empathy, and compassion for others are developed, creating opportunities for cross-cultural communication and caring in the classroom.

There is also convergence between teaching for transformative frameworks and the tenets of relational teaching. Both are predicated on building respectful relationships, empathizing with others, addressing injustices in education, and improving teaching and learning through a decentered curriculum. Despite the challenging content and contentious issues that often arise in this course, I never lose sight of the importance of staying "in relationship" with students who are grappling with issues of diversity. I respect differences and model openness to diverse perspectives, as noted in my course evaluations: "The instructor models compassion and creates a safe space to address the difficult topics in this course. I feel comfortable sharing yet am challenged as well to rethink my ideas about teaching and learning" (Course Evaluations, 2017). Through relational teaching, the TCs and I navigate the challenges and dissonance we experience as a class by implementing reflective practice, establishing safety in the classroom, and promoting inquiry in place of judgment. I strive to model integrity between my beliefs and actions as a teacher educator (Palmer, 1998) in order to emphasize the importance of that relationship as well. Relational teaching also warrants that relationships be constructed between theory and practice, whether through curricular arrangements (Sivia & MacMath, 2016) or situating learning within schools (O'Connor, 2016).

CONCLUSION AND IMPLICATIONS

When Gloria Ladson-Billings (1995) stated "we are not in this fight to win, but to struggle," I better understand what this might mean for teacher education. Teaching transformative frameworks (diversity pedagogy, critical pedagogy, and peace education) for social justice *invites* the struggle. By teaching in the ways described in this chapter, and drawing on lived experiences and experiential knowledge that is centered on racial and social justice (Solorzano, 1997; Huber & Solorzano, 2015), I have attempted to show how to navigate the struggles that TCs face in today's diverse contexts. Preparing socially just teachers means they must know how to view schools critically and with an intentionality about changing practices and challenging injustices. They must embrace diversity and value knowing their students through balanced and empowering relationships. They must develop culturally relevant and responsive curriculum for/with their students (Gay, 2002) to counter racism and discrimination. They must foster peaceful coexistence and a value for freedom. The synergies between teaching transformative frameworks and mindful and relational teaching have been made clearer for me through this self-study of my practices. Thus, I am hopeful that teacher educators can use the ideas in this chapter to prepare TCs to engage in this struggle and develop the capacities to address diversity, calmly, thoughtfully, with love and empathy, and with a desire to know and relate to their own future students.

REFERENCES

Apple, M. (2004). *Ideology and curriculum* (3rd Ed.). New York: Routledge.
Bar-Tal, D. (2002). The elusive nature of peace education. In G. Salomon & B. Nevo (Eds.), *Peace education: The concept, principles and practice in the world*. Mahwah, NJ: Lawrence Erlbaum.
Baxan, V., Ragoonaden, K., & Sivia, A. (2016). Conceptualizations of diversity and inclusion in an urban teacher education program: A case study of teacher capacity development. In M.

Hirschkorn & J. Mueller (Eds.). *What should Canada's teachers know? Teacher capacities: Knowledge, beliefs and skills*. Ottawa, ON: Canadian Association for Teacher Education.

Berry, A. K., & Loughran, J. J. (2005). Teaching about teaching: the role of self-study. In C. Mitchell, S. Weber, K. O'Reilly-Scanlon (Eds.), *Just who do we think we are? Methodologies for autobiography and self-study in teaching* (pp. 168–180). London: Routledge.

Berry, A. K. (2007). *Tensions in teaching about teaching: Understanding practice as a teacher educator*. Dordrecht, NL: Kluwer Academic Publishers.

Boutte, G. S. (2012). Urban schools: Challenges and possibilities for early childhood and elementary education. *Urban Education, 47*(2), 515–550.

Bullock, S. M. (2009). Learning to think like a teacher educator: Making the substantive and syntactic structures of teaching explicit through self-study. *Teachers and Teaching: Theory and Practice, 15*(2), 291–304.

Clandinin, J., & Connelly, M. (1995). *Teachers' professional knowledge landscapes*. New York: Teachers College Press.

Clarke, A., & Erickson, G. (2004). The nature of teaching and learning in self-study. In J. J. Loughran, M. L. Hamilton, V. K. LaBoskey, & T. L. Russell (Eds.), *International handbook of self-study of teaching and teacher education practices* (pp. 41–68). London, UK: Kluwer Academic.

Cochran-Smith, M. (2004). The problem of teacher education. *Journal of Teacher Education, 55*(4), 295–299.

Cullen, M. (2011). Mindfulness-based interventions: An emerging phenomenon. *Mindfulness, 2*(3), 186–193.

Cummins, J. (2000). *Language, power, and pedagogy: Bilingual children in the crossfire*. Bristol, UK: Mulitilingual Matters.

Darling-Hammond, L. (2000). How teacher education matters. *Journal of Teacher Education, (51)*3, 166–173.

Delpit, L. (2006). *Other peoples' children: Cultural conflict in the classroom*. New York: New Press.

Egbo, B. (2009). *Teaching for diversity in Canadian schools*. Toronto, ON: Pearson.

Egbo, B. (2019). *Teaching for diversity in Canadian schools* (2nd Ed.). Toronto, ON: Pearson.

Flook, L., Goldberg, S. B., Pinger, L., Bonus, K., & Davidson, R. J. (2013). Mindfulness for teachers: A pilot study to assess effects on stress, burnout, and teaching efficacy. *Mind, Brain, and Education, 7,* 182–195.

Freire, P. (1970). *Pedagogy of the Oppressed*. New York, Continuum.

Freire, P. (1998). *Teachers as cultural workers: letters to those who dare teach*. Boulder, CO: Westview Press.

Gay, G. (2002). Preparing for culturally responsive teaching. *Journal of Teacher Education, 53*(2), 106–116.

Gay, G. (2003). *Becoming multicultural educators: Personal journey towards professional agency*. San Francisco: Jossey-Bass.

Giroux, H. (2011). *On critical pedagogy*. New York: Continuum.

Gruenewald, D. (2003). Foundations of place: A multidisciplinary framework for place conscious education. *American Educational Research Journal, 30*(3), 619–654.

Hamilton, M. L. (1995). Confronting the self: Passion and practice in the act of teaching or my Oz-dacious journey to Kansas! *Teacher Education Quarterly 22*(3), 29–42.

Hamilton, M. L., & Pinnegar, S. (2015). *Knowing, becoming, doing as teacher educators: Identity, intimate scholarship, inquiry*. Bingley, UK: Emerald Publishing.

hooks, b. (1994). *Teaching to transgress: Education as the practice of freedom*. New York: Routledge.

Huber, L. P., & Solorzano, D. G. (2015). Racial microaggressions as a tool for critical race research. *Race Ethnicity and Education, 18*(3), 297–320.

Iram, Y. (Ed.). (2006). *Educating toward a culture of peace*. Charlotte, NC: Information Age.

Jackson, T. O., & Boutte, G. S. (2018). Exploring culturally relevant/responsive pedagogy as praxis in teacher education. *The New Educator, 14*(2), 87–90.

Kitchen, J. (2005). Conveying respect and empathy: Becoming a relational teacher educator. *Studying Teacher Education, 1*(2), 195–207.

Kitchen, J. (2006). Reflecting on the feedback loop in reflective practice: A teacher educator responds to reflective writing by preservice teachers. *Proceedings of the Sixth Annual International Conference on Self-study of Teacher Education Practices*, 147–151.

Kitchen, J. (2009). Relational teacher development: Growing collaboratively in a hoping relationship. *Teacher Education Quarterly, 36*(2), 45–62.

LaBoskey, V. K. (2004a). The methodology of self-study and its theoretical underpinnings. In J. J. Loughran, M. L. Hamilton, V. K. LaBoskey, & T. Russell (Eds.), *International handbook of self-study of teacher education practices* (pp. 817–869). Dordrecht: Kluwer Academic Publishers.

LaBoskey, V. (2004b). Moving the study of self-study research and practice forward: Challenges and opportunities. In J. Loughran, M. L. Hamilton, V. LaBoskey, & T. Russell (Eds.), *International handbook of self-study of teaching and teacher education practices* (pp. 817–869). Dordrecht: Kluwer.

Ladson-Billings, G. (1995). Toward a theory of culturally relevant pedagogy. *American Educational Research Journal, 32*(3), 465–491.

Ladson-Billings, G. J. (2005). Is the team all right? Diversity and teacher education. *Journal of Teacher Education, 56*, 229–234.

Loughran, J. (2007). Developing a pedagogy of teacher education. *British Journal of Educational Technology, 38*(4), 381–396.

Lucas, T. & Villegas, A. (2013). Preparing linguistically responsive teachers: Laying the foundation in preservice teacher education. *Theory Into Practice, 52*(2), 98–109.

MacKinnon, A. M., & Bullock, S. M. (2016). Playing in tune: Reflection, resonance, and the dossier. In D. Garbett & A. Ovens (Eds.), *Enacting self-study as methodology for professional inquiry* (pp. 291–296). Herstmonceux, UK: S-STEP.

Martin, A. (2018). Professional identities and pedagogical practices: A self-study on the "becomings" of a teacher educator and teachers. In D. Garbett & A. Ovens (Eds.), *Pushing boundaries and crossing borders: Self-study as a means for researching pedagogy*. Herstmonceux, UK: S-STEP.

McDonald, M. A. (2005). The integration of social justice in teacher education: Dimensions of prospective teachers' opportunities to learn. *Journal of Teacher Education, 56*(2), 418–435.

McKenzie and Scheurich. (2004). Equity traps: A useful construct for preparing principals to lead schools that are successful with racially diverse students. *Educational Administration Quarterly, 40*(5), 601–632.

McLaren, P. (2015). *Life in schools: An introduction to critical pedagogy in the foundations of education*. New York: Paradigm.

Mogadime, D. (2011). An Ethnography of two teachers' antiracist and critical multicultural Practices. *Brock Education, 21*(1), 33–52.

Montgomery, K. (2013). Pedagogy and privilege: The challenges and possibilities of teaching critically about racism. *Critical Education, 4*(1), 1–22.

Munby, H., & Russell, T. (1994). The authority of experience in learning to teach: Messages from a physics methods class. *Journal of Teacher Education, 45*(2), 86–102.

Nieto, S. (2004). *Affirming diversity: The sociopolitical context of multicultural education*. Boston: Allyn and Bacon.

Noddings, N. (2002). *Starting at home: Caring and social policy*. Berkeley: University of California Press.

O'Connor, K. (2016). A pedagogy of place: Promoting relational knowledge in science teacher education. *Teacher Learning and Professional Development, 1*(1), 44–60.

Palmer, P. (1998). *The courage to teach: Exploring the inner landscapes of a teacher's life*. San Francisco: Jossey Bass.

Pinar, W. (2004). *What is curriculum theory?* Mahwah, NJ: Lawrence Erlbaum Associates.

Pinnegar, S., & Hamilton, M. L. (2009). *Self-study of practice as a genre of qualitative research: Theory, methodology, and practice*. Dordrecht, NL: Springer.

Pinnegar, S., & Hamilton, M. L. (2014). Intimate scholarship in research: An example from self-study of teaching and teacher education practices methodology. *Learning Landscapes, 8*(1), 154–170.

Ragoonaden, K. (2015a). Mindful education and well-being. In K. Ragoonaden (Ed.), *Mindful teaching and learning: Developing a pedagogy of well-being* (pp. 17–31). Lanham, MD: Lexington Books.

Ragoonaden, K. (2015b). Self-study of teacher education practices and self-study: The fifth moment in a teacher educator's journey. *Studying Teacher Education, 11*(1), 81–95.

Ragoonaden, K. O., Sivia, A., and Baxan, V. (2015). "Teaching for diversity in teacher education: Transformative frameworks." *The Canadian Journal for the Scholarship of Teaching and Learning, 6*(3), 145–169.

Reeves, J. & LeMare, L. (2017). Supporting teachers in relational pedagogy and social emotional education: A qualitative exploration. *International journal of emotional education, 9*(1), 85–98.

Roeser, R. W., Skinner, E., Beers, J., & Jennings, P. A. (2012). Mindfulness training and teachers' professional development: An emerging area of research and practice. *Child Development Perspectives, 6*(2), 167–173.

Schoeberlein, D. & Sheth, S. (2009). *Mindful teaching and teaching mindfulness.* Somerville, MD: Wisdom Publications.

Schön, D. A. (1987). *Educating the Reflective Practitioner.* San Francisco, CA: Jossey-Bass.

Sheets, R. H. (2005). *Diversity pedagogy: Examining the role of culture in the teaching-learning process.* Boston: Pearson.

Shor, I. (1992). *Empowering education: Critical teaching for social change.* Chicago: University of Chicago Press.

Sivia, A., & MacMath, S. (2016). Examining the university-profession divide: An inquiry into a teacher education program's practices. *The Canadian Journal for the Scholarship of Teaching and Learning, 7*(2), 1–17.

Sivia, A. K. (2017). *Discord and dissonance: Living through and learning from a teacher educator's memories* (Unpublished doctoral dissertation). Simon Fraser University, Burnaby, B.C.

Sleeter, C. (2001). Preparing teachers for culturally diverse school: Research and the overwhelming presence of Whiteness. *Journal of Teacher Education, 52*(2), 94–106.

Sleeter, C. E. (2012). Confronting the marginalization of culturally responsive pedagogy. *Urban Education, 47*(3), 562–584.

Solorzano, D. G. (1997). Images and world that wound: Critical race theory, racial stereotyping, and teacher education. *Teacher Education Quarterly, 24*(3), 5–19.

Toh, S. H. & Cawagas, V. F. (2010). Peace Education, ESD and the Earth Charter: interconnections and synergies. *Journal of Education for Sustainable Development, 4*(2), 167–180.

Van Manen, M. 1997. *Research lived experience.* London ON: The Althouse Press.

Villegas, A. M. (2007). Dispositions in teacher education: A look at social justice. *Journal of Teacher Education, 58*(5), 370–380.

Villegas, A. M., & Lucas, T. (2002). Preparing culturally responsive teachers: Rethinking the curriculum. *Journal of Teacher Education, 53*(1), 22–31.

Villegas, A. M., & Lucas, T. (2007). The culturally responsive teacher. *Educational Leadership, 13*(22), 33–58.

Wolk, S. (1998). *A democratic classroom.* New York: Stenhouse Publishers.

Chapter Six

Embedding Lived Indigenous Perspectives in Teacher Education

Co-constructing Mindful Pathways for Truth, Reconciliation, and Social Justice

Terry-Lee Beaudry,
Kevin Kaiser, and Karen Ragoonaden

UNPACKING THE WHY

These are the narratives of many, ours and theirs, of learning and unlearning, of storying and re-storying, of standing by and witnessing our journeys toward *w*holistic understandings of the Truth and Reconciliation Commission's Calls to Action, pressing toward respectful, reciprocal, relevant, and responsible ways of being and doing. In doing so, we are sharing our experiences of embedding lived Indigenous perspectives in teacher education. Taking our lead from scholarly literature in Diversity Pedagogy, Social Justice and Mindfulness, we explore the collaborations supporting our pathways toward truth and reconciliation.

KAREN'S STORY: LEARNING ABOUT THE TRC

In June 2015, the Truth and Reconciliation Commission (TRC) of Canada released an Executive Summary along with ninety-four calls to action regarding reconciliation between Canadians and Indigenous peoples. The purpose of the commission was to document the history and intergenerational impacts of the Canadian Indian residential school system on Indigenous children and their families. While the Commission concluded that the Indian residential school system amounted to cultural genocide, the recommendations focused on redressing the legacy of residential schools and advancing the process of reconciliation. As stated in the TRC, "now that we know about residential schools and their legacy, what do we do about it?" (p.vi).

Our chapter responds to the question, *what do we do about it*? Framed as an example of relational mindfulness, we explore contextual factors, key institutional and faculty specific supports including best practices for conceptualizing and developing pathways for mindfully acknowledging First Nations, Inuit and Métis Peoples of British Columbia, Canada. Specifically the TRC Call for Action, Education as Reconciliation # 62 is the focus of our discussion.

> 62. We call upon the federal, provincial, and territorial governments, in consultation and collaboration with Survivors, Aboriginal peoples, and educators, to:
> i. Make age-appropriate curriculum on residential schools, Treaties, and Aboriginal peoples' historical and contemporary contributions to Canada a mandatory education requirement for Kindergarten to Grade 12 students.

As educators, the TRC Calls to Action sparked an urgency to decolonize K–12 and post-secondary educational institutions by prioritizing the reconceptualization of curriculum, embedding holistic understandings of Canada's past with contemporary perspectives of Indigenous peoples, and co-constructing new pathways toward truth and reconciliation. This marks a time in Canada's history where past histories are acknowledged, pressing educators to reimagine and re-story teaching and learning along with a shared responsibility toward social justice education through the revelation of truths and commitment to reconciliation.

Reimagining Teacher Education: A New Beginning

Soon after the release of the TRC (2015) report, the Ministry of Education in British Columbia (BC) Canada, released a new curriculum (2016), specifically promoting the insertion of Indigenous perspectives into K–12 curricula. Following the steps of the Ministry of Education, the University of British Columbia's Okanagan School of Education (OSE) took action to reconcile with past historical omissions. Recognizing that the university was built on the unceded land of the Syilx Okanagan Peoples, the OSE invited Knowledge Keepers from the Okanagan Nation Alliance (ONA) to participate in the reimagining of the teacher education program. Members of the ONA, Westbank First Nation, the Okanagan Indian Band, and members of the Métis Federation, came alongside faculty, teachers, educational leaders, and community members to cocreate a vision, prioritizing the indigenization of curriculum as an important component of the newly-imagined teacher education program. Named, INSPIRE (in situ scholar practitioner inquiry to reimagine education), the program is representative of a university community alliance built on respectful, reciprocal, relevant, and responsible relationships with First Nation, Inuit and Métis Peoples of Canada (Kirkness & Barnhardt, 1991; Macintyre Latta et al., 2018).

As mindful community discussions evolved about how best to co-construct the INSPIRE program, colleagues from Indigenous communities proposed a "wholistic approach" to the teacher education program. Pidgeon, Archibald, and Hawkley (2009) conceptualized the *w*holistic Indigenous Framework emphasizing the interconnectedness of the intellectual, physical, emotional, and spiritual elements of human development. Adopting a wholistic approach, mindful considerations were given to the connections and relations of family and community as well as the impact of institutional and political influences in the development of the teacher education program.

With the vision of creating a rich tapestry of understandings, the Indigenous Knowledge Keepers imagined threads of indigeneity interwoven throughout the teacher education program. This approach required a shared commitment among all faculty to embed authentic Indigenous history, traditional teachings, and contemporary perspectives within their coursework. However, this shared commitment was not without its issues. It was recognized that this new approach would be complex, instilling new vulnerabilities for faculty and teacher candidates.

We recognized that this wholistic approach to indigenizing all aspects of coursework would require mindful attitudes and dispositions, like being present, paying attention in a particular way, on purpose and nonjudgmentally, to the unfolding of experience moment to moment (Kabat-Zinn, 2012). This attentiveness is at the heart of mindfulness practices, and to a certain extent, the *First Peoples Principles of Learning*, bringing clarity to a way of knowing while inspiring a way of being.

TERRY'S STORY: EMBEDDING FIRST PEOPLES PRINCIPLES OF LEARNING

Along with community consultations, the curricular document, The *First Peoples Principles of Learning* served as important guidelines for the INSPIRE program (First Nations Education Steering Committee, 2008). The principles represent an attempt to identify common elements in the varied teaching and learning approaches that are prevalent in First Peoples societies. They include nine belief statements:

- Learning ultimately supports the well-being of the self, the family, the community, the land, the spirits, and the ancestors.

- Learning is holistic, reflexive, reflective, experiential, and relational (focused on connectedness, on reciprocal relationships, and sense of place).
- Learning involves recognizing the consequences of one's actions.
- Learning involves generational roles and responsibilities.
- Learning recognizes the role of Indigenous knowledge.
- Learning is embedded in memory, history, and story.
- Learning involves patience and time.
- Learning requires exploration of one's identity.
- Learning involves recognizing that some knowledge is sacred and only shared with permission or in certain situations.

Establishing an Indigenous Education Council (IEC)

As faculty and local Indigenous community members considered how to embed Indigenous content, history, and perspectives into the teacher education curricula, the idea of reestablishing an Indigenous Education Council (IEC), consisting of local Knowledge Keepers, Indigenous scholars, and faculty, to support efforts to cocreate authentic learning experiences anchored in traditional and ancestral knowledges, emerged. With the release of the TRC (2015), BC's New Curriculum (2016), and the new teacher education program, INSPIRE (2017), it was time to reconnect with community members (MacIntyre Latta et al., 2017).

Mindful Applications of Reimagining Education

Once the IEC was established, the first forthcoming recommendation focused on bringing the teacher candidates, all non-Indigenous, on to the ancestral lands of the Syilx Okanagan Peoples. With the consent of the Westbank First Nation (WFN), the first day of the INSPIRE program was spent participating and engaging in a traditional welcome. On that warm, Okanagan summer afternoon, over one hundred people (strangers to each other) held hands, in a circle, denoting a sense of equality and a new beginning of deep learning and experiences for all. Members of WFN spoke of the territory, their values, and traditional beliefs, encouraging open dialogue and questions from the faculty and teacher candidates. The truths that were revealed on the first day spoke to the importance of the learning ahead and foreshadowed a compelling theme of sense-making in relation to identity.

> This is my first time on the Westbank First Nation Reserve even though I have lived in the Okanagan for 26 years. I believe this is the beginning of a long and important journey and relationship. I believe this journey must take place slowly and be filled with integrity and respect. (OSE Teacher Candidate, 2017)

> I've spent the majority of my life in the Okanagan and have never heard the language before today. This was an experience I will always carry with me. (OSE Teacher Candidate, 2017)

> This journey will be hard. I'm not sure where I am going or meant to go nor an I sure how to get there. (OSE Teacher Candidate, 2017)

Feedback from that very first day reflected a deep sense of gratitude for the opportunity to participate in a traditional opening on WFN land. This was the beginning of authentic, Indigenous in situ learning, highlighting the importance of a sense of place, for all learners, and the beginning of a journey involving collaborative storying and re-storying.

From Reimaging Education to Re-storying Education

As we progressed from reimaging education through INSPIRE, we also recognized the importance of re-storying Indigenous histories, content and perspectives into the teacher education curricula. Re-storying social justice practices are one way to approach reconciliation by recognizing local narratives and documenting authentic historical realities as a form of resistance aimed at revisionist history. Within this context, story work and re-storying offered numerous opportunities to learn and relearn, again and again, becoming an active and dynamic curriculum planning and development involving Elders, knowledge holders, and community members (Archibald, 2008; Hare, 2011; Ragoonaden et al., 2009).

The storying and re-storying experiences below are representative of mindful teachings and learnings instigating connections to self and society, between the TRC Calls to Action (2015), BC's New Curriculum (2016), the First Peoples Principles of Learning, and the INSPIRE teacher education program (2017).

Learning Requires Exploration of One's Identity

Within a circle, teacher candidates began to share their personal cultural identities and family ancestries. Reading and referencing the stories from British Columbia's Indigenous communities provoked rich, engaging discussions that often lead to personal introspection, exposing person biases and unveiling new truths learned.

> As I read and hear Indigenous perspectives, traditional and contemporary, my truth is I have much to learn. I was very ignorant before starting this program when it came to understanding Indigenous perspectives but I have learned so much about truth and reconciliation, shaping a new identity for me—that is to be an ally going forward.
> (OSE Teacher Candidate, 2018)

Learning Involves Recognizing that Some Knowledge is Sacred and Only Shared with Permission or in Certain Situations

Facilitated by Elders, faculty, and teacher candidates were invited onto the Westbank First Nation Beach where Elders facilitated traditional circle teachings and a water ceremony, marking the importance of honoring and caring for the water as a "giver of life" (Okanagan National Alliance Water Declaration, 2014). Hearing the traditional songs, stories, and teachings firsthand from Elders was a profound experience for all present, marking the importance of in situ learning. Teacher candidates learned from Elders the sacredness of ceremony and many regarded it an honoring and privilege to be gifted this opportunity. This beginning sense of connectedness to community revealed the power of quieting our voices to hear the teachings of local Elders and community share their stories.

> The water ceremony not only allowed me to experience a deeply spiritual aspect of community building; it cleansed and prepared me for the upcoming year. In conversations with Elders after the ceremony, I shared with them challenges that I'm struggling with. They gave me instructions for conducting my own water ceremony for ten days. I am now re-energized, grounded—ready to embark on this journey of personal transformation. (OSE Teacher Candidate, 2018)

Learning Recognizes the Consequences of One's Actions

Teacher candidates engaged in coursework and participated in various iterations of cultural sensitivity training through presentations on identity, stereotypes, bias, and the effects of residential schools and colonization. The KAIROS Blanket Exercise,[1] for example, facilitated by local Indigenous secondary school students, unpacked the history of Indigenous peoples. As historical truths were revealed, Elders provided support to those in a high emotional state.

> My truth and reconciliation [after this learning] is to stop friends from talking negatively about First Nations peoples. I will use my new knowledge, gifted to me, to inform others (about what is true). (OSE Teacher Candidate, 2018)

Learning is Embedded in Memory, History, and Story

From Indigenous storytelling sessions, connected to Indigenous literacy methodologies, to panel discussions (consisting of chief and council members, Knowledge Keepers, residential school survivors, Indigenous entrepreneurs and artists, and non-Indigenous educators), these learning sessions were co-constructed to teach through personal narratives. Personalized stories revealed historical experiences with residential schools to contemporary perspectives on self-governing nations, Indigenous treaty rights, and United Nations Indigenous rights. After a panel discussion, teacher candidates were asked: What has resonated with you today?

One teacher candidate wrote:

> I pledge to practice the concept of Métissage in my future classroom, in which all stories are respected and valued equally. I hope to work with all students in non-judgemental ways and respect their prior knowledge and ways of knowing. (OSE Teacher Candidate, 2018)

Learning Involves Generational Roles and Responsibilities

The opportunities for teacher candidates to learn in community has led to new relationships and connections with Elders, Knowledge Keepers, and community members. This concept of generational connectedness was interwoven throughout several courses and in situ experiences.

> I really liked pairing the multi-generational cultural knowledge with artistic practice—profound learning. (OSE Teacher Candidate, 2018)

After ten months of threading Indigenous teachings and learnings throughout coursework and in situ experiences, one teacher candidate wrote:

> I feel so grateful that Indigenous peoples in the community have been such a central part of our [teacher education] program and have taken the time to tell us their stories and their experiences with reconciliation. Deep learning has come from these hands-on experiences and connections with community. (OSE Teacher Candidate, 2018)

KEVIN'S STORY: SYNTHESIZING OUR LEARNING: INDIGENOUS IMMERSION WITHIN A LOCAL CONTEXT

I am a Stellate'en First Nation member working on the unceded territory of the Syilx Okanagan Nation. I continued with the thread of re-storying Indigenous content, histories, and perspectives in an outdoor, experiential Summer Institute course offered to teacher candidates and service teachers. I served to scaffold the learning from the courses held during the academic year, supporting teacher candidates as they deepened their learning, co-constructing multiple pathways to authentically embed Indigenous teachings and learnings in K–12 curriculum. The course titled, *Living the First Peoples Principles of Learning in the Okanagan Context*, invited a profound exploration of Indigenous ways of being and ways of doing. The course provided pathways for non-Indigenous teachers working with First Nation or Métis youth to develop the necessary confidence to design culturally responsive learning.

While some historical knowledge about the intergenerational trauma of the Indian Residential Schools was required, the course focused on the Indigenous wholistic and ecological ways of teaching and learning.

To move forward with the Truth and Reconciliation Calls to Action in Education, it is important to examine education from varying perspectives, creating an education ecosystem of change practitioners. For this reason, the course continued the focus on the First Peoples Principles of Learning (FPPL), describing what a First Peoples approach to learning *is*, what it *supports, involves, recognizes*, and *embeds* (FNESC, 2008). These principles are meant to be experiential and not a structured set of lessons or unit plans. Westernized teachers need to develop their understanding of place and context so that the principles align what is relevant and timely for their students and communities (Chrona, 2014). For example, developing shared learnings about the mythical Ogopogo of Lake Okanagan, known as N'ha-a-tik, the Spirit of the Lake to the Okanagan People, can provide non-Indigenous teachers with a context to understand local and placed-based First Nations perspectives.

A part of this process includes mindful investigations of everyday lives through contemplative experiences (with attention to our inner lives) and relational experiences (with attention to our social, cultural, and historical connections). To support this collective and collaborative inquiry, I introduced participants to methods of reflective life writing (Hanson, 2017; Kelly, 2010). Through life writing, participants described, curated, and individually and collectively engaged in ongoing sense-making, all the while reflecting on: *Who am I? Where am I? Who are we together in this place each day?*

ENGAGING IN RELATIONAL MINDFULNESS AND INDIGENOUS LEARNING

As the stories unfolded, life experiences came to the foreground of reflecting on identity and positionality in society. This type of identity work is important especially when learning how to work with Indigenous communities and youth. Circle discussions, known as Talking Circles, supported this reflection. This framework allowed teachers and teacher candidates to see who they are and what they bring to their learning path and how to move even deeper into Indigenous ways of knowing. An important component in this process is the building of trust between non-Indigenous educators and Indigenous communities. By co-constructing protocols for respectful dialogue, truths emerged providing a safe place to question, share vulnerabilities, and scaffold learning to create deeper understandings.

The Talking Circles followed specific protocols to ensure that all voices were heard, enabling trust to be built. Some of the protocols for the talking circles were created by the participants themselves, and it was remarkable how close they were to traditional protocols.

- Positive comments only. Be mindful of your words.
- Talk truths about how you feel or things that you experienced.
- Share from your heart, remain true to yourself. Talking circles are not a place for untruths.
- Leave space for others to be truthful.

To facilitate deeper connections, an online talking circle took the form of a blog to provoke teacher candidates' reflections on the learnings of the day. The guiding questions elicited deep inquiry and new sense-making:

- How can educators develop an awareness of self and others in ways that increase their capacity to attend to the needs and interests of their students?
- What does it mean to enliven the redesigned curriculum with an understanding of First Peoples Principles of Learning?
- How does this understanding support opportunities for critical/creative thinking and personal/social exploration in their classroom?

Expectations for the online circle included following the threads of written conversation that are most meaningful to each participant and comment on contributions from peers. The blog was not intended to be laborious or overly lengthy in responses.

During this time, the teacher candidates were also exposed to authentic experiences on the land that included meeting with Elders and hearing firsthand their experiences in school. These days were always heavy with deep, meaningful conversations. All participants were given the time and space to reflect on these interactions. The Elders were open and honest, remaining mindful on how the sharing of personal stories may trigger emotional responses. To ensure everyone felt safe, we started each day with a talking circle to go over what we were about to experience.

> I feel so blessed to be around all these amazing future educators. There is real compassion and care for students and each other that can be felt when talking in circle. (OSE Teacher Candidate, 2018)

In our interactions with the Elders, teacher candidates learned the importance of creating safe spaces wherever they go because the time students have in their classrooms might be the only safe space they will have all day.

> This course was very eye opening for me, on a personal and professional level. It made me realize how much of my own story I still have to untangle. Since

we started this course I have been on the phone with my dad every night, sometimes for hours just to sort through some feelings. (OSE Teacher Candidate, 2018)

By taking teachers and candidates out onto the land to pick traditional medicines as well as cook and eat traditional foods, the participants realized ways in which traditional Indigenous ways are embedded within a contemporary context.

Building strength within students requires the teacher to possess the capacity to build solid relationships by focusing on how important parents are to children, how important a safe home is to raising children, and how important opportunity is for all students. This way, we are setting up conditions to learn how Indigenous students may have felt and reacted when these things were taken away from them through Residential Schools, the 60s Scoop (a practice that occurred in Canada of taking, or "scooping up," Indigenous children from their families and communities for placement in foster homes or adoption), children in care, and incarceration.

Education has come a long way in the past few years, and the need to provide culturally-relevant education for Indigenous and non-Indigenous educators has never been more important (Ragoonaden & Mueller, 2017). One of the skills all educators need to possess is the ability to identify authentic Indigenous resources for the classroom and imagine how they might engage students with the resources. This involves more than a Google search. This requires an authentic knowledge of the history and contemporary issues surrounding Indigenous communities. This understanding enables educators to also focus on the beautiful part of Indigenous culture without appropriating the culture, and allow all people to appreciate the culture. The key to avoiding appropriation is to consult with the local Band and/or community Knowledge Keepers first to determine appropriate local resources and to seek permission to use these resources.

One of the most common questions teacher candidates ask is why the need to mandate Indigenous content in the redesigned BC curriculum? The easy answer is to create safe spaces for Indigenous learners to thrive. To emphasize the importance of relevancy in learning, learning was presented in a variety of contexts beyond the traditional classroom. In doing so, the conditions were set for teacher candidates to engage in collaborative inquiry with Elders and Knowledge Keepers.

Creating a Mindful Awareness: Where We Are ... Where We Need to Go

> What had once seemed intimidating and scary now seems attainable. I am grateful to be part of a teacher education program that prioritizes Indigenous education. (OSE Teacher Candidate, 2018)

This chapter has attempted to respond to the TRC's (2015) seminal question: *Now that we know about the residential schools and their legacy, what do we do about it?* As we three come to the end of our story, we reflect on how this mindful journey has facilitated connections between history, land, and people. By being present and aware of embodied conceptions of self, within the discourse of teacher education, new ways of being and new ways of doing have emerged. As we continue to journey together, there are particular in situ teachings which have disrupted and shifted mindsets, provoked new learnings, and deepened commitments to truth and reconciliation. Faculty, students, and community members have engaged in learning together, fostering deeper understandings of Indigenous history, identities and local epistemologies of the Okanagan territory; and yet, we would all agree that we have not arrived. What we do know is that the more we explore, in situ, the authentic identities of Indigenous peoples, the more we unpack our own truths and biases, provoking new opportunities for Indigenous and non-Indigenous educators to learn together (Macintyre et al., 2017). This commitment to learning the truths will deepen our own sense of identity. Only then will we be fully ready to engage in reconciliation, moving us beyond knowing and understanding to a way of being—inclusive, culturally responsive, and committed to equity, setting the conditions for all Indigenous and non-Indigenous learners to thrive mindfully and purposefully. By sharing our experiences of embedding lived Indigenous perspectives in teacher education, we acknowledge the challenges and the rewards of critical transformative pedagogies aimed at creating fair, equitable, and just ways of being and ways of doing.

We, Terry, Kevin, and Karen, recognize and honor the opportunity to live, work, and learn on the unceded territory of the Syilx Okanagan People.

NOTE

1. The KAIROS Blanket Exercise™ is an experiential history lesson, codeveloped with Indigenous Elders, Knowledge Keepers, and educators promoting truth, understanding, respect, and reconciliation among Indigenous and non-Indigenous peoples.

REFERENCES

Archibald, J. (Q'um Q'um Xiiem). (2008). *Indigenous storywork: Educating the heart, mind, body, and spirit*. Vancouver, BC: UBC Press.

Battiste, M. (2014). *Decolonizing education: Nourishing the learning spirit*. Saskatoon: Purich Publishing.

Battiste, M., & Henderson, J. (2009). Naturalizing Indigenous knowledge in Eurocentric education. *Canadian Journal of Native Education, 32*(1), 5–18.

British Columbia Ministry of Education and First Nations Education Steering Committee (2008). English 12 First Peoples Integrated Resource Package (2008). Retrieved from http://www.bced.gov.bc.ca/irp/pdfs/english_language_arts/2008eng12_firstppl.pdf.

British Columbia Ministry of Education (2013–2014). Transforming curriculum and instruction. Retrieved from: https://curriculum.gov.bc.ca/.

Chrona, J. (2014). Learning ultimately supports the well-being of the self, the family, the community, the land, the spirits, and the ancestors. Retrieved from https://firstpeoplesprinciplesoflearning.wordpress.com.

Corntassel, J., is, C.-w.-., & T'lakwadzi. (2009). Indigenous storytelling, truth-telling, and community approaches to reconciliation. *ESC: English Studies in Canada, 35*(1), 137–159.

First Nations Eucation Steering Committee (2008). *Teacher resource guide: English 12 First Peoples*. West Vancouver, British Columbia.

Hanson, K. (2017). *A mindful teaching community: Possibilities for teacher professional development*. Landham, MD: Lexington.

Hare, J. (2011). They tell a story and there's meaning behind that story: Indigenous knowledge and young Indigenous children's literacy learning. *Journal of Early Childhood Literacy, 12*(4) 389–414.

Kabat-Zinn, Jon. (2012). *Mindfulness for beginners: Reclaiming the present moment and your life*. Boulder, CO: Sounds True, Inc.

The Kairos Blanket Exercise. (n.d.). Retrieved from https://www.kairosblanketexercise.org/.

Kelly, V. (2010). Finding face, finding heart, and finding foundation: Life writing and the transformation of educational practice. *TCI (Transnational Curriculum Inquiry), 7*(2), 82–100.

Kirkness, V. J., & Barnhardt, R. (1991). First Nations and higher education: The four R's respect, relevance, reciprocity, responsibility. *Journal of American Indian Education, 30*(3), 1–15.

Kitchenham, A., Fraser, T., Pidgeon, M., & Ragoonaden, K. (2016). *Aboriginal education enhancement agreements: Complicated conversations as pathways to success*. Victoria, BC: BC Ministry of Education. Retrieved from: http://www2.gov.bc.ca/assets/gov/education/administration/kindergarten-to-grade-12/aboriginal-education/research/aeea_report.pdf.

Macintyre Latta, M., Cherkowski, S., Crichton, S., Klassen, W., & Ragoonaden, K. (2018) Investing in communities of scholar-practitioners. *Teacher Learning and Professional Development. 2(1)* 32–44.

Macintyre Latta, M., Hanson, K., Ragoonaden, K., Briggs, W., & Middleton, T. (2017). Accessing the curricular play of critical and creative thinking. *Canadian Journal of Education 4*(3) 1–28.

Okanagan Nation Alliance. (2018). Okanagan Nation Alliance 2017–2018 Report. Retrieved from https://www.syilx.org/about-us/operations/annual-reports/.

Okanagan National Alliance Water Declaration, 2014. Retrieved from https://www.syilx.org/about-us/.

Pidgeon, M., Archibald, J.-A., & Hawkey, C. (2014). Relationships matter: Supporting Aboriginal graduate students in British Columbia, Canada. *Canadian Journal of Higher Education, 40*(1), 1–21.

Ragoonaden, K., Cherkowski, S., Baptiste, M., & Després, B. (2009). Sntrusntm i7 captikwlh: Unravel the story, the Okanagan way. *Alberta Journal of Educational Research, 55*(3), 382–396.

Ragoonaden, K., & Mueller, L. (2017). Culturally responsive pedagogy in higher education: Indigenizing curriculum. *Canadian Journal of Higher Education, 47*(2), 22–46. http://journals.sfu.ca/cjhe/index.php/cjhe/article/view/187963.

Ragoonaden, K., Macintyre Latta, M., Hanson, K., Draper, R., & Coble, J. (in press). Broadening, burrowing, storying and re-storying Indigenous narratives: A holistic exploration of an arts based curricular experience. *Alberta Journal of Educational Research.*

Truth and Reconciliation Canada. (2015). *Honouring the truth, reconciling for the future: Summary of the final report of the Truth and Reconciliation Commission of Canada.* Winnipeg: Truth and Reconciliation Commission of Canada.

Chapter Seven

A Relational Approach to Collaborative Research and Practice among Teacher Educators in Urban Contexts

Jane McIntosh Cooper, Leslie M. Gauna, Christine E. Beaudry, and Gayle A. Curtis

We call ourselves Las Chicas Críticas (The Critical Girls), an identifying marker capturing our ongoing and evolving collective identity. Chicas Críticas captures our shared commitment to social justice pedagogy, grounded in common practical experience in urban K–16 teaching contexts, along with our identities as women connected to Latinx presence in Texas. Latinx is used as a gender-neutral word for people of Latin American descent (Merriam-Webster, 2019). We have worked and written together for over eight years in various roles: graduate students, authors, team teachers, peer support, co-researchers, and friends. Recently, we turned our reflection on our lived experience together to strengthen our practice. We realize as we have transitioned into post-doctoral instructors in higher education that our work together has sustained and nurtured us. This chapter highlights our reflections on how our work together sustains and fulfills us as teacher educators.

We have previously analyzed how we co-constructed knowledge about classroom practices through self-study, while in this piece we look more closely at our Chicas relationship. Self-study is recognized as an approach for "developing new understandings and producing new knowledge about teaching and learning" through teachers studying their practices (Hamilton & Pinnegar, 1998, p. 243). Turning our collective critical eye to the relational and sustaining qualities of our group, we found Kitchen's (2016) characteristics of Relational Teacher Education (RTE) to be useful "lenses through which to think about [ourselves], practice and engagement" (p. 170). For this chapter, we extend the concept of RTE as an analytical framework in distilling the distinctive features of our peer collaboration. Our aim is to strengthen aspects of our individual and collective identities and to reinforce our commitment to social justice aims in teacher education practices. Specifically, we use several of Kitchen's (2016) RTE characteristics that resonated with us: (1) understanding the professional landscape, (2) having and conveying respect and empathy, and (3) understanding one's own personal practical knowledge to frame and situate the experiences that have occurred in our ongoing group collaborations. By delving into the depths of these interactions, we aim to improve our relationships with each other, with the students in our classrooms, and with others in the professional community.

METHODS

This self-study of our collaborative approach emerges from our eight-year longitudinal investigation of critical perspectives in teacher education, which has resulted in several presentations and publications (e.g., Cooper, Beaudry, Gauna, & Curtis, 2018; Cooper, Gauna, & Curtis, 2016). We now seek to extend our "reflection on practice . . . and move to wider communication and consideration of ideas, i.e., the generation and communication of new knowledge and understandings" (Loughran & Northfield, 1998, p. 15). We recognize that multiple perspectives are integral to transforming practice and ongoing dialogue is crucial to the meaning-making process in our experiences (Hamilton, Pinnegar, & Davey, 2016). Data used for this study was collected Summer 2017–Fall 2018. As a group, we met weekly (online or face-to-face) to share reflections (Schön, 1983), collaboratively interrogate individual practices as a way of storying and re-storying our experiences (Craig, 1997), and continue to refine our data and outcomes. Audio-taped meetings, shared database meeting notes, written journal reflections, and classroom artifacts were data sources.

Interim texts represented major transformations in our thinking and practice (Tidwell et al., 2012) and were often based on critical incidents (Tripp, 1993/2012). Exemplars chosen were jointly analyzed for inter-participant reliability (Connelly, Clandinin, & He, 1997). Interim field texts were inductively coded (Charmaz, 2006) individually, then collectively as each identified points of convergence and dissonance with perceived values of relational practice (LaBoskey, 2004).

Exemplars chosen for inclusion represent shared experiences of group practice (Lyons & LaBoskey, 2002), lending trustworthiness to this work (Mishler, 1990). These exemplars are "elaborated so that members of a relevant research community can judge for themselves 'trustworthiness' and the validity of observations, interpretations, etc." (Lyons & LaBoskey, 2002, p. 20). Furthermore, we ground our work in the authority of experience (Munby & Russell, 1994). Exemplars are somewhat fictionalized to protect anonymity.

LAS CHICAS CRÍTICAS: AN EVOLVING IDENTITY

We look historically at the Chicas group identity to distill relevant aspects and patterns of relationship. At our university's College of Education, we came together in graduate school with shared commitments and knowledge of critical values and theory. While, many colleagues shared this stance, what bound us together was a firm ethical commitment and priority to enact these values in our classroom practices.

In our early collaboration, we were graduate students beginning to make connections to our critical commitments, lived experiences as teachers, and budding individual research agendas. In this early stage of our collaboration we functioned as colleagues and mentors who "walked alongside" each other (Curtis, 2013). During that time, we began meeting weekly to support our writing. Through the process, we came to understand and value the others' personal practical knowledge (Connelly & Clandinin, 1988), or "the experiential knowledge that is embodied in them as persons and is enacted in their classroom practices and in their lives" (Connelly & Clandinin, 1994, p. 149).

After receiving our doctoral degrees, we began collaborating in response to our common educational demands, particularly around the areas of classroom practice, research, and professional dispositions. We continued weekly meetings focused more systematically on problems of practice while implementing critical values in classroom settings. We struggled with isolation as new work experiences distanced us from one another. We began recording meetings to document ideas, themes, and instances for reference. We learned more about shared commitment to enact challenging critical and social justice curriculum. In short, Chicas Críticas developed into a knowledge community (Craig, 1992, 1995).

As faculty, in our latest phase of group development, we have become more focused by merging our classroom and research demands through systematic study of the integration of our critical values into our classroom practices. Over the past three years we have conducted several cycles of self-study on our practice. First, we identified the core critical values we individually and collectively shared: co-construction of knowledge and deconstruction of commonly held ideas (Cooper, Gauna, & Curtis, 2016). We collected data and met to unpack findings from our conversations and student reflections. Findings suggested strategic changes within classroom practices in the areas of assessments, classroom dialogue, and feedback (Cooper, Beaudry, Gauna, & Curtis, 2018). Our continued collaboration over several stages of inquiry is significant, leading to unanticipated insights about our relationship.

We entered this collaborative space to investigate our work of social justice, broadly, and critical pedagogy, specifically. We found that we have also grown in our relationships with each other and our students. Kitchen (2009) suggests that time is a necessary function for relationship in RTE, mirroring Chicas' finding that extended time in collaboration is necessary to enact critical pedagogy in the classroom (Cooper, Beaudry, Gauna, & Curtis, 2018). As we examine our eight years together, extending RTE to peer collaboration, we will distill specific features of our collaborative space that have helped us grow in relationship. We hope to give voice and honor to the depth of experience, growth of knowledge, and deep relationship of the Chicas Críticas.

EXAMINING OUR INTERACTIONS THROUGH THE LENS OF RELATIONAL TEACHER EDUCATION

We chose a representative exemplar dilemma from fall 2018 to focus our reflections and analysis on relational practice. Participants in the exemplar are blinded for anonymity. In our third iteration of classroom changes in response to previous research findings (Cooper, Beaudry, Gauna, & Curtis 2019), we enacted democratic assessment practices. Changes included: purposeful emphasis on measuring growth rather than outcomes, student-determined rubrics and grades, and differentiated iterative feedback. Accompanying these practices were concerted modifications in teaching methods that included extended time for students to work collaboratively, transparency of purposes by the instructor (Cooper, Beaudry, & Gauna, 2018), and vulnerability (Gauna, Cooper, & Beaudry, 2019) to strengthen relationships.

The following exemplar reflects a dilemma that occurred in the midst of these curricular changes.

> *Chicas Teller: After my first round of grading, a student sent an email distressed that his grade was not fair. He had seen other students' work and they received better grades than his while completing less work. He stated that I was "biased" against him and penalizing him. I was completely devastated. I used methods and strategies that our previous research showed would be effective and align to my values. I immediately called one of my Chicas. (September 2018)*

This problem of practice becomes a core experience, or window into our interactions. Below we will unpack responses to this dilemma as a reflection point using modified versions of RTE.

Engaging Our Professional Landscapes

Our deep knowledge of each other's professional landscapes, emerging from our work together, is a keystone to timely and meaningful feedback, resonating with Kitchen's RTE (2009). One of the first responses to the dilemma shared was

> *Listener/Responder: It is really challenging for them [our students] to see that effort is not reflected in the amount of words that they put on the page, or that all grading is subjective, even if it appears standardized. (September 2018)*

Here, we examine how common understandings of three landscapes—our college classrooms, teacher education programs, our joint research—provide valuable tools for strong relationships. Responses to the above dilemma that ensued in Chicas meetings reflected the deep shared knowledge of these professional landscapes.

The college classroom for this dilemma has unique characteristics, knowledge of which makes strong mentorship possible (Kitchen, 2009). The population of this college is comprised of diverse, lower- to middle-income urban students from the surrounding major city—an epicenter of national educational reform, emphasizing standardized outcomes. As critical educators, the Chicas' research involves deconstructing this standardizing context of reform and its impacts upon teaching practices (Cooper, Beaudry, & Gauna, 2019). We understand that effects of standardized measures upon our students include narrowed curriculum (Mehta, 2013), making it more difficult for students to adjust to seemingly radical approaches to assessment enacted in our classes. We also know that standardized reform efforts affect our urban students' K–12 experiences more critically and negatively, as compared to other contexts (Au, 2009). A common practical struggle in our critical classrooms has been to engage students in deconstructing their own educative experiences. The responder above alludes to this knowledge of the common landscape. This shared knowledge becomes a basis for our conversations together.

There is also a shared professional landscape for the Chicas Críticas, which is evident in unpacking the exemplar dilemma. Our roles in university can be isolating and high-stakes (Gauna, Cooper, & Beaudry, 2019). Enacting critical ideals, like democratic assessments, can add to this sense of isolation. While there are many in common cause with the stance of social justice discourse broadly, there is often less comfort with radical approximations of Freire's (2005a) ideals of student-led curriculum. Pressures on teacher education programs from policy makers and philanthro-businesses are narrowing curriculum in university settings (Zeichner, 2018), demanding alignment of outcomes in college classrooms (Cochran-Smith, 2018). This pressure leaves few adherents of radical practices, like democratic assessments. Pressures to conform to norms conflicting with our critical values, leaves the Chicas vulnerable. One negative review from a student can have much import in this context. Shared knowledge of this aspect of the professional landscape became apparent as the mentoring between the Chicas began:

> *Listener/Responder: What are you going to do?*
>
> *Teller: I think I will email him back and try to explain it to him in the email, tell him not to worry . . . so that . . .*
>
> *Listener/Responder: You need to meet with him face to face to discuss, just send an email to set up a time to meet and be empathetic, you don't want to have anything in writing that he might misconstrue.*

It is clear from this interaction that a common understanding of the landscape allows for direct peer mentoring. Knowing the university setting as one where there is not always trust or camaraderie allows for the conversation to go directly to solving the problem of practice.

At the time of this incident, the Chicas Críticas had engaged in several years of investigation into critical practices. Aspects studied collaboratively included impacts of standardized and standardizing curriculum on practice, investigation on critical thinking, and multiple perspective on deconstruction and methods that support social justice aims in classroom practices (Cooper, Beaudry, Gauna, & Curtis, 2018). This previous research context becomes the in situ landscape of this interaction. As the dilemma continued to be discussed in the Chicas Críticas weekly meeting, understanding the research landscape became central to ensuing discussions.

> *Listener/Responder: How transparent were you about your grading practices before you sent out the grades?*
>
> *Teller: I thought I was extremely clear, I'm never sure how well students receive that, or how clear it comes across.*
>
> *Listener/Responder: Students struggle with receiving hard feedback, sometimes I hold the grades until just before I see them in class, so we can talk about it together, and ask them how well they think they would do the first time they practice. (September 2018)*

Transparency was one of several research goals the Chicas emphasized this semester. This conversation is based on the intimate knowledge or the research landscape.

We extend Kitchen's (2009) RTE characteristic of understanding the professional landscape to analyze our peer-to-peer engagement. From the analysis of specific conversations, the common understandings of our three landscapes is a basis from which we engage in mentoring. While the time aspect of our collaboration is clearly key to the depth of shared knowledge, it is the common commitment to continuously engage in critical inquiry into the three knowledge landscapes—research, classroom practices, professionalism—that accounts for its value for individual members. The Chicas become a model for our pedagogy in classrooms for our students, with collaborative inquiries into professional landscapes becoming standard teaching tools. Examples include student group collaborations into problems of student teaching practice, class conversations on school observations, and peer reviews of personal research topics. We hope these methods will give space for students to discover how deep understanding of professional landscape can improve their practice and relationships.

Understanding One's Personal Practical Knowledge

We understand Connelly and Clandinin's (1988) concept of personal practical knowledge to mean one's unique experiential knowledge that, while constantly changing, is embodied by the individual and enacted in one's teaching and daily lived experiences. The Chicas enact RTE reflectively, to be aware of our "moral commitments . . . [and past] personal experiences in order to address challenges of classroom teaching" (Kitchen, 2009, p. 188). The understanding of our personal practical knowledge is the basis for clearly understanding our purposes for curricular decisions. We seek clarity of individual and collective ideals and values through the telling/retelling of individual experience over time (Olson, 1995), enacting these commitments in our pedagogy. This includes democratic assessments as highlighted in the exemplar dilemma. A reaction during the phone call was to use personal practical knowledge to empathize with the Teller as the Listener/Responder recalled times when similar events occurred:

> *Teller: I was devastated that students challenged both my identity as someone who would conflate behavior with academics . . . especially given where I have worked.*
>
> *Listener/Responder: . . . it's really hard when students challenge your identity. (September 2018)*

By valuing the personal practical knowledge of the Teller and having clear resonances with the practical experiences that forms our identity, the Listener/Responder builds on these notions to give support.

The conversation then turned to reminding the Teller how caring an educator she was, that we knew that she understood the importance of preserving student "intellectual safety" through grading procedures. Reflecting on this, the Teller wrote:

> *Teller: Then the conversation turned to her reminding me of my stance toward students and how caring an educator I was. That she understood how much I cared that student "intellectual safety" was preserved through my grading procedures. She respected my practice when she validated the care I had put into developing the methods I employed in that classroom . . . and many times we enacted them together. (Journal entry, September 2018)*

The Teller was validated when our shared history of developing alternative assessment methods were brought to light. Shared personal practical knowledge jointly formed through efforts to revise and build curriculum became the basis for mentorship.

The above conversations demonstrate how the RTE characteristic of understanding personal and collective practical knowledge enables us to explore two main functions of our group: (1) to reflect upon and examine our past, and (2) to strive for an environment that fosters collaboration and reflection (Kitchen, 2016). We look at our past because as Kitchen (2009) reminds us, we "enter the profession . . . not as blank slates but as persons shaped by a wealth of past experiences" (pp. 187–188).

The students' claim of bias in the exemplar dilemma affirmed core beliefs of power relationships for the Chicas. As critical researchers we investigate how practices can be oppressive for students, specifically assessment practices. This common personal practical knowledge was the initial impetus to create democratic assessment practices. The claim of bias became a large threat to our declared shared (and individual) identity, as student placed us in the role of oppressor. Considering that our "practice as . . . teacher educator[s] was grounded in the lessons learned" (Kitchen, 2009, pp. 187–188), our previous research finding on transparent classroom practices was a way to help students make sense of the purposes of our practice. It now became a way for us to make sense of this perceived attack on our identity. In this situation, it meant the need to explain, first to each other and eventually to the student, the criteria for the grading. The next step, as one of the Chicas Críticas suggested, was to be willing to be vulnerable and transparent when meeting the student one-on-one:

> *Listener/Responder: Remember what you told me last time I had to talk to the class? You stated to not be afraid of straightforward person-to-person*

communication with students and you talked about being vulnerable. (October 2018)

Our individual and shared practical knowledge grounded our relationship.

An environment that fosters collaboration and reflection is necessary to clarify personal and co-construct collective practical knowledge. We also consider ourselves "radical" pedagogues, or "individuals who [are] not afraid to confront, to listen, to see the world unveiled . . . not afraid to meet the people or to enter into dialogue with them" (Freire, 2005, p. 39). Our dialogues have not been pain-free. From our collective experiences we know that collaboration requires trust and we have purposefully put the relationship before the often challenging intellectual and sometimes moral work we do together. We have initiated a "check-in" before our meetings, allowing each member to "speak our mind" about pressing issues, personal or professional, or just sharing joys from our work. This prioritizing of the relational has been embedded in or practice, by taking time at the beginning of class to allow for students to "check-in" with each other and with us at the beginning of class.

Through interrogation of our shared Chicas Críticas past, we clarified and co-constructed our personal practical knowledge that informs our multiple identities. To foster the ultimate goals of professional collaboration it is necessary to create an environment that puts the personal first, which we strive to enact in our own classroom and group practices. These classroom environments based on relationship reflect on students' personal practical knowledge as an essential characteristic of building relationships with us, the instructors, and among students. As such, we foster individual and group reflection of their life past experiences through a variety of mediums—writing, enactments, visual expressions, and dialogues—to enable collaborations (Cooper, Beaudry, & Gauna, 2019). Learning about each other's experiences or willingness to understand our personal practical knowledge of self and others can lead to respect and empathy for each other.

Having and Conveying Respect and Empathy

Kitchen (2016) emphasizes that commitments to respect and empathy for preservice teachers are "at the heart of RTE" (p. 180). This resonates with observations from others that emphasize that relationship is at the heart of teaching and must be grounded in ethics of care (Noddings, 1984, 2005). This applies to our peer collaboration as well. Being mindful of caring practices within these relationships foster group well-being (Ragoonaden, 2015), and are central to critical and responsive approaches to teaching and learning (Freire, 2005; Gay, 2010). As Kitchen (2016) observes:

> Although commitment to respect and empathy requires no specialized skills, it is difficult to achieve because the teacher educator needs to take the time and effort to listen to each of their stories in order to help them address professional challenges in ways that are meaningful to them . . . so that they appreciate the efforts made on their behalf. (p. 180)

Having and conveying respect and empathy are shared values recognizing the centrality of caring relationships in our roles as critical teacher educators and members of the Chicas. As we strive to acknowledge and affirm the diverse identities, experiences, personal practical knowledge, and professional landscapes reflected in our preservice teachers, we do so in our relations with each other. It is crucially important, not just that educators care for their students, but also that students interpret these sentiments as intended and *feel* cared for in these interactions. Therefore, we enact practices that allow for each other to feel respect and empathy.

In our group, voicing empathy around problems of practice is often heard as common concerns are shared. Soon after the original incident the Responder(s) showed respect just by allowing time for discussing the incident. The following is reflective of empathy, revolving around the original incident:

Teller: I can't believe that he would claim bias . . .

Responder: Remember that student that I clashed with last semester? The one who told me I was dismissive of his point of view. It was so bad . . . I didn't know what to say . . . you told me that he had a point. (October, 2019)

Empathy is expressed, hereby bringing up shared issues, it makes the Teller feel less alone. In this instance, the responder and teller share in having students challenge their teacher identity. This incident also shows how by starting with empathy, the group is able to move past the conundrum of the issue toward shared critical reflection and resolution. Conveying respect and empathy are central to our relationship.

One image that gets to the core of how the Chicas have and convey respect and empathy is the metaphor of "remando" (to row) (Chicas, work in progress). This phrase illustrates our recognition of the ongoing shifting of commitments and availability of each member at given times in our work together. We are supportive about the contributions each are able to make, based on availability and interest, as well as what unique contributions the members are able to enact. In our long work together, we, as individuals, have experienced displacement, marital challenges, health scares, and professional crises, as well as more mundane dilemmas, like our above story, which can inhibit productivity in our collaborations. These challenges impact not only the individual, but the entire group.

We seek to each take our turn rowing, in ongoing collaborative activities, with the understanding that we will strive to pick up the oars when someone unexpectedly encounters a challenge that may necessitate that she ride along as the remaining members continue to row our Chicas boat forward. As part of our practice, we make concerted efforts to take turns driving projects based on individual interest and individual expertise, bilingual education, critical pedagogy and policy reform. In doing so, we convey respect both for the capacity and interests for one another as researchers, as well as empathy for varied and shifting personal and professional contexts.

While responses to our exemplar dilemma clearly demonstrate empathy, we have found that we are more effective when we plan for and focus on demonstrating it more purposefully. To this end, we have embedded strategies in scheduled meetings, like the "check-ins" and an "Intentional Dialogue" protocol (Hendrix & Hunt, 2005) to paraphrase each other's statements that need clarification or elicit disagreement. Using protocols promotes attentive listening and empathetic responses that focus on retelling to confirm what has been said, asking clarifying questions, and using "I" statements to qualify perspectives and feedback. It shows that to facilitate co-construction of knowledge, not only is talking important (Freire, 2005; Guilfoyle, Hamilton, Pinnegar, & Placier, 2004) but listening is important as well.

Mirror our own goals of empathizing with each other, we know we must convey this respect and empathy to our students through practice developed purposefully. How we transparently convey respect and empathy in practice with preservice teachers stems from the relational approaches we practice in our collaborative group For example, we provide multiple opportunities for students to share their experiences to make connections to learning. We emphasize dialogue and collaboration, promoting attentive listening and thoughtful response. We also engage with our students in personal conversations joining them in their own inquiries whenever possible. Collectively, we emphasize the importance of promoting a classroom community that reflects collaborative and constructivist approaches to teaching and learning that are grounded in caring and valuing each participant.

The exemplar dilemma challenged the values of respect and empathy that we hold collectively. The challenge asserting bias is clear demonstration that the students did not *feel* respected or empathized. Despite the development of practices, respect for students as valued decision makers, and empathy for their personal and professional landscapes, the conveyance of these values did not reach its subject. We acknowledge that it is not unusual for this kind of misunderstanding to arise among the Chicas as well. Many times feelings of respect, empathy, and even love for each other get overwhelmed by the events of the moment, and we do not feel valued by the other. Therefore, we are not surprised by the students' claim of bias but are disheartened by it. As always, continuing to engage in the process of relationship-making, to try other avenues of conveying respect and empathy, is central to the work we do together. This is the strategy our Teller employed with this student, restating the feelings that the student expressed, listening to the student's fears, and reminding the student about the core values and purposes that the Chica had in the classroom.

ENHANCING RELATIONSHIPS IN TEACHER EDUCATION

We found RTE (Kitchen, 2009) characteristics to be meaningful analytical lenses through which to examine dilemmas of our collaborative practice, augmenting our understanding of our relational work together and how that work impacts our critical classroom practices. We have found that to grow in a relationship we need to understand that the respect, empathy, and care we feel is not always conveyed consistently across contexts. That said, we find that RTE demands mindfulness (Ragoonaden, 2015), ensuring that respect, empathy, and care are cornerstones of our work, together and with our students. Urban teacher education programs, and urban K–12 school sites have pledges to diversity and integration. Lessons from our collaborative work together hold great signifigance examined through this critical lens.

This self-study revealed that personal practical knowledge needs empathy, respect, and mindfulness to enhance professional relationships. The personal practical knowledge formed within urban K–16 landscapes has taught us that many students struggle with the invisible curriculum of school sites. Critical educators scaffold these students, providing direct, explicit rules to navigate the expectations of the institution. Our own urban college students need scaffolding to engage in novel and seemingly radical curriculum, like democratic assessments that we practice. We have learned that relational scaffolding is also needed to prepare students to adjust to their new roles in collaborative classrooms. As roles within the Chicas' landscapes have shifted, we relied on each other for support, understanding, and empathy to be explicitly given and scaffolded during challenging times. Recognizing parallels with our students' experiences, coupled with our self-study, we embed scaffolding of relational practice in our college classrooms.

Commitment to show up, even when uncomfortable, was an unexpected insight in this study. We often say that the Chicas function like a marriage. Continuing to show up and engage with each other, despite competing claims, is central. Although we share many common values, we often find personal challenges to the intimacy of our relationship. The work we do is intellectually, emotionally, and even ethically challenging. It is not surprising that given the level of dissonance that can be experienced within our group, we might want to disengage. Showing up becomes an act of bravery. We see here an empathy with our students, who may also find it difficult to engage fully in our classroom experiences. We commit to this work because of the value it brings based on our vocations as critical educators.

The Chicas' interactions are predicated on our shared critical love. At its best, it is a love that is "lively, forceful, and inspiring, while at the same time, critical, challenging, and insistent" (Darder, 1998, p. 2). The insistent nature of critical values requires risk-taking within classrooms also, aligned with Freire's (2005a) notion that teachers' struggles "involves their capacity to challenge their students . . . so that students understand the need to create coherence between discourse and practice" (p. 27). We use our Chicas group as an opportunity to align our own discourse and practice. We deconstruct educational power structures and advocate for justice alongside our students. We draw on the Chicas' shared knowledge of the landscape in order to inform and sustain this radical work with our students. We understand that critical and radical work of enacting critical practices, like democratic assessments, is risky. Our group sustains us despite the possibilities of censure. Most of our students will soon be teaching in similarly contested spaces. Our collaboration is a model for our students to navigate their own future contexts, as they enact their values in their practices.

Enacting self-study, iteratively, over time and embracing relational practice is a model for other working groups. The Chicas function as a "hub," where the multiple roles of teacher educator, researcher, and friend are not just embraced, but are central to development and productivity. Intellectual growth is often allowed when we push ourselves personally. Intellectual or work conflicts are often resolved through relational responses. We are reminded that the *personal* practical knowledge (Connelly & Clandinin, 1995) of our varied identities unfold over time (Craig, 2007). We bring the totality of our humanity with us into educative spaces. The Chicas unite and elevates varied identities allowing us to live our "best-loved selves" as we enact our practices together, in the classroom and professionally (Schwab, 1954; Craig, 2007). As a hub of multiple identities, the Chicas' work together defines our individual and collective identities, while simultaneously sustaining and nurturing them. Potential collaborative groups should be mindful of how to acknowledge and affirm the multiple identities of its members.

Classroom practices that reflect the findings here include: honing group discussions through stronger empathetic protocols, explicit instruction on relational practice, differentiating our affect for students, taking even more time to hear and make connections to our students' personal practical knowledge and landscapes, while reminding ourselves to listen first. We find that when successful our students desire to enact similar relational practices in their own future classrooms. For example:

> You welcome us to sit where we are comfortable and make us feel accepted and appreciated. You take the time to ask us about things that are going on in our lives and do a great job of connecting our lives to your life. It is important to allow students to feel safe and comfortable, and make sure their basic needs are met so higher learning can take place. As a future educator I will do my best to mimic the manner you conduct the beginning of class, allowing time to talk to everyone, and make everyone feel welcome and comfortable. (Student reflective journal, Spring 2019)

While we hope that all students would feel this way, we can fall short. We are often thwarted in our efforts to show students our "best-loved selves." However, the rewards of entering bravely into relationship with each other consistently have been unparalleled. Although students do not see our collaboration first hand, we hope our students come to see the relational practices we have honed together as a model for their future practice. Bringing mindful respect, empathy, and care into teaching is a radical act of educational renewal, especially within many constrained urban contexts of teaching we and our students will face. Our work together as Las Chicas Críticas has been central to our ongoing efforts to enact this renewal.

REFERENCES

Au, W. (2009). *Unequal by design: High-stakes testing and the standardization of inequality.* New York: Routledge.

Bullough, R. V. (2005). Teacher vulnerability and teachability: A case of a mentor and two interns. *Teacher Education Quarterly, 32*(2), 23–39.

Charmaz, K. (2006). *Constructing grounded theory: A practical guide through qualitative analysis.* London, UK: Sage.

Cochran-Smith, M., Carney, M. C., Keefe, E. S., Burton, S., Chang, W., Fernandez, M. B., Miller, A. F., Sanchez, J. G., & Baker, M. (2018). *Reclaiming accountability in teacher education.* New York: Teachers College Press.

Connelly, F. M., & Clandinin, D. J. (1988). *Teachers as curriculum planners: Narratives of experience.* New York: Teachers' College.

Connelly, F. M., & Clandinin, D. J. (1995). *Teachers' professional knowledge landscapes.* New York: Teachers' College.

Connelly, F. M., & Clandinin, D. J. (1994). Telling teaching stories. *Teacher Education Quarterly, 21*(1), 145–158.

Connelly, F. M., Clandinin, D. J., & He, M. F. (1997). Teachers' personal practical knowledge on the professional knowledge landscape. *Teaching and Teacher Education, 13*(7), 665–674.

Cooper, J. M., Beaudry, C., Gauna, L. (2019). Teacher education reform: A genealogy of practice and its implications. American Educational Research Association Annual Meeting, Toronto, Ontario, Canada.

Cooper, J. M., Beaudry, C., Gauna, L. & Curtis, G. A. (2018). Bridging theory and practice: Exploring the boundaries of critical pedagogy through group self-study. In D. Garbett & A.

Ovens (Eds.), *Pushing boundaries and crossing borders: Self-study as a means for knowing pedagogy* (pp. 160–173). Herstmonceux, UK: S-Step.
Cooper, J. M., Gauna, L., & Curtis, G. A. (2016). Desenredando (unknotting) the threads of our educator practice: Elucidating the drive and essence of our present teacher education curriculum and practice. In D. Garbett and A. Ovens (Eds.), *Enacting self as methodology for professional inquiry* (pp. 379–386). Herstmonceux, UK: S-Step.
Craig, C. J. (1992). *Coming to know in the professional knowledge context: Beginning teachers' experiences.* (Unpublished dissertation). Edmonton, Alberta, Canada: University of Alberta.
Craig, C. J. (1995). Knowledge communities: A way of making sense of how beginning teachers come to know in their professional knowledge contexts. *Curriculum Inquiry, 25*(2), 151–175.
Craig, C. J. (1997). Telling stories: Accessing beginning teacher knowledge. *Teaching Education, 9*(1), 61–68.
Craig, C. J. (2004). The dragon in school backyards: The influence of mandated testing on school contexts and educators' narrative knowing. *Teachers College Record, 106*(6), 1229–1257.
Craig, C. J. (2007). Illuminating qualities of knowledge communities in a portfolio context. *Teachers and Teaching: Theory and Practice, 13*(6), 617–636.
Curtis, G. A. (2013). *Harmonic convergence: Parallel stories of a novice teacher and a novice researcher.* (Unpublished doctoral dissertation). University of Houston, Houston, Texas.
Darder, A. (1998). Teaching as an act of love: In memory of Paulo Freire. American Educational Research Association Annual Meeting, San Diego, CA.
Fenstermacher, G. D. (1994). The knower and the known: The nature of knowledge in research on teaching. In L. Darling-Hammond (Ed.), *Review of Research in Education*, 20 (pp. 3–56). Washington, DC: American Educational Research Association.
Freire, P. (2005a). *Pedagogy of the oppressed*, (30th anniversary ed.). New York: Continuum. (Originally published in 1970.)
Freire, P. (2005b). *Teachers as cultural workers: Letters to those who dare to teach.* Boulder, CO: Westview.
Gauna, L., Beaudry, C., Cooper, J. M. (2019). Dialogue as a critical pedagogy for contested topics: The case of guest speakers for LGBTQ issues. American Educational Research Association Annual Meeting, Toronto, Ontario, Canada.
Gauna, L., Cooper, J. M., Beaudry, C. (2019). Sustaining critical practice in contested spaces: Teacher educators resist narrowing definitions of curriculum. American Educational Research Association Annual Meeting, Toronto, Ontario, Canada.
Gay, G. (2010). *Culturally responsive teaching: Theory, research and practice.* 2nd ed. New York: Teachers College Press.
Guilfoyle, K., Hamilton, M. L., Pinnegar, S., & Placier, P. (2004). The epistemological dimensions and dynamics of professional dialogue in self-study. In *International handbook of self-study of teaching and teacher education practices* (pp. 1109–1167).
Hamilton, M. L., & Pinnegar, S. (1998). Conclusion: The value and the promise of self-study. In M. L. Hamilton, S. Pinnegar, T. Russell, J. Loughran, & V. LaBoskey (Eds.), *Reconceptualizing teaching practice: Self-study in teacher education* (pp. 235–246). London, UK: Falmer.
Hamilton, M. L., Pinnegar, S., & Davey, R. (2016). Intimate scholarship: An examination of identity and inquiry in the work of teacher education. In J. Loughran & M. Hamilton (Eds.), *International handbook of teacher education* (pp. 181–237). Singapore: Springer.
Hendrix, H., & Hunt, H. L. (2005). *Imago relationship therapy: Perspectives on theory* (Vol. 1). New York: Jossey-Bass.
Kelchtermans, G. (1996). Teacher vulnerability: Understanding its moral and political roots. *Cambridge Journal of Education, 26*, 307–323.
Kelchtermans, G. (2005). Teachers' emotions in educational reforms: Self-understanding, vulnerable commitment, and micropolitical literacy. *Teaching and Teacher Education, 21*(8) 995–1006.

Kitchen, J. (2005). Conveying respect and empathy: Becoming a relational teacher educator. *Studying Teacher Education, 1*(2), 195–207.

Kitchen, J. (2009). Relational teacher development: Growing collaboratively in a hoping relationship. *Teacher Education Quarterly, 36*(2), 45–62.

Kitchen, J. (2016). Looking back on 15 years of relational teacher education: A narrative self-Study. In J. William & M. Hayler (Eds.), *Professional learning through transitions and transformations: Teacher educators' journeys of becoming* (pp. 167–182). New York: Springer.

LaBoskey, V. K. (2004). The methodology of self-study and its theoretical underpinnings. In J. J. Loughran, M. L. Hamilton, V. K. LaBoskey, & T. Russell (Eds.), *International handbook of self-study of teaching and teacher education practices* (pp. 817– 869). Dordrecht, Netherlands: Springer.

Latinx. (2019). In *Merriam-Webster.com*. Retrieved from https://www.merriam-webster.com/words-at-play/word-history-latinx

Loughran, J. J., & Northfield, J. (1998). A framework for the development of self-study practice. In M. L. Hamilton (Ed.), *Reconceptualizing teaching practice: Self-study for teacher education* (pp. 7–18). London, UK: Falmer.

Lyons, N., & LaBoskey, V. K. (Eds.). (2002). *Narrative inquiry in practice: Advancing the knowledge of teaching*. New York: Teachers College.

McLaren, P. (2008). This fist called my heart: Public pedagogy in the belly of the beast. *Antipode, 40*(3), 472–481.

Mehta, J. (2013). *The allure of order: High hopes, dashed expectations and the troubled quest to remake American schooling*. New York: Oxford.

Mishler, E. (1990). Validation in inquiry-guided research: The role of exemplars in narrative studies. *Harvard Educational Review, 60*(4), 415–442.

Munby, H., & Russell, T. (1994). The authority of experience in learning to teach: Message from a physics methods classroom. *Journal of Teacher Education, 25*(2), 89–95.

Noddings, N. (1984). *Caring: A feminine approach to ethics and moral education*. 2nd ed. Berkeley: University of California Press.

Noddings, N. (2005). *The challenge to care in schools: An alternative approach to education*. 2nd ed. New York: Teachers College Press.

Olson, M. R. (1995). Conceptualizing narrative authority: Implication for teacher education. *Teaching and Teacher education, 11*(2), 119–135.

Ragoonaden, K. (2015). Mindful education and well-being. In K. Ragoonaden (Ed.), *Mindful teaching and learning: Developing a pedagogy of well-being* (pp. 17–32). Lanham, MD: Lexington Books.

Schön, D. A. (1983). *The reflective practitioner: How professionals think in action*. New York: Basic Books.

Schwab, J. J. (1954). Eros and education: A discussion of one aspect of discussion. *The Journal of General Education, 8*(1), 51–71.

Tidwell, D., Farrell, J., Brown, N., Taylor, M., Coia, L., Abihanna, R., Strom, K. (2012). Presidential session: The transformative nature of self-study. In J. Young, L. Erickson, & S. Pinnegar (Eds.), *Extending inquiry communities: Illuminating teacher education through self-study* (Proceedings of the Ninth International Conference on Self-study of Teacher Education Practices, pp. 15–16). Provo, UT: Brigham Young University.

Tripp, D. (2012). *Critical incidents in teaching: Developing professional judgement*. New York: Routledge. (First published in 1993.)

Zeichner, K. M. (2018). *The struggle for the soul of teacher education*. New York: Routledge.

Chapter Eight

Responding to Cries of Pain through Literature

A Mindful Approach to Preparing to Teach Children of War

Barbara McNeil

Each year, many school-aged children and their families flee pain and suffering produced by war and find refuge in Canada. Ensuring the sensitive transition and integration of children of war into the life of Canadian classrooms and school communities is an ethical and professional responsibility embraced by teachers. A way to promote ongoing teacher awareness, responsiveness, and efficacy to children of war is through the mindful and sensitive use of carefully selected pieces of children's and young adult literature. Literature opens eyes and can provide nuanced understandings of war and its emotional, psychological, physical, and material impact on children. Examples of this literature include: *Child in Prison Camp* (Takashima, 1971); *Children of War: Voices of Iraqi Refugees* (Ellis, 2009); *Dear World: A Syrian Girl's Story of War and Plea for Peace* (Alabed, 2017); *The Bite of the Mango* (Kamara, 2008); and *We are Displaced: My Journey and Stories from Refugee Girls Around the World* (Yousafzai, 2019).

This chapter is an unabashed attempt to respond to the "cries of pain" (Weil, 1977) that dwell within children of war, and to stem their reproduction in Canadian classrooms through thoughtful interventions by mindful (Hick and Furlotte, 2009), caring, compassionate and informed teachers. Weil (1977) states that we need to respond to cries of pain even if they are founded on—as they often are with children—misunderstanding. Factual autobiographical narratives such as Kamara's (2008) and Yousafzai's (2019), of girls of war, indicate that the cries of pain they emitted were not based on the children's misunderstandings. Rather, their cries were/are based on situated and embodied lived experiences of war. They were/are based on the real material conditions of war that proved to be devastating for the children, their families, communities, and their countries.

In the following, I use significant excerpts from Kamara's autobiographical account of being a refugee child of war in *The Bite of the Mango* to telescope Weil's (1977) belief that,

> At the bottom of the heart of every human being, from the earliest infancy until the tomb, there is something that goes on indomitably expecting, in the teeth of all experience of crimes committed, suffered, and witnessed, that good and not evil will be done to him. It is this above all that is sacred in every human being. (1977, p. 315)

Understanding the "sacred in every human being" is at the core of deploying factual texts such as Kamara's. This example of young adult literature compellingly and unforgettably speaks to us of the cries of pain (Weil, 1977) of children of war. In Kamara's and other biographies (e.g., *We are Displaced: My Journey and Other Stories from Refugee Children around the World*, Yousafzai, 2019), children of war use their own voices to share their pre-immigration experiences, the broader social relations and cultural practices in and through which they emerged, and their overall historical and contemporary ways of thinking and understanding the world (Furo, 2011, p. 104). I argue that listening to the voices of children of war through their own narratives, contributes to teachers' compassionate interpretation and incorporation of a pedagogy of voice and understanding that are beneficial to the mindful, sensitive, and successful transition of children of war into Canadian and other classrooms.

In *The Bite of the Mango*, Kamara (2008), aided by Susan McClelland, tells her searing and tumultuous story of a contextually, normative early childhood. And, then a mid-girlhood burnished by multiple abuses, fright, pain, terror, and push-back against the ravages brought on by the civil war of the 1990s that was particularly devastating for the people of rural Sierra Leone—especially their children. In addition, Mariatu shares the details of a girlhood punctuated with evidence of succor and caring as well as mindful, responsible, and positive human intervention.

SUMMONING MINDFUL DISPOSITIONS AND PRACTICES

Mindfulness as a conceptualization "can be described as the human capacity for observation, participation, and acceptance of life's moments from a loving, compassionate stance" (Ragoonaden, 2015, p. 17). Citing several authors/scholars (Albrecht et al., 2012; Kabat-Zinn, 1990; Shapiro, Carlson,

Astin, & Freedman, 2006), Ragoonaden (2015) underscores that "core mindfulness concepts includes: intention, attention, and attitude" (p. 19). I am drawn to mindfulness thinking and practices precisely because of the emphasis placed on compassion, intention, attention, and attitude. Thus, mindfulness—"mindful education" is summoned because it "is one valuable way to help teachers and students integrate and embody the lessons of anti-oppression pedagogy" where it can be "integrated to deepen introspection and inquiry" (Berila, 2016, p. 13). When learned, internalized, and operationalized, Berila notes that the contemplative practices of contemplative pedagogy, enable students to "cultivate emotional intelligence, learn to sit with difficult emotions, recognize deeply entrenched narratives they use to interpret the world, cultivate compassion for other people, and become more intentional about how they respond in any given moment" (2016, p. 15). In the following exploration and analysis, I draw on the foregoing practices to highlight their capacity to "transform dialogue about power, oppression, and privilege [to engender] more relational, empathic, and reflective experiences" in the interest of social justice and the reduction of suffering/oppression in schools and in society (Berila, 2016, p. 15).

In addition, I utilize the work of Hick and Furlotte (2009) who see "mindfulness as a particular way of paying attention" (p. 6) and consequently draw attention to the importance of the "dialogue between mindfulness and social justice approaches." In linking social justice approaches to pedagogical sites in Canada, my intention is to engender greater mindful awareness of children of/from war to avoid further pain/oppression and to reduce the possibility of adding to their suffering and traumatization—especially those from non-dominant ethnic, linguistic, racial, or religious groups. Consequently, the focus on mindfulness will be centered throughout my analysis and when teacher agency is discussed later in the chapter, where I hope to illustrate relationship between mindfulness and social change through the items of consideration, I respectfully propose to readers/teachers (Hick & Furlotte, 2009, p. 6).

A MINDFUL AND CONTEMPLATIVE READING: *THE BITE OF THE MANGO*

Mariatu was twelve years old, when war came to Sierra Leone. She and members of her family were driven from their rural homes by rebels. While on the move, they come upon a village under siege by rebels. Mariatu hears gunshots, is roughed up, and witnesses the intentional killing of a human being. Witnessing such a scenario, Mariatu starts to cry as she had "never seen anyone die before, let alone be killed" (Kamara, 2008, p. 30). She is forced to watch the torching of the villagers' houses while listening to the cries of horror and pain of people deliberately trapped inside by the rebels. Next, she sees the beheading of a woman carrying a baby tied to her back as she tried to escape a burning house, the cruel silencing of the village by the rebels, and the murder of a pregnant woman as her husband and others watched helplessly. And, she also observes "girl rebels," participating in the killing, and destruction of the village.

Now under the control of rebels, Mariatu is compelled to say that she enjoyed what she witnessed. Fear permeated her being, and she is asked to choose her punishment in the form of: "which hand do you want to lose first?" (Kamara, 2008, p. 39). She pleaded for mercy from her captors but to no avail. Mariatu's body began to sway, she was held in place by the boys and then the machete came down on her right arm. It took more than one attempt to cut it off. Mariatu's eyes did not stay closed, they popped open and she watched her precious severed limb as it flailed and is eventually stilled. This was not all. The young captors took her other arm and achieved their terrible purpose after three attempts. Mariatu sank to the ground and before her eyelids closed, she saw the boys "giving each other high-fives as they laughed." Inebriated, they were happy because they believed they had succeeded in their misguided mission of removing her ability "to vote" for the president, because she now had no hands.

After reading Mariatu's harrowing experiences, teachers are in possession of difficult knowledge. Teachers, as Berila (2016) suggests, can choose "to feed the part of ourselves that can create more empowering worlds through mindfulness practices" (p. 20). This includes deep self-reflection, analyzing our feelings, and being compassionate and kind. These practices offer more than analysis; they encourage mindfulness of what is happening in the body and it is this that has been explicitly absent from critical discourses. Mindfulness practices acknowledge the embodied nature of oppression, unlike critical pedagogy.

Berila (2016) explains that the "reflection contemplative pedagogy allows is an internal one that explores an individual's emotional, physiological, and cognitive responses. As such, it provides an added dimension to the analytical and structural analysis emphasized in anti-oppression pedagogy" (p. 20). Teachers need to know and do this work (mindfulness-based pedagogy) prior to leading students to do so. Thus, if "students are to really reflect on their roles in systems of oppression, they, [along with their teachers] need to cultivate the tools for recognizing and understanding their internal and external reactions to that growing [critical] awareness" afforded by mindfulness (Berila, 2016, p. 20). I contend that the reading in class of *The Bite of the Mango* enables such critical awareness and enhances opportunities for teachers and students to be open, reflective, and vulnerable to the lives of those in the classroom and beyond, and to engage with them with greater capacities for tenderness. Berila (2016) for instance asserts that, mindfulness teaches us how to recognize patterns in ourselves, including mental tapes that play and the embodied effects they have. We begin to see not only what happens in our intellects but also how it rests in our bodies: what triggers our fears, resentments, and insecurities (p. 21).

Hence, prior to reading the text, students should be prepared for what Berila identifies as *"experiential inquiry."* Through "experiential inquiry" with the use of engrossing/transfixing literature such as *The Bite of the Mango*, teachers, and eventually students, can be guided to cultivate and take on the role of *witness*. It is to this, I now turn (2016, p. 21).

WITNESSING AND BEING MINDFUL TO LIFE-FORCE IN CHILDREN OF WAR

"Witnessing is one of the mindfulness practices that allows one to be fully in an experience and simultaneously bigger than it" (Berila, 2016, p. 21). This is what happened to me after immersing myself in Mariatu's book. Allowing myself to be alongside Mariatu, I incorporated her story in my mind and body. Following, is my written testimony, utilizing the contemplative practice of journaling, of what I witnessed about life-force after reading. . . .

As reader/onlooker/witness, I noted the nettle of suffering Mariatu was forced to gaze at, and then the heart-breaking, body hacking cruelties that she was put through, and found evidence of her splendid life-force (Houston, 1980; Temple, 2012). Life-force is the metaphysical, life-giving well-spring that propelled Mariatu to face "down death by daring to hope" (Angelou 1991, p. 206–207, cited in Temple, 2012, p. 28). Therefore, I observed that when Mariatu realized what happened to her, she drew on her inner resources—and was able to accept what transpired, and that she simultaneously adopted a "loving compassionate stance" toward herself. It is such a stance that fueled her life-force—the desire to live, to go on—a "mindful mode of self-care" (Hick, 2008, cited in Hick & Furlotte, 2008, p. 7). This illustrated evidence of a powerful mindfulness and "introspection"—one through which Mariatu recognized, understood and befriended her new self and in so doing, learned about: her resiliency, power to live, and desire for life. This is consonant with Ragoonaden's (2015) conceptualization of mindfulness as the "human capacity for, among other capacities . . . acceptance of life's moments from a loving, compassionate stance" (p. 17). Mariatu's narrative voice evoked my deep compassion.

I was not the same after the experience of witnessing, and did not want to be; I wanted to be better, bigger, and agentic. And so, instead of being "consumed" by the lived through experience of my reading transaction (Rosenblatt, 1971), I "stepped back" (Berila, 2016, p. 21), reflected/introspected deeply on it and decided to write about the impact of being beckoned by

Mariatu's memoir—to witness and testify on and about it for myself as teacher and for others too.

I did so in the interest of making change for children like Mariatu who come to our classrooms every day from geographies and localities steeped in the strife and misery of war. I could not and did not want to look away from her splendid life-force. Some of my witnessing is captured above in a close reading/writing technique purposed to try and articulate what allowed Mariatu to get up and keep going after the trauma of what she witnessed and felt during and after the amputation. I wanted to capture for myself and for teachers who will have children, and learners who will have peers like Mariatu in the classroom. Thus, as Berila (2016) suggests, I did/do not want readers, teachers, and learners to take my word for it. I yearn(ed) for them to try to see what happened (p. 21) and to *witness* the life-force in Mariatu and most likely, other children who come to us from war through hers/their immersing narrative(s).

WITNESSING HUMANITY AND COMPASSION ALONG THE JOURNEY OF FLIGHT

As teachers, we teach stirring books like *The Bite of the Mango* using mindful and contemplative practices in order to witness, lessen oppression, and enlarge the perspectives of our students. For example, Berila contends that this "mindful embodied learning is a crucial component to anti-oppression pedagogy because it teaches us how to meet our responses with clarity and compassion" (p. 22). Mindful reading of Mariatu's memoir asks us to identify and name compassion in order to acknowledge it in action so that we can cultivate and use it carefully to address pain/oppression/suffering.

For instance, in the memoir, the sighting of an adult male after journeying through the forest alone at night following the amputation, signaled hope to the lonely child, so long bereft of companionship and compassion from others. Urgently needing his humanity, Mariatu hailed him. He, fearful that she could be a decoy for rebels, ran away. She caught up to him at an abandoned village and walked slowly toward him. At first, he turned toward her in distrust, asking her what she wanted. Mariatu confessed to being sick and hungry and it is at this pivotal moment that she encountered a familiar act of humanity and compassion. The man looked at her, felt her cry of deep pain, bent down, picked up a mango and passed it to her. When she was unable to raise her arms to take the fruit, he beheld the condition of her body: her hands were cut off. Angry at this outrage against a child, the man accounted for his initial fear, explained his own bitter tale of war, and encouraged Mariatu to seek medical attention in the nearest town. The man's humanity and compassion gushed forth and culminated in his holding up the fruit to Mariatu's mouth for her to eat. I argue that from a mindful and contemplative perspective, we need to create a gap between reaction and response (Berila, 2016, p. 22) to acknowledge that even in sites of war, hope through humanity and compassion (acts of life-saving and other kindnesses) exist, and that these contribute to survival and maintenance of the markers of humanity.

The instance described above, emphasized Mariatu's compassion for her new emerging self (Germer & Neff, 2013). Though appreciative of the man's actions, Mariatu refrained from eating from his hand. Somehow she knew she needed to demonstrate an act of self-reliance, of some independence in order to make it in the world with her new reality. So, guided by the compassionate man, who placed the mango between the folds of fabric she wore, Mariatu was able to take a few bites of the mango on her own (hence the title of the book). It was at this moment, soon after the forced amputation that she began to yeast an orientation toward compassionate self-reliance and independence as a way of making it in the world without her hands. I argue that this is an instance of "biopsychological" mindfulness (Hick & Furlotte, (2009, p. 6), along with awareness of her material circumstances—a dialectic that is always operational in lived experiences.

After the first bites of the mango, Mariatu told the man of her heart's desire: "I want to go home" she said. This was indeed a cry of pain—borne from a desire to return to safety, to the comfort of home. This is the longing, the tragedy, and the conundrum of children of war. Many cannot return to their pre-war notions of home and this knowledge is hard to assimilate, comprehend, and accept. Often, such are the circumstances of children of war, and teachers need to be fully alert to, and be mindful of them, and compassionate toward this particular cry of pain (geographies, places, and spaces of deep attachment now out of reach)—a pain that says, I cannot go back to what I knew and understood of home. This is difficult knowledge that teachers and students need to witness, "sit with" (Berila, 2016, p. 15), and then compassionately move on to consider other possibilities for/of home.

And so, as *witness* to Mariatu's experience, I commiserated as she journeyed toward the hospital in Port Loko for care, and when she eventually came across a village. Upon entering, Mariatu greeted the women she saw. The women were instantly suspicious and fearful that she was a "decoy" sent by the rebels to distract them for the purposes of unleashing destruction. Thus, the normative mothering of these Sierra Leonean women was not offered instantaneously; it was skewed and distorted by war—both the girl and the women were caught up in a kind of "black female pain" (hooks, 2016, para. 11) attributable to patriarchy, colonialism, and capitalism. Though delayed, the mothering was activated when Mariatu begged for help and collapsed in the arms of one of the women. Beholding the severity of her injuries, the women wasted little time in getting her back on her feet so that she could get the medical attention she needed in Port Loko. This situation is resonant of Langer's (1989, cited in Hick & Furlotte, 2009, p. 8) view that mindfulness is not just about paying attention. It is also making a conscious effort to be "in the moment" and not to ignore the external environment (Hick & Furlotte, p. 8).

In the above, I have taken care to highlight the succor and ministrations offered to Mariatu by the ordinary folk she chanced upon as she fled marauding rebels in the countryside, to show that in the presence of the atrocities inflicted on children during the civil war, there were also loving-kindness, compassion, and care, illustrating that the war did not, and could not, eliminate all of the society's core values regarding relationality and interdependence—resonant, for instance, of the Buddhist conceptualizations of relational process (Kuttner, 2012). Kuttner states that in Buddhism, mindfulness means taking part in, and being mindful of, the process of dependent co-arising, being in the relation and in the situation as it co-arises, without any attachment to the "self" as a seemingly separate entity (p. 328). Hence, those who offered compassion and care along Mariatu's journey were mindful of the need and ontological responsibility to do so. This is what draws me to mindfulness as a pedagogical approach; it calls for pause, reaction, and response (Berila, 2016, p. 22).

Evidence of this can be found in what happened to Mariatu while in Camp Aberdeen (a refugee center). She learned that "Bill," a man from Canada, was motivated to help her and her family after seeing a picture of her that had been taken by a journalist. In the picture she was holding her son on the sensationalized cover of a newspaper. This beckoned Bill's empathy and rational compassion (Bloom, 2016), and he intentionally sponsored Mariatu to Canada. He heard her cries of pain. Once in Canada, Bill connected Mariatu to the Sierra Leonean community and together they helped her attain refugee status and citizenship. Bill's decision shows conscious intervention in the life of another in order to lessen suffering and oppression. His actions indicate that we can indeed intervene to enact positive change and is an opportunity for "[b]ringing mindfulness to [l]ayered discussions in the classroom" (Berila, p. 160) about national and provincial refugee and immigration policies.

SILENCED DISCOURSES

Believing "mindfulness concepts include: intention, attention, and attitude" (Ragoonaden, 2015, p. 19), I draw on them here because in the monograph, I detected silence about an important yet troubling aspect of schooling: racism—part of the daily experience of nonwhite students in Canada (Codjoe, 2001; Dei, 2008; Hamilton, 2007; James, 2012; 2017; Pirbhai-Illich, 2010/2011; Richards, 2014; Truth and Reconciliation Commission, 2015). Though

I understand why explicit discussion of racism in Canadian schools might be silenced in a memoir that, among other possibilities, positions Mariatu as a grateful and successful black West African war refugee, unwilling to critique her country of refuge, my own and others' experience of racism, awareness, use of critical race theory (CRT) (Aylward, 1999), commitment and mindful attention to anti-oppressive education, along with being an *ally* of children of war, require exposure of the silenced dialogue about racism and the inequities it produces in schools. I argue that in relation to racialized children of war, socially just schooling requires "[p]olitical awareness . . . [because] through unawareness [of race and schooling,] we unconsciously participate in the reproduction of societal structures" (Berila, 2016, p. 12), which are still very much shaped by racial hierarchies.

Work of Canadian educators such as Codjoe (2001), Hamilton (2007), James (2012, 2017), and Smith, Schneider, and Ruck (2005) incisively document the painful impact of race on the schooling experiences of African-Canadians. Therefore, I urge teachers to mindfully respond to Feagin's (2006) contention that an ongoing set of "White racial frames" continue to influence experiences and achievement of racial minorities, and hence the necessity for privileging educational equity/justice for all. One way to disrupt such hegemonic influence is through literature and the pedagogies selected to engage them in schools. Relatedly, Berila (2016) advises, that "pedagogy could be much deeper if we brought it to an embodied level" since we "hold our lived experiences in our bodies and in our psyches." Hence, we can practice and teach our students to "cultivate nonjudgmental compassion for what we are experiencing "(p. 81). In addition, we can mindfully choose to learn, practice, and teach our students which storylines to release, to let go—for instance, those negative "White racial frames" identified by Feagin, those that cause the most harm—those that cause oppression to self and others (Berila, p. 81–82). Despite racial silence in Mariatu Kamara's story, teachers of nonwhite children of war need to teach through the lens of race since it is a salient feature of schooling that affects the psycho-emotional well-being and academic achievement of many children of color—including those of war.

SUMMARY

The discussion above was motivated by a desire to engender greater acknowledgment and mindful, critical awareness by teachers, of the needs of refugee children of war through autobiographical narratives. In the above, I called for the sensitive use of children's and young adult literature, underlined the usefulness of Mariatu's memoir to lay bare the narratives teachers need to know to effectively attend to the needs of children of war. Now, I proffer the following *considerations* for teaching children of war based on the reading of *The Bite of the Mango* by Mariatu Kamara.

Consideration One

After reading Kamara's memoir, teachers may be tempted to locate the challenges, deprivations, and extreme suffering of children of war in others, in countries far away. Thus, empirically based accounts/stories of children of war who seek refuge in Canada should be read in tandem with monographs depicting the long history of victimization of children in Canada—especially those who were/are not white. A gripping example of the Canadian government's and people's complicity in hurting children during war is the deliberate victimization of Japanese-Canadian children and their families during World War II, as distilled in Takashima's (1971) *Child in Prison Camp*, a memoir of her family's internment in a camp in British Columbia. This is worth reading to reduce *stereotype threat* (Steele & Aronson, 1995) toward children of war from Africa or Asia. In this way, we bear and cultivate the *witness* (Berila), and acknowledge our own complicity in hurting children during war.

Consideration Two

Another way to compassionately and mindfully serve children of war is to select and utilize factual texts in a variety of formats to deepen learning about their backgrounds. Kumashiro (2004) champions the practice of moving beyond repetition of stories we have traditionally told so as to include the "experiences and perspectives and contributions" of the "marginalized" (p. 52–53). Examples of this could include the prolonged use of forced, harsh, and demeaning residential school treatment of Indigenous children, as documented by the Truth and Reconciliation Commission (2012) in: *They Came for the Children: Canada, Aboriginal Peoples and the Residential Schools*. In a paper related to the treatment of Aboriginal children by the Canadian state, de Leeuw (2009) cogently argues that "various discourses carefully constructed Aboriginal peoples as children, thus providing ideological cornerstones to governmental and ecumenical strategies seeking legitimations to expand territory and manage Indigenous people's cultures, bodies, minds, and spirits" (p. 124). Additionally, de Leeuw states that, "as embodiments of extant Indigeneity, Indigenous children were threats to settler-colonial imaginations. So something had to be done with Aboriginal children (p. 124).

Also, Canada's role in contemporary wars and their impact on the displacement of thousands of people needs scrutiny. Teachers can link biographical literature to documentary films and trusted maps to show that no nation is entirely innocent. For instance, the Canadian Broadcasting Corporation (2018) reported, "Canada has committed millions of dollars of aid to Yemen, which is gripped by a brutal civil war and what the UN calls the worst humanitarian crisis on the planet. . . . But the Canadian government also continues to sell arms to Saudi Arabia—even though airstrikes carried out by the Saudi-led coalition waging war against Houthi rebels have killed thousands of Yemeni civilians" (para. 1). This complicity can be countered through ethical action on behalf of children of war in classrooms and beyond.

My advocacy here rests on the belief that teachers want to end oppression and will, once aware of them, choose tools and practices conducive to such aspirations. Therefore, ongoing curriculum diversification is needed and as Kumashiro (2004) suggests, "teachers and students need to engage in a type of analysis that raises questions about what is included" (p. 52).

Learning, listening, and bearing witness require much more than understanding factual texts at the "cognitive level" (Berila, p. 102). Based on compelling ideas absorbed from Berila, I implore teachers to adopt the practice of deep listening to the stories of children of war from a "place of receptivity that is open, attentive, and calm" (Berila, p. 104). Deep listening aimed at reducing and eliminating oppression for children of war in our classrooms, "means being receptive to new perspectives and truly focused on trying to hear what someone else is trying to say, both on the surface level of content and on the deeper level of intention"—in order to hear their cries of pain and desire for belonging, relationality, growing, learning, and overall success at school (Berila, 2016, p. 104–105). As well, I exhort teachers to become increasingly, and mindfully, cosmopolitan in their outlook, outreach, and outwardness to enable even deeper introspection and sensitive responsiveness.

Consideration Three

Immersion in biographical literature reveals that children of war need much more than curricula focused on skill development and technical literacy. Children of war require explicit articulation of relational pedagogies of care (Noddings, 1996; 2005), critical pedagogy (McLaren, 2009; hooks, 1994; 2003) for incisive exploration of relations of power, domination and subordination, mindful education (Berila, 2016; Long & Christian, 2015; Ragoonaden, 2015; 2017a; 2017b) and what Plummer (2005) calls "critical humanism"—a teaching language as well as an approach tied to democratic thinking, storytelling, moral progress, redistribution, justice, and good citizenship for full and continuous actualization as well as empowerment.

Mindfulness practices such as compassionate dialogue with others that "helps us learn to bridge our inner and outer landscapes with the compassionate awareness that much of our suffering tends to come into relief through our relationships with others" are essential (Barbezat & Bush 2014, p. 146, cited in Berila, p. 108). The mindfulness practices of deep listening for instance, encourages listening from a place of receptivity, inquiry and with the goal of relieving the suffering of others (Berila, 2016, p. 113). And since all students need and want to be heard deeply, this is the ethical, loving-kindness work we are called to do every day in classrooms everywhere.

The Buddhist worldview from which Berila builds her conceptualizations of loving-kindness and mindful education centers relationality as ontologically human (Kuttner, 2012). Contrary to "traditional Western" perspective, the Buddhist worldview, sees the perception of the self as an illusion that creates human suffering (Kuttner, p. 327), hence the need for enacting loving relationships.

Additionally, research by Singh et al. (2013) indicate that when teachers were provided mindfulness training, followed by mindfulness practice, it resulted in greater teacher efficacy with learners. The study revealed that "[w]ith mindfulness training" there was reduced teacher "emphasis on child behaviours . . . [t]hey noticed that their responses arose from within, without thinking and without planning." With regard to children who were perceived to be misbehaving, the teachers found that after the training, they were able to "be with the child's misbehaviors"—a practice that, in hindsight, they identified as calm abiding in the present moment with whatever behavior the children engaged in" (p. 225). In general, the teachers in the study "believed a positive personal transformation was taking place in their lives as they continued meditating during the mindfulness phase and beyond," and this augers well for what mindfulness meditation can contribute to thoughtful, caring, and compassionate relationality, which is beneficial for children of war. An important salient point is Singh et al.'s observation that their research participants "noted that training in mindfulness meditation was not to enable them to better manage the children, but to produce changes in themselves that invariably affected those they interacted with on a daily basis" (Singh et al., 2013, p. 225–226). Overall, mindfulness practices have much to contribute to enhancing teachers' relationship with those in their care.

Consideration Four

By turning to children's/young adults' memoirs of war, teachers will find strong evidence of the power of expressive practices—e.g., music therapy, theater, storytelling, drawing—providing psychosocial, biopsychological aid, de-traumatization, and precious moments of relief for children of war. In *Child in Prison Camp*, Takashima (1971), guided by her Buddhist faith, illuminated her images with soft yellow light. In so doing, she exhibits "an inner awareness of [her] own spiritual and moral condition" (Ingram, 1974, p. 344), while attending to the beauty of the natural world surrounding the camp. In this way, Takashima offered powerful resistance to the oppressors—proof that she did not allow the traumatic experience to "consume" her, thereby denying her tormentors full victory over hers, and the mind, body, and spirit, and that of the interned Japanese Canadians. I theorize that the lighted/illuminated paintings in *Child in Prison Camp* symbolize the embodied light-force that emanated from the Buddhist faith of the Takashima family—the source of their endurance, loving-kindness, resilience, and triumph.

Also, when memoirs are read in conjunction with research reports such as Hedenreich's (2005), and Long and Christian's (2015), teachers acquire a strong evidentiary basis for using "mindful self-regulation" practices along with "recreational and expressive activities such as "music, arts, writing, and story-telling" (p. 131). Additionally, Long and Christian's study is complementary to expressive practices because of their global orientation toward "mindfulness as a self-regulatory factor that can mitigate processes underlying the injustice-retaliation relationship" (p. 8) to which we are all vulnerable. Thus, there are compelling reasons for promoting student mindfulness that draws on training in fairness principles (Long & Christian, p. 9) and arts such as dancing, writing, singing, and so forth, in order to mitigate or reduce retaliation as a response to perceived injustices. Moreover, work by Canadian researchers such as Rousseau et al. (2005) corroborate children's narratives about the substantive benefits of creative expression, and are important for teachers to investigate and apply to their practices. Also, I draw attention to similar, and distinctive, contemplative practices from the Tree of Contemplation (Berila, 2016, p. 5) purposed to relieving the suffering of others (e.g., journaling, beholding, dialog).

Another reason for the mindful, intentional, incorporation of expressive practices such as drama, dance, drawing, drumming, guided repetitive chanting, and other forms of art-making is that they are embodied or tap into and draw on that which is held in, pent up, and imprinted on minds and bodies. These and other related contemplative and mindfulness practices (e.g., walking meditation) are essential for children not yet able to speak or write in the dominant languages of Canadian schools and are empowering and enabling for children of war and others who are differently abled. They offer some relief and release for and through the body—they help to make visible that which we cannot yet see or hear.

Consideration Five

Teachers of children of war need to continuously acquire *new theories* and diverse ethical as well as social justice practices from different parts of the world. From a mindfulness and social justice perspective (Hick & Furlotte), this points to the necessity for *enlarged* perspectives (Miller, 2010), and critical consciousness—what Freire (1970) refers to as conscientização. A vital component of this is teaching compassionately through a variety of critical lenses: such as race, social class, disability, gender, sexuality/ies, migration, and pedagogies of refuge to name only a few of the identity locations/markers that are to be found in classrooms and in society. Given their importance and complexities, teachers are encouraged to give serious consideration to integrating mindfulness training and related practices based on research evidence (Semple, Lee, Rosa & Miller, 2010) that such practices are instrumental in promoting well-being through stress reduction, increased resiliency, and improvement in scholastic achievement for children with "attention and anxiety problems" (p. 226). For many children of war, these are precisely what is needed.

To conclude this section, I draw attention to Berila's (2016) assessment that "[s]ocial justice work has to happen at the collective level of institutionalized change: altering our laws, our practices, our criminal justice systems, our educational systems, our media portrayals" (p. 172) and that it also needs to "happen at the level of the individual, as we unlearn prejudicial ideologies and oppressive ways of being" (p. 173). This is why I embrace Berila's view that there needs to be "an awareness of our individual responses to power, oppression, and privilege," and that consequently, an "embodied unlearning" is crucial. Mindfulness and contemplative practices are vital to this undertaking. Moreover, it would be unhelpful and unproductive to deny that "oppression affects us on a cellular level" (Berila, 2016, p. 172); and since oppression affects us all, we need to deepen, and enrich our pedagogies with mindfulness and contemplative practices in the interest of interrupting suffering and creating a better world for children of war and for us all.

Consideration Six

My final offering for teachers' consideration relates to post-structuralist notions of *citation* and *supplementation* that permeate Kumashiro's (2000; 2004) theory of anti-oppressive education. Awareness of *citation* and *supplementation* allows teachers and students to acknowledge that we are all likely to *cite* and repeat harmful stories about the Other (e.g., blame, demonize, dehumanize), especially if we perceive the Other as being responsible for the suffering that occurs in wars. Children of war, similar to other children in our classrooms, may come with entrenched binaries—negative ideas about who is good (innocent) and who is not (the demon), who the oppressor is and who s/he/ze is not. It is very possible that there will be war refugee children from varying sides of the differing sites of combat around the world. In such scenarios, teachers need enabling tools that foster compassion, reconciliation, healing, and loving-kindness for the well-being of all. Critical—mindful—awareness of the power of learned harmful discourses, cautions us about their repetition, their citation. This challenges us to consider and look deeply at what is silenced or back-grounded when they are repeated so that we can see their partiality and limitations and what could be supplemented to disrupt the harm of oft-cited, partial discourses.

Post-structuralist ideas about *supplementation* draws attention to the possibilities of altering, reworking, and re-signifying denigrated identities to move away from a cycle of harm that is often a feature of material and psychic war, and toward social justice. Concrete evidence of this promising possibility is illustrated in *The Bite of the Mango*, where Mariatu supplemented the partial discourses she carried about the boy soldiers who amputated her arms with a broader, more nuanced and compassionate understanding, after reading Beah's (2007) disclosures about his oppressive and painful life as a boy soldier in *A Long Way Gone*. Through reading his autobiography, Mariatu heard his cries of pain and responded with full humanity—a willingness to empathize with, be mindfully compassionate, and forgive boy and girl soldiers of war. Hers is a testimony of the construction of human nature from a mindfulness orientation in which "[h]umans are [construed to be] naturally generous, kind, and caring" (p. 12).

In addition to valuing post-structuralist conceptualizations of *citation* and *supplementation*, my journey with mindfulness and contemplative practices has afforded rich new insights that come from Buddhism. As Kumashiro (2005) indicates, these can be deployed in secular ways in classrooms. From Ha Vinh Tho (2009), I learned the following:

> True insight into the nature of suffering, interdependence, and non-self can bring about peace, reconciliation, and healing, but it cannot come from intellectual reasoning alone. It needs to be nourished by life experience, by mindfulness in everyday life, by meditation....
>
> Meditation is looking deeply into reality as it is, both in us and around us. It is training ourselves not to react immediately with sympathy or antipathy: I like, I dislike, I want, I don't want, I grasp, I reject. But rather to create an open space, free of judgment, free of notions and preconceived ideas, allowing reality to unfold and reveal itself in our heart and mind. By doing this, insight and compassion arise naturally, effortlessly, for they are the very nature of our deeper being.

In the foregoing are examples of discourses needed in classrooms to engender living together well by highlighting the universality of suffering and how it can be mediated through contemplation on our common humanity, our need for each other, and how "insight and compassion for each other can be called forth through mediation to reduce suffering and pain." Thus, the foregoing discourses expressed by Tho (2009), are the ones we most need to hear, articulate, be mindful of, and practice daily in every classroom serving children arriving from localities of civil and other wars/armed conflict, and hostilities as well as those who have lived under the boot heels of multiple forms of dehumanizing colonial oppression for centuries.

In conjunction with the above, I advocate the mindfulness practice of loving-kindness that originates from the Buddhist traditions. According to Berila (2016), the "idea is to send love, friendship, and kindness to ourselves and people around us, starting with the people for whom it is easy to wish well-being and ending with those we may have a difficult time forgiving" (p. 144). Here, I quickly bring in Berila's reminder that wishing well for a perceived oppressors "does not mean we do not hold them accountable for the oppression they have enacted," "[i]nstead it is to both heal ourselves and to refuse to reproduce the tools of oppression by finding new ways of relating to one another." Such, as she indicates, is a "practice about connecting to the part of ourselves that connects with others. It is not about how that person feels or what that person does; it is about how we relate to them and others, how we want to be in the world" (Berila, 2016, p. 144).

Therefore, in addition to bringing teachers' attention to the post-structuralist concepts of *citation* and *supplementation*, I implore enactment of a "pedagogy that concentrates on the contemplative and ethical minds of their students" through "contemplative ideologies" (p. 217). And to this I recommend inclusion of loving-kindness experiential practices along with reading quality memoirs and biographies by and about children of war for ethical global citizenship, and transformation.

CONCLUSION

By uncovering the journeys of a child of war (Mariatu Kamara) in this chapter and bearing mindful witness to hers and the stories of others (Shizuye Takashima) thorough memoirs—a particular type of biographical literature, I underscored the need to operationalize pedagogies that are sensitive to their lived experiences, cries of pain, displacement, anxiety, suffering, and hope for a better future. These pedagogies privilege the ethic of care in teacher-student interactions, are acutely aware of relations of power in such interactions, and mindful of the ongoing dialectic contradictions between the school as a site of domination and subordination as well as its transformative possibilities in the interest of equity and justice. In addition, I spotlighted the importance of marshalling anti-oppressive pedagogies and incorporating mindfulness contemplative and meditative practices as ways of enacting and envisioning school experiences that would reduce the layers of trauma already carried/embodied by children of war in order to lessen oppression and suffering for self and others.

Furthermore, I indicated the exigency for pedagogies that go deeper than analyzing—to foreground and enact embodied pedagogies that bring intentional appreciation to feeling compassion, and to be more fully cognizant of the embodied nature of oppression, trauma, of suffering, and also of resilience and transformation. I concluded by explicitly calling for conscious, mindful attention/responsiveness to critical race theory as a way of acknowledging mainstream Canadian classrooms as white dominant spaces in which nonwhite children of war are likely to experience marginalization and subordination based on race and other markers of difference. As well, I exhorted teachers to reach beyond traditional practices by enhancing them with other lenses—"non-western ways of knowing and being" (Berila, 2016; Kumashiro, 2004; Mahani, 2012; Oliha, 2012) such as the Buddhist ideas of contemplative and mindfulness practices lovingly underscored in the six items of considerations proposed to teachers/readers after analyzing Mariatu Kamara's moving and unforgettable narrative.

Overall, I stressed the power of personal narratives (e.g., memoirs) to enlarge our perspectives and position us to be witnesses to the embodied experiences of children of war. I argued that the prudent use of biographical literature about the painful pre-immigration, refugee experiences of children of war can broaden and deepen teachers' critical awareness, mindful attentiveness, and emotional responsiveness to such learners. In addition, I encouraged kind and loving recognition of the rich socio-cultural resources, cultural capital, and experiences that the children bring to their classrooms. Ultimately, this chapter was borne from my heart's longing and desire for my colleagues and I to more mindfully, sensitively, and compassionately enable sensitive transitions and successful integration of children of war into Canadian classrooms in the interest of reducing oppression and suffering, and for living together well, moment by moment.

REFERENCES

Abebe, T. (2008). Earning a living on the margins: Begging, street work and the socio-spatial experiences of children in Addis Ababa. *Human Geography*, *90*(3), 271–284.

Alabad, B. (2017). *Dear world: A Syrian girl's story of war and plea for peace*. New York: Simon & Schuster.

Albrecht, N. J., Albrecht, P. M., & Cohen, M. (2012). Mindfully teaching in the classroom: a literature review. *Australian Journal of Teacher Education*, 37(12).

Angelou, M. (1991). *All god's children need travelling shoes*. New York: Vintage Books.

Angelou, M. (1991). I dare to hope (poem). *New York Times*. Retrieved from: https://archive.nytimes.com/query.nytimes.com/gst/fullpage-9D0CE1DE173FF936A1575BC0A967958260.html, June 16, 2019.

Aylward, C. A. (1999). *Canadian critical race theory: Racism and the law*. Halifax: Fernwood Publishing.

Barbezat, D. P., & Bush, M. (2014). *Contemplative practices in higher education: Powerful methods to transform teaching and learning*. New York: Jossey Bass.

Beah, I. (2007). *A long way gone: Memoirs of a boy soldier*. New York: Sarah Crichton Books.

Berila, B. (2016). *Integrating mindfulness into anti-oppression pedagogy: Social justice in higher education*. New York: Routledge.

Buber, M. (1965). *Between man and man*. New York: Macmillan.

Canadian Broadcasting Corporation (CBC), (Radio). (2018, November 23 and 25). "Do we stand by our principles, or are we happy being double-faced?": Canada's contradictory position on Yemen. Retrieved from, https://www.cbc.ca/radio/thesundayedition/november-25-2018-the-sunday-edition-with-michael-enright-1.4911588/do-we-stand-by-our-principles-or-are-we-happy-being-double-faced-canada-s-contradictory-position-on-yemen-1.4917752.

Codjoe, H. (2001). "Public enemy" of black academic achievement: The persistence of race and schooling in the experience of black students. *Race, Ethnicity, and Education, 4*(4), 344–375.

Dei, G. J. (2008). Beware of false dichotomies: Revisiting the idea of "Black-Focused" Schools in Canadian contexts. *Journal of Canadian Studies/Revue d'études Canadiennes*.

Dei, G. J., & Asgharzadeh, A. (2001). The power of social theory: The anti-colonial discursive Framework. *Journal of Educational Thought, 35*(3), 297–323).

de Leeuw, S. (2009). "If anything is to be done with the Indian, we must catch him very young": Colonial constructions of Aboriginal children and the geographies of Indian residential schooling in British Columbia, Canada. *Children Geographies, 7*(2), 123–140.

Delgado, R., & Stefancic, J. (Eds.). (2000). *Critical race theory: The cutting edge*. Philadelphia: Temple University.

Dunn, P. A. (2013). Disabling assumptions: Challenging stereotypes about disability for a more democratic society. *English Journal, 103*(2), 94–96.

Ellis, D. (2009). *Children of war: Voices of Iraqi refugees*. Toronto: Groundwood Books.

Feagin, J. R. (2006). *Systemic racism: A theory of oppression*. New York: Routledge.

Freire, P. (1970). *Pedagogy of the oppressed*. New York: Seabury.

Furniss, E. (1995). *Victim of benevolence: The dark legacy of the Williams Lake residential school*. Vancouver, BC: Arsenal Pulp Press.

Furo, A. (2011). What is in a voice? A pedagogy of voice for museums. *Journal of Curriculum Theorizing, 27*(1), 104–116.

Geres, K. (2010). *Using digital narratives with refugee and immigrant youth to promote literacy, healing and hope*. Saskatoon, SK: Dr .Stirling McDowell Foundation for Research into Teaching.

Germer C. K., & Neff, K D. (2013). Self-compassion in clinical practice. *Journal of Clinical Psychology, 69*(8), 856–867.

Gholami K. & Tirri, K. (2012). Caring teaching as moral practice: An exploratory study on perceived dimensions of caring. *Education Research International*, 2012, 1–8.

Goleman, D. (2008). *Introduction to building emotional intelligence: Techniques for cultivating inner strength in children*. Boulder, CO: Sounds True.

Hamilton, S. (2007). *The little black school house*. Halifax, NS: Maroon Films.

Heidenreich, V. (2005). Music therapy in war-effected areas. *Intervention, 3*(2), 129–134.

Hick, S. F. (2008). A Personal Journey to Mindfulness: Implication for Social Work Practice. *Reflections: Narratives of Professional Helping, 14*(2), 16–28.

Hick, S. F., & Furlotte, C. R. (2009). Mindfulness and social justice approaches: Bridging the mind and society in social work practice. *Canadian Social Work Review, 28*(1), 5–24.

hooks, b. (1994). *Teaching to transgress: Education as the practice of freedom*. New York: Routledge.

hooks, b. (2016, May). Femme: Feminista. The bell hooks Institute. Retrieved from: http://www.bellhooksinstitute.com/blog, June 17, 2019.

hooks, b. (2018). *Teaching community: A pedagogy of hope*. New York: Routledge.

Houston, J. (1980). *Life force: The psycho-historical recovery of the self*. New York: Dell Publishing.

Immigration, Refugees and Citizenship Canada. (2018). Annual report to parliament on Immigration. Retrieved from https://www.canada.ca/en/immigration-refugees-citizenship/corporate/publications-manuals/annual-report-parliament-immigration-2018/report.html.

Ingram, P. O. (1974, December). The symbolism of light and pure land Buddhist soteriology. *Japanese Journal of Religious Studies, 1*(4), 331–345.

James, C. E. (2012). Students "at Risk": Stereotypes and the schooling of Black boys. *Urban Education, 47*, pp. 464–492.

James, C. E. (The Jean Augustine Chair in Education, Community & Diaspora). (2017). *Towards race equity: The schooling of Black students in the greater Toronto Area*. Toronto: York University.

Kabat-Zinn, J. (1990). *Full catastrophe living: Using the wisdom of your body and mind to face stress, pain, and illness*. New York: Delacorte.

Kabat-Zinn, J. (2013). *Full catastrophe living: Using the wisdom of your body and mind to face stress, pain, and illness* (2nd Ed.). New York: Dell.

Kamara, M. (with Susan McClelland). (2008). *The bite of the mango*. Toronto, ON: Annick Press.

Kittay, E. F. (1999). *Love's labour: Essays on women, equality, and dependency*. New York: Routledge.

Kumashiro, K. (2000). *Toward a theory of anti-oppressive education. Review of Educational Research, 70*(1), 25–53.

Kumashiro, K. (2004). *Against common sense: Teaching and learning toward social justice*. New York: Routledge.

Kuttner. R. (2012). In theory: Cultivating dialogue: Fragmentation to relationality in conflict Interaction. *Negotiation Journal*, 315–335.

Ladson-Billings, G. (2005). The evolving role of critical race theory in educational scholarship. *Race Ethnicity & Education, 8*(1), 115–119.

Langer, E. J., & Moldoveanu, M. (2000). The construct of mindfulness. *Journal of Social Issues, 56*(1), 1–9.

Long, E. C., & Christian, M. S. (2015, March 9). Mindfulness buffers retaliatory responses to injustice: A regulatory approach. *Journal of Applied Psychology*. Advance online publication. http://dx.doi.org/10.1037/apl0000019.

Lynch-Brown, C. Tomlinson, C. M., & Short, C. (2011). *Essentials of children's literature* (7th ed.). Boston: Pearson.

MacIntyre, A. (1984). *After virtue: A study in moral theory*. Notre Dame, IN: University of Notre Dame Press.

Mahini, S. (2012). Promoting mindfulness through contemplative education. *Journal of International Education Research, 8*(3), 215–222.

McLaren, P. (2009). Critical pedagogy: A look at the major concepts. In A. Darder, M. P. Baltodano, and R. D. Torres (Eds.), *The critical pedagogy reader* (pp. 61–83). New York: Routledge.

Miller, R. (2010). *Yoga Nidra: A meditative practice for deep relaxation and healing*. Boulder, CO: Sounds True.

Noddings, N. (2010). Moral education in an age of globalization. *Educational Philosophy and Theory, 42*(4), 390–396.

Noddings, N. (2005). Caring in education, *The encyclopedia of informal education*. http://infed.org/mobi/caring-in-education/. Retrieved: June 17, 2019.

Noddings, N. (2002). Caring, social policy, and homelessness. *Theoretical Medicine, 23*, 441–454.

Noddings, N. (1996). The cared-for. In S. Gordon, P. Benner and N. Noddings, *Caregiving: Readings in knowledge, practice, ethics, and politics* (pp. 21–39). Philadelphia: University of Pennsylvania Press.

Noddings, N. (1988). *Caring: A feminine approach to ethics and moral education*. Berkeley, CA: University of California Press.

Noddings, N. (1984/2003). *Caring: A feminine approach to ethics and moral education*. Berkeley: University of California Press.

Oliha, H. (2012). Critical Questions: The impact and import of the contradictions and epistemic denials in the field of intercultural communication research, theorizing, teaching, and Practice. *The International Communication Gazette, 74*(6), 586–600.

Perumal, J. C. (2013). Pedagogy of refuge: education in a time of dispossession. *Race Ethnicity and Education, 16*(5), 673–695.

Pirbhai-Illich, F. (2010/2011). Aboriginal students engaging and struggling with critical multiliteracies. *Journal of Adolescent and Adult Literacy, 54*(4), 257–266.

Plummer, C. (2005). Critical humanism and queer theory: Living with tensions. In N. K. Denzin and Y. S. Lincoln (Eds.), *The Sage handbook of qualitative research* (3rd ed.) (pp. 357–373). Thousand Oaks, CA: Sage.

Ragoonaden, K. (Ed). (2015). *Mindful teaching and learning: Developing a pedagogy of well-being*. Lanham, MD: Lexington Books.

Ragoonaden, K. (2017a). smartEducation: Developing stress management and resiliency techniques. *LEARNning Landscapes, 10*(2), 241–255. http://www.learninglandscapes.ca/index.php/learnland/article/view/813.

Ragoonaden, K. (2017b). A pedagogy of well-being: Introducing mindfulness to first year access students. *Journal of Contemplative Inquiry 4*(1), 1–28.

Richards, B. N. (2014). Ethnic identity on display: West Indian youth and the creation of ethnic boundaries in high school. Ethnic and Racial Studies 37(6), 978–997.

Rosenblatt, L. M. (1971). On a Review of Louise Rosenblatt's "Literature as Exploration." *The Journal of Aesthetic Education, 5*(3), p. 188–190.

Rousseau, C. et al. (2005). Creative expression workshops in school: Prevention programs for immigrant and refugee children. *The Canadian and Adolescent Psychiatry Review, 14*(3), 77–80).

Semple, R. J., Lee, J., Rosa, D., & Miller, L. F. (2010). A randomized trial of mindfulness-based cognitive therapy for children: Promoting Mindful Attention to enhance social-emotional resiliency in children. *Journal of Child and Family Studies, 19*(2), 218–229.

Shanks, L., & Schull, M. J. (2000). Rape in war: The humanitarian response. *Canadian Medical Association Journal* (CMAJ), *163*(9), 1152–1156.

Shapiro, S. L., Carlson, L. E., Astin, J. A., & Freedman B. (2006). Mechanisms of mindfulness. *Journal of Clinical Psychology, 62*(3), 373–386.

Singh, N. N., Lancioni, G. E., Winton, A. S. W., Karazsia, B. T., & Singh, J. (2013). Mindfulness training for teachers changes the behavior of their pre-school students. *Research in Human Development, 10*(3), 211–233.

Smillie, I. (2000). Getting to the heart of the matter: Sierra Leone, Diamonds, and Human Security. *Social Justice, 27*, 4, 24–31.

Smith, A., Schneider, B. H., & Ruck, M. D. (2005). "Thinking About Makin' It": Black Canadian students' beliefs regarding education and academic achievement. *Journal of Youth and Adolescence, 34*(4), 347–359.

Smith, M. K. (2004). Nel Noddings, the ethics of care and education. In *Encyclopedia of informal education*, www.infed.org/thinkers/noddings.

Steele, C. M., & Aronson, J. (1995). Stereotype threat and the intellectual test performance of African Americans. *Journal of Personality and Social Psychology, 69*(5), 797–811.

Sterling, S. (1992). *My name is Seepeetza*. Toronto: Groundwood Books.

Temple, C. N. (2012). The cosmology of Afrocentric womanism. *The Western Journal of Black Studies, 36*(1), 23–32.

Takashima, S. (1971/1992). *A child in prison camp*. Toronto, ON: Tundra Books.

Tho, H. V. (2009). War conflict and healing: A Buddhist perspective. *War Conflict and Healing, 51* (Summer). Retrieved from: https://www.mindfulnessbell.org/archive/2015/02/war-conflict-and-healing, June 17, 2019.

Truth and Reconciliation Commission of Canada. (2012). *Truth and Reconciliation Commission of Canada: Interim report*. Winnipeg, Manitoba.

Uwiringiyimana. S. (2017). *How dare the sun rise: Memoirs of a war child*. New York: Harper Collins.

Walkerdine, V. (1990). *Schoolgirl fictions*. London: Verso.

Ward, J., & Marsh, M. (2006). Sexual violence against women and girls in war and its aftermath: Realities, responses, and required resources. Symposium on sexual violence in conflict and beyond. Brussels, Belgium.

Weil, S. (1977). Human personality. In G. A. Panichas (Ed.), *Simone Weil reader*, (pp. 313–339). Mt. Kisco, NY: Moyer Bell.

Women's International Network News. (2003). Sierra Leone: Human Rights Watch details sexual atrocities in civil war. *WIN News, 29*(2), 53.

Yousafzai, M. (2019). *We are displaced: My journey and stories from refugee girls around the world*. New York: Little, Brown Books for Young Readers.

Conclusion

Karen Ragoonaden

Our book, *Mindful and Relational Teacher Approaches to Social Justice, Equity, and Diversity in Teacher Education* presents our collective views exploring relational knowing as crucial to meaningful interactions examining critical pedagogies in contemporary schooling. Our perspectives focus on developing new paradigms for relating to self, the other, and society at large, integral perspectives in the practice of teacher education. Like Owen-Smith (2018), we identify mindfulness practices as metacognitive exercises and first person investigations exploring awareness, concentration, insight, empathy and compassion. Within the perspective of mindful attention, exercises in reflection, listening, dialogue, journaling, self-inquiry, and silence have been applied to our own contexts and experiences. Many of these practices, already situated in social justice scholarly literature, are defined as transformative, critical, experiential, and engaged learning. We recognize that while critical social justice pedagogues develop strategies that respond to omitted histories, positionality, and inaction, mindfulness practices can provide opportunities to delve into deeper reflection about marginalized voices and perspectives and about the social construction of knowledge rooted in and shaped by specific positions and interests.

Sensoy and DiAngelo (2014), addressing the importance of building and maintaining trust, recognize that guidelines are fundamental to creating community and safe spaces. Within the context of social justice scholarly literature, they also note the embodied aspect of assignments where personal connections to readings or other texts are encouraged. Guidelines, developed by the instructor and shared with the group or cocreated with the participants from the group, usually include the following: respectful listening, nonjudgment, listening and respecting all opinions, respecting the right of others to disagree, creating time and space for all voices, and assuming good intentions.

Yet, Sensoy and DiAngelo (2014) warn that these guidelines do not always consider the power relations between mainstream and marginalized students. As an example, they cite discussions where students dominate by reinforcing knowledge as neutral, universal, and objective, thereby silencing the voices of others. In these contexts, the challenge for instructors is to navigate and to facilitate complex relations of power and resistance and to address them in intentional, strategic, and critical ways. Sensoy and DiAngelo advocate for news ways of developing critical reflective stances and interrogating the dynamics of oppression and privilege. We, the authors of this edited book, advance that the secular mindfulness practices described in this volume may provide this direction.

As we explored how mindfulness practices can benefit social justice initiatives, we came back to Burrows's (2011) concept of "relational mindfulness" as potential support for educators as they struggle to maintain equanimity in intense learning environments. Specifically, the chapters in this book considered how relational mindfulness can provide educators with the necessary disposition and skills to negotiate controversial and emotionally charged learning contexts. Understanding that mindfulness interventions distinguish between reacting and responding to intense emotional situations, we posit that these secular interventions have the capacity to build relational competence among educational professionals. The challenge presented is when to introduce, and how to practice relational mindfulness as part of one's professional way of being. Developing an open, calm receptivity along with a realistic attitude about long-held opinions, assumptions, and biases toward the self and others, the relational mindfulness approaches described by all the authors aim at creating supportive, calming, and nonjudgmental environments where unlearning and relearning expand and flourish.

Within this context, the authors of each chapter reflected on their experiences with student resistance to discussions relating to social justice. Recognizing that resistance to equity, diversity, and inclusion (Berila, 2014; Burack, 2016; Sensoy & DiAngelo, 2014) is present in teacher education, the authors discussed how introducing race, social class, gender, war, and trauma in K–12 is often fraught with discomfort and angst. Of import are the collaborative insights that emerged our own perspectives nourished by hard-earned experiences within normalized paradigms of racialized and gendered oppression. We were all questioning how mindfulness can inform discussions of inclusion and diversity in teacher education and how these types of transformative pedagogies can contribute to a more compassionate and equitable society.

Berila (2016) emphasizes that a more equitable, caring, kind world will only emerge if we find news ways of relating to one another. As Noddings

(2003; 2005) states this is the challenge of twenty-first-century teacher education. This transformative process requires honesty, authenticity, openness, an ability to sit with discomfort, and a willingness to unlearn oppression. As with all our experiences with education and diversity, some discomfort is necessary, particularly since existing inequalities emerge once the discussion begins. Berila (2014; 2016) and Noddings (2003; 2005) note that oppression needs to be unlearned by examining normalized practices, and in particular, interrogate the social systems in which we all participate. While this deep inquiry can be disconcerting and uncomfortable, mindfulness practices offer pathways that facilitate this inquiry.

bell hooks (1994) refers to this deep inquiry into social justice, equity, and diversity as an engaged pedagogy, emphasizing well-being, openness, discernment, and care of the soul. This well-being involves a knowledge of oneself and an accountability for one's actions, as well as a deep self-care, for both students and educators. She states that *engaged pedagogy* is an education for how to live in the world. We agree.

Orr (2002) suggests that mindfulness practices can foster change not only on the intellectual level but also within the heart, body, and spirit, usually where most resistance lies. Within the context of mindful pedagogy, a holistic approach to teaching and learning can provide the parameters to build this foundation of *engaged pedagogy*.

We recognize that most social justice courses engage in variations of anti-oppression pedagogy, like critical pedagogy, feminist pedagogy, anti-racist pedagogy. While these approaches typically challenge Western educational thought, Adichie (2009) warns us about being grounded in *the danger of the single story* as does Palmer (1998) with his concern about the *universal story*. Reiterating Noddings (2003; 2005), Palmer (1998) states unequivocally that good teaching comes from the integrity of the teacher, and from the relation between teacher and student. He discredits the presence of the *universal* tale and calls for an acknowledgment and a validation of the plurality of contemporary society where diverse stories can be told and heard.

Activist and social justice oriented educators engage in anti-oppression pedagogy to disrupt normalized claims of universality by validating and acknowledging for local, place-based and situated knowledges from multiple perspectives. Within the framework of anti-racist pedagogy, critical pedagogy, and feminist pedagogy, the chapters in this book describe how teacher candidates and service teachers are called upon to learn and to unlearn taken-for-granted knowledge at deep cognitive and affective levels, impacting the sense of self and revolutionizing their understandings of history, society, politics, and economy—which is why deep emotions are often triggered.

Acknowledging that Dewey (1938) called for teachers to engage in reflective action and that Schön (1983) depicted professional practice as a cognitive process of posing and exploring questions relating to pedagogy, the mandates laid out in social justice scholarly literature stream adhere, as we do, to the epistemological traditions of pedagogical knowledges. Notably, Hanson (2005) emphasizes teaching as a moral and intellectual practice positioned as an opportunity to construct meaningful experiences.

Several of our chapters propose that secular mindfulness techniques can provide safe spaces for institutions, educators, and students to consider the impact of enlarged awareness of self and society, nurturing informed choices without guiding or imposing those choices. As an example, Magee (2016 in Ergas, 2019) introduces mindfulness practices to first year Law students as a way to educate future lawyers in social sensitivity and awareness to how racial biases can shape their professional work. Orr (2004) refers back to the work of Eastern and Western philosophers, Dogen, Nagarjuna, and Wittgenstein, who theorize humans as holistic, relational, as part of the natural order with a complex intellectual and cultural developing. Appreciating that these epistemologies provide a therapeutic understanding of the constructed gulf between the mind and body, feeling and spirit, ideas and life, and self and the other, we conclude our tome by referring to the broader applications of mindfulness, equity, and diversity to the scholarship of teaching and learning.

We recognize Murphy (2019), who states that the most powerful mindfulness strategy is the educator's own practice. In light of this statement, we acknowledge that the chapters in this volume involve teacher educators "paying attention on purpose, in the present moment, and non-judgmentally to the unfolding of experience moment by moment" (Kabat-Zinn, 1990, p. 4) as they grapple with issues of diversity, equity, and social justice. The stories of these dedicated educators offer a diverse range of ways in which mindfulness and relational teaching can improve teacher preparation and make schools more responsive to the multiple realities emerging from our rapidly globalized world, using kindness and compassion as anchors on the journey to equality.

REFERENCES

Adichie, C. (2009). On the danger of a single story [Video file]. http://www.ted.com/talks/chimamanda_adichie_the_danger_of_a_single_story.ht

Berila, B. (2014). Contemplating the Effects of Oppression: Integrating Mindfulness into Diversity Classrooms. *Journal of Contemplative Inquiry, 1*, 55–58.

Berila, B. (2016). *Integrating mindfulness into anti-oppression pedagogy: Social justice in higher education.* New York: Taylor & Francis.

Burack, C. (2014). Responding to the challenges of a contemplative curriculum. *Journal of Contemplative Inquiry, 1*, 35–53.

Burrows, L. (2011). Relational mindfulness in education. *ENCOUNTER, Education for meaning and social justice, 24*(4), 24–29.

Dewey, J. (1938). *Experience and education.* New York: Collier Books.

Ergas, O. (2019). Education and mindfulness practice: Exploring a dialog between two traditions. *Mindfulness*. Retrieved from https://doi.org/10.1007/s12671-019-01130-w.

Hanson, D. (2005). Creativity in teaching and building a meaningful life as a teacher. *The Journal of Aesthetic Education, 39*(2), 57–68.

hooks, b. (1994). *Teaching to transgress: Education as the practice of freedom*. New York: Routledge.

Kabat-Zinn, J. (1990). *Full catastrophe living: Using the wisdom of your body and mind to face stress, pain, and illness*. New York: Dell.

Magee, R. V. (2016). Reacting to racism: Mindfulness has a role in educating lawyers to address ongoing issues." *ABA Journal* p. 26. LegalTrac. Retrieved from http://link.galegroup.com/apps/doc/A464758817/LT?u=ubcolumbia&sid=LT&xid=fa34671a.

McLaren, P. (1989). *Life in schools: An introduction to critical pedagogy in the foundations of education*. Toronto: Irwin Publishing.

Miller, J. P. (1994). *The contemplative practitioner: Meditation in education and the professions*. Toronto: OISE Press.

Murphy, S. (2019). *Fostering mindfulness: Building skills that students need to manage their attention, emotions, and behavior in classrooms and beyond*. Markham, ON: Pembroke.

Noddings, N. (2003). *Caring: A feminine approach to ethics and moral education*, (2nd ed.). Berkeley: University of California Press

Noddings, N. (2005). Caring in education. *The encyclopedia of informal education*, Retrieved from www.infed.org/biblio/noddings_caring_in_education.htm.

Orr, D. (2002). The uses of mindfulness in anti-oppressive pedagogies: Philosophy and praxis. *Canadian Journal of Education/Revue canadienne de l'education, 27*(4), 477–497.

Owen-Smith, P. (2018). *The Contemplative mind in the scholarship of teaching and learning*. Bloomington: Indiana University Press.

Palmer, P. J. (1998). *The courage to teach: Exploring the inner landscape of a teacher's life*. San Francisco: Jossey-Bass Publishers.

Schön, D. (1983). *The reflective practitioner: How professionals think in action*. San Francisco: Jossey-Bass.

Sensoy, Ö., & DiAngelo, R. (2014). Respecting differences? Challenging the common guidelines in social justice education. *Democracy and Education, 22*(2). Retrieved from https://democracyeducationjournal.org/home/vol22/iss2/1/.

Index

agents of change, 74
American Educational Research Association, 2
anti-oppression pedagogy: Berila on, 133, 134, 136; variations of, 155
anti-racist pedagogy, 155
anxiety: gratitude over, 24; overcoming, 55; of teacher educators, 49
assessment practices: competencies for fair, 71–72; democratic, 119, 122; oppression from, 122
attention: to citation and supplementation, 144–145, 146; to class dynamics, 49; as core mindfulness concept, 95, 133; at heart of RTE, 17; mindfulness as, 2
attitude, 95, 133
authority of experience, 15–16

Bateson, G., 3
Bateson, M. C., 3
Beah, I., 145
Berila, B.: on anti-oppression pedagogy, 133, 134, 136; on emotional intelligence, 133; on experiential inquiry, 135; on Loving Kindness practice, 146; on mindful practice, 39, 40, 134–135; on oppression, 33, 144, 154–155
The Bite of the Mango (Kamara): on children of war, 132; mindful reading of, 133–135; teaching considerations based on reading, 139–146; witnessing humanity and compassion in, 136–138; witnessing life-force in, 135–136
Bode, P., 73
Buddhism: Chinese, 44; insights from, 145–146; Loving Kindness practice of, 146; mindfulness in, 138; *sati* in, 3
Bullock, Shawn, 2
Burack, C., 33–36, 39, 40

Canada: illusion of inclusive society in, 64; IRS System in, 9, 101–102; privileged identity in, 65–66; race and diversity in, 62, 64–74; race context in, 63; teaching for diversity in, 61; TRC of, 9, 101, 101–102, 111, 140. *See also* children of war; Indigenous peoples
care: dialogic inquiry for locating, 50–51; embodiment of, 18–19; for intellectual safety of students, 122; Noddings on, 5–6; relationships of authenticity and, 6; teaching grounded in, 123. *See also* compassion
check-in process, 123, 125
Las Chicas Críticas: critical love of, 127; curriculum dilemma for, 118; identity evolution of, 117–118; meaning of, 115; personal practical knowledge of, 121–123; professional landscapes of, 119–121; relationship enhancement in teacher education, 126–128; respect and

empathy from, 124–126; RTE for examining, 118–126; storying and re-storying of, 116
Child in Prison Camp (Takashima), 140, 142–143
children of war: attention to citation and supplementation for, 144–145, 146; *Child in Prison Camp* on, 140, 142–143; cries of pain within, 131–132; critical humanism for, 141; deep listening for, 141, 142; discourse of silence regarding, 138–139; expressive practices for, 142–143; literature for understanding, 131, 146–147; mindfulness meditation for, 142; mindful reading on, 133–135; teaching considerations for, 139–146; victimization of, 140; witnessing and mindful to life-force in, 135–136; witnessing humanity and compassion toward, 136–138
Chinese Buddhism, 44
Chinese Daoism, 44–45
Church and State, separation of, 36, 39–40
citation, 144–145, 146
class dynamics, 49
Cochran-Smith, M., 66–67, 72
collaborative research: findings, 126–128; methodology, 116–117; reasoning for, 118; RTE for, 115–116. *See also* Las Chicas Críticas
Community Ethnography, 84–86
compassion: attitude allowing for, 95; from life-force, 135; from meditation, 145–146; mindfulness emphasizing, 132–133; peace education for integrity and, 90; witnessing humanity and, 136–138
Confucianism, 44, 45
conscientization, 32
contemplative practices. *See* mindful practices
conventional pedagogy, 34–35
The Courage to Teach (Palmer), 4, 83–84
Cranton, P., 68
critical consciousness, 61, 143–144
critical friendship, 20
critical humanism, 141

critical knowledge base: on race and diversity, 64–66; transformation, 66–74
critical love, 127
critical pedagogy: practices, 70–71; reflection on teaching, 86–89; as transformative framework, 86
critical race theory (CRT): social justice commitment of, 62–63; work grounded in, 80–81
CRP. *See* culturally relevant pedagogy
CRT. *See* critical race theory
culturally inclusive curriculum, 88–89
culturally relevant pedagogy (CRP): diversity pedagogy contingent on, 83; role of, 81
culturally responsive pedagogy, 79, 81, 94–95
culture: of fear, 50; of silence, 72–74, 138–139
curriculum: Las Chicas Críticas dilemma with, 118; culturally inclusive, 88–89; formal, 81; hidden, 86–88; holistic education concerned with, 4; INSPIRE program for indigenization of, 102–103; multicultural education, 43; smartEducation, 37–38; social justice for re-imagining, 93–94; societal, 81; symbolic, 81; TRC Calls to Action for re-conceptualizing, 102

deep listening, 141, 142
de Leeuw, S., 140
Delpit, Lisa, 69–70
democratic assessment practices, 119, 122
demographics, 43
Dewey, John: *Experience and Education* by, 24–25; progressive education of, 4
dialogic inquiry, 50–51
DiAngelo, R., 153–154
discourse of silence: on race and diversity, 72–74; on racism, 138–139
dissonance, 92–93
diversity: Canada teaching for, 61; dialogic inquiry for locating care despite, 50–51; peace education correlation with, 89; race and, 62, 64–74; recognition of, 52–53; reflection on, 35; resistance to, 14; as strength, 85–86

diversity pedagogy: conscientization and, 32; mindful practices for, 39, 40; reflection on teaching, 83–86; as transformative framework, 83
dysconscious racism: countering of, 61; King on, 65

Ellsworth, E., 39, 40
embodiment: of care, 18–19; of learning, 39
emotional intelligence, 133
empathy: Las Chicas Críticas expressing respect and, 124–126; commitment to, 124; conveying respect and, 23–24; peace education fostering, 90, 91–92; reflection developing respect and, 94; Rogers on, 6; for TCs, 22–23
engaged pedagogy, 33, 40, 155
equity: meritocracy impacting, 65; resistance to, 14; in Trump era, 2; U.S. issues with wealth and, 47
Experience and Education (Dewey), 24–25
experiential inquiry, 135
expressive practices, 142–143

fear, 50
feminist pedagogy, 155
First Peoples Principles of Learning (FPPL): course on, 107–108; as guidelines for INSPIRE program, 103–104
formal curriculum, 81
FPPL. *See* First Peoples Principles of Learning
fragmentation, 3
Freedom to Learn (Rogers), 6

Gay, G., 79, 81
gender, 31, 32, 40, 143–144
generational connectedness, 107
globalization, 43
gratitude: over anxiety, 24; for Indigenous culture participation, 105, 107
guilt, 66

hard talk, 72
Ha Vinh Tho, 145–146
healing: meditation for, 145–146; mindfulness for, 1

heart: of RTE, 17; sacredness of human, 132; of teaching, 123; teaching with, 92
hidden curriculum: power connection to, 86–87; TCs exposed to, 87–88
higher education, 32–34
Hinduism, 3
holistic approach: curriculum concern of, 4; INSPIRE program as, 102–103; mindful practice aligned with, 94–95
The Holistic Teacher (Miller), 4
hooks, bell: on engaged pedagogy, 33, 40, 155; on race and racism, 52
humanity: life-force in, 135–136; sacredness of, 132; witnessing compassion and, 136–138
humility, 27

identity: Las Chicas Crítica evolving, 117–118; guilt from race, 66; Indigenous cultural interactions impacting, 108; Indigenous perspectives shifting, 105; Latinx, 115; privileged, 21, 23, 33, 52–53, 65–66; queer, 20–21; reclaiming integrity and, 18, 83–84; students challenging teacher, 121; of teacher educators, 43; transformative frameworks impacting, 93; trauma from marginalized, 32–33
Identity Bags, 84, 85–86
ideology, 64–66
IEC. *See* Indigenous Education Council
inclusiveness: culturally inclusive curriculum for, 88–89; of literature, 88; multicultural education for, 13–14
inclusive society: illusion of, 64; mindfulness for, 8
Indian Residential School (IRS) System: as cultural genocide, 101–102; trauma of, 9
Indigenous Education Council (IEC), 104
Indigenous Knowledge Keepers, 102–103
Indigenous peoples: children of, 140; FPPL for, 103–104, 107–108; generational connectedness of, 107; INSPIRE program, 102–103, 103–104, 104–107; in IRS System, 9, 101–102; KAIROS Blanket Exercise, 106, 111n1; mindful awareness of, 111; nature as sacred to, 3; relational mindfulness for

learning about, 108–110; responsiveness to needs of, 9; storying and re-storying of, 105–107; Talking Circles, 108–109; TRC on, 9, 101, 101–102, 111, 140; WFN, 104–105
inequity hunters, 87
inquiry: dialogic, 50–51; experiential, 135
INSPIRE program: FPPL as guidelines for, 103–104; for re-imagining teacher education, 102–103; storying and re-storying with, 105–107; WFN working with, 104–105
integration, 3
integrity: good teaching from, 155; peace education for compassion and, 90; reclaiming identity and, 18, 83–84
intellectual safety, 122
intention, 95, 133
Intentional Dialogue protocol, 125
intersections, 34–35
intimate scholarship, 82
IRS System. *See* Indian Residential School System

Journal of Contemporary Issues in Education, 61

Kabat-Zinn, Jon, 1, 16, 36–37
KAIROS Blanket Exercise, 106, 111n1
Kamara, Mariatu: *The Bite of the Mango* by, 132; *A Long Way Gone* read by, 145; mindful reading on, 133–135; teaching considerations based on writing of, 139–146; witnessing humanity and compassion toward, 136–138; witnessing life-force of, 135–136
King, Martin Luther: on dysconscious racism, 65; on social justice, 13
knowledge: authenticity of Indigenous, 110; landscapes, 121; personal practical, 19, 20–21, 47–49, 56, 121–123; relationship between power and, 86; sharing of sacred, 106
Komagata Maru Incident, 90–91

Ladson-Billings, Gloria, 68, 96
landscapes: professional, 119–121; of teacher education, 22

Latinx identity, 115
Levine-Rasky, C., 65
liberal elites, 22
life-force, 135–136
literature: inclusiveness of, 88; for transformative frameworks, 80–81. *See also* children of war
A Long Way Gone (Beah), 145
Loving Kindness practice, 146
Lucas, T., 70–71

marginalized identity, 32–33
materialism, 4
MBSR program. *See* Mindfulness-based Stress Reduction program
meditation: for healing, 145–146; mindfulness, 142
meritocracy, 65
Miller, J. P., 4
Milner, H., 63–64, 68, 69, 72–73
mindful awareness: of Indigenous peoples, 111; relational teaching as, 5–6
mindfulness: as attention, 2; in Buddhism, 138; compassion emphasized in, 132–133; core concepts of, 95, 133; definition of, 1, 94; humility from, 27; for inclusive society, 8; of life-force in children of war, 135–136; meditation, 142; methodology for relational knowing and, 46–47; for pattern recognition of self, 135; personal narrative of relational knowing and, 44–46; relational, 38–39, 108–110, 154; relational approach and, 5, 45; RTE demanding, 126; for social justice teacher education, 6–10; strategy, 156; tradition of, 3–5; as way of being, 16
Mindfulness-Based Stress Reduction (MBSR) program, 1, 36–37, 37
mindful practices: Berila on, 39, 40, 134–135; challenges to introducing, 33–34; controversial nature of, 36; conventional pedagogy integrated with, 34–35; of deep listening, 141, 142; for diversity pedagogy, 39, 40; empowerment from, 134; essentialness of, 3; in higher education, 32–34; holistic approach aligned with, 94–95; as metacognitive exercises, 153; for

oppression, 144; RTE as, 16–18; safety regarding, 35–36; self-reflection in, 31–32, 32; smartEducation, 36–38, 39–40; suggestions for integrating, 40; transformative frameworks as, 95–96; as transformative pedagogy, 31, 40; trauma induced memories triggered by, 35; when and how to introduce, 34; of witnessing, 135–138
mindful reading, 133–135
moral commitments, 121
morality, 26–27
multicultural education: curriculum, 43; goal of, 13–14
mysticism, 3

nature, 3
Nieto, S., 73
Noddings, Nel, 84; on care, 5–6; on oppression, 154–155

Okanagan School of Education (OSE), 102–103
oppression: anti-oppression pedagogy, 133, 134, 136, 155; from assessment practices, 122; conscious intervention to lessen, 138; meritocracy and, 65; mindful practice for dealing with, 144; self-reflection for understanding, 33; unlearning of, 154–155. *See also* children of war
OSE. *See* Okanagan School of Education

pain: cries of, 131–132; MBSR designed for intense, 36–37. *See also* children of war
Palmer, Parker J.: Courage to Teach program of, 4; on good teaching, 155; on identity and integrity, 18, 83–84
peace education: reflection on teaching, 89–92; as transformative frameworks, 89
pedagogy: anti-oppression, 133, 134, 136, 155; anti-racist, 155; conventional, 34–35; critical, 70–71, 86–89; CRP, 81, 83; culturally responsive, 79, 81, 94–95; diversity, 32, 39, 40, 83–86; engaged, 33, 40, 155; feminist, 155; moral commitments enacted in, 121;

relational, 2, 9–10, 94; of sensations, 39–40; transformative, 31, 40
personal narratives: of mindfulness and relational knowing, 44–46; power of, 147
personal practical knowledge: of Las Chicas Críticas, 121–123; recognition of, 56; reflection for, 19; understanding of own, 20–21, 47–49
positionality: Indigenous cultural interactions impacting, 108; self-reflection for examining, 45–46
power: of expressive practices, 142–143; hidden curriculum connection to, 86–87; of personal narratives, 147; of race as social construct, 63; relationship between knowledge and, 86; teachers shaping relations of, 70, 154
practitioner research, 13–14
preservice teachers: commitment to helping, 24–25; critical knowledge base and ideology of, 64–66; critical knowledge base transformation for, 66–74; dialogic inquiry for, 50–51; feedback from, 54–55; reflective journaling by, 52–53, 56
privileged identity: acknowledgment of, 21; in Canada, 65–66; reflective journaling on, 52–53; resistance to, 33; Step into the Circle activity on, 23
professional landscapes, 119–121
progressive education, 4

queer identity, 20–21

race: CRT on, 62–63, 80–81; guilt from identity of, 66; hooks on, 52; illusion of inclusive society regarding, 64; power of, as social construct, 63; the teaching self connection to, 68
race and diversity: critical knowledge base transformation for addressing, 66–74; discourse of silence on, 72–74; hard talk on, 72; ideology and critical knowledge base, 64–66; neglect of, 62
racial and cultural literacy, 69–70
racism: discourse of silence on, 138–139; dysconscious, 61, 65; hooks on, 52; pervasiveness of, 63–64; reflective

journaling on, 52–53
receptivity: from deep listening, 141, 142; to relationship growth, 25–26, 54–55
reflection: Community Ethnography for, 84–86; on critical pedagogy, 86–89; on diversity, 35; on diversity pedagogy, 83–86; empathy and respect developed through, 94; on hidden curriculum, 87–88; Identity Bags for, 84, 85–86; importance of, 20; on Komagata Maru Incident, 90–91; on past experiences, 122; on peace education, 89–92; for personal practical knowledge, 19; on queer identity, 20–21; on refugee student stories, 91–92; self, 31–32, 32, 33, 45–46; of TCs, 19
reflective journaling, 19, 25–26, 52–53, 54, 56
reflective life writing, 108
refugees: of Komagata Maru Incident, 90–91; student stories, 91–92. *See also* children of war
relational approach, 5, 45
relational knowing: definition of, 6; for meaningful interactions, 16–17; methodology for mindfulness and, 46–47; personal narrative of mindfulness and, 44–46
relational mindfulness: definition and benefits of, 38–39; development of, 154; for Indigenous learning, 108–110
relational pedagogy: manifestation of, 94; for RTE, 2; for trauma, 9–10
relational scaffolding, 126
relational teacher education (RTE): Las Chicas Críticas examination through, 118–126; for collaborative research, 115–116; mindfulness demand from, 126; as mindful practice, 16–18; relational pedagogy for, 2; seven characteristics of, 15, 20–26; social justice through, 20–26; for TCs, 14–15
relational teaching: as mindful awareness, 5–6; principles of, 94; transformative frameworks as, 95–96
relationships: authentic and caring, 6; being real for building, 85; Las Chicas Críticas enhancing teacher education, 126–128; at heart of teaching, 123; between power and knowledge, 86; receptivity to growing in, 25–26, 54–55; relational teaching principles for founding, 94; respect and empathy as central to, 124; of trust, 18; with what is actually so, 1

religion: of Buddhism, 3, 44, 138, 145–146; of Daoism, 44–45; dialogic inquiry on, 50–51; of Hinduism, 3; respect of, 56; separation of Church and State, 36, 39–40
remando metaphor, 124–125
research summary, 7–10
respect: Las Chicas Críticas expressing empathy and, 124–126; commitment to, 124; conveying empathy and, 23–24; KAIROS Blanket Exercise for promoting truth and, 106, 111n1; for opinions, 53; reflection developing empathy and, 94; of religion, 56; for TCs, 22–23
Rogers, Carl: on empathy, 6; on experience as highest authority, 2, 17
RTE. *See* relational teacher education

sacredness: of humanity, 132; of knowledge, 106; of nature, 3
safety: climate of trust and, 14; feeling of acceptance and, 128; guidelines for building trust and, 153–154; intellectual, 122; regarding mindful practice, 35–36
sati, 3
self-reflection: in mindful practice, 31–32, 32; positionality examined with, 45–46; for understanding oppression, 33
self-study of teacher education practices (S-STEP): benefits of, 19; definition of, 82; recognition of, 115
Sensoy, Ö., 153–154
Sharma, Manu, 20
silence, discourse of, 72–74, 138–139
Skerrett, A., 64
smartEducation. *See* Stress Management and Resiliency Techniques
smrti, 3
snowball writing, 91
social change, 66–67

social justice: attending to, 18–19; CRT commitment to, 62–63; curriculum re-imagined through teaching, 93–94; dialogic inquiry for teaching, 50–51; King on, 13; mindfulness for teacher education on, 6–10; reflective journaling for teaching, 52–53; resistance to discussion of, 154; through RTE, 20–26. *See also* transformative frameworks

societal curriculum, 81

S-STEP. *See* self-study of teacher education practices

standardized tests, 71–72

State and Church, separation of, 36, 39–40

Step into the Circle activity, 23

stereotype threat, 140

storying/re-storying: of Las Chicas Críticas, 116; of Indigenous peoples, 105–107

Stress Management and Resiliency Techniques (smartEducation), 36–38, 39–40

supplementation, 144–145, 146

symbolic curriculum, 81

Takashima, Shizuye, 140, 142–143

Talking Circles, 108–109

"Talking race and racism", 52

teacher candidates (TCs): attention given to, 17; calling of, 79; caution against labeling, 14; challenges and barriers to, 79–80; climate of safety and trust for, 14; Community Ethnography for, 84–86; culturally inclusive curriculum for, 88–89; embodiment of care for, 18–19; FPPL course for, 107–108; hidden curriculum exposed to, 87–88; Identity Bags for, 84, 85–86; as inequity hunters, 87; INSPIRE program for, 102–103, 103–104, 104–107; Komagata Maru Incident studied by, 90–91; living alongside, 7–8, 15; reflection of, 19; refugee student stories studied by, 91–92; respect and empathy for, 22–23; RTE for, 14–15; storying and re-storying experiences of, 105–107; Talking Circles participation of, 108–109; thank you note from, 26. *See also* preservice teachers

teacher education: improvements of own practice in, 21–22; INSPIRE program for re-imagining, 102–103; mindfulness for social justice, 6–10; racial and cultural literacy for, 69–70; relationship enhancement in, 126–128; for social change, 66–67; struggles, 96; the teaching self in, 67–69; understanding landscape of, 22. *See also specific topics*

teacher educators: anxiety of, 49; attention to class dynamics, 49; feedback on performance of, 54–55; identity of, 43; reflective journaling by, 54

the teaching self, 67–69

technical-rationalism, 4

transformative frameworks: advocacy for, 8–9; critical pedagogy as, 86; diversity pedagogy as, 83; lessons learned from, 92–94; literature for, 80–81; methodological approach to teaching, 82–83; as mindful practice and relational teaching, 95–96; peace education as, 89; research questions for, 80; for teacher education struggles, 96

transformative pedagogy, 31, 40

transformative practices: barriers to, 65; critical consciousness development leading to, 61

trauma: of IRS System, 9; from marginalized identity, 32–33; mindful practice triggering memories of, 35; relational pedagogy for, 9–10. *See also* children of war

TRC. *See* Truth and Reconciliation Commission

Trump, President, 2

trust: climate of safety and, 14; for collaboration, 123; guidelines for building safety and, 153–154; relationships of, 18; Talking Circles for building, 108–109

truth: of integration, 3; KAIROS Blanket Exercise for promoting respect and, 106, 111n1; Talking Circles and, 108–109

Truth and Reconciliation Commission (TRC): Calls to Action, 101, 101–102;

IRS System reporting by, 9; response to, 111; *They Came for the Children* by, 140

United Nations Universal Declaration of Human Rights, 89
United States (U.S.): demographics of, 43; wealth and equity issues in, 47
urban teaching context, 115, 119, 126. *See also* Las Chicas Críticas
U.S. *See* United States

Villegas, A. M., 70–71

wealth, 47
Weil, Simone, 131, 132
West bank First Nation (WFN), 104–105
witnessing: humanity and compassion, 136–138; life-force, 135–136

Yemen, 140–141

About the Contributors

Christine Beaudry, EdD, is an assistant professor of social studies education at Nevada State College. She teaches courses in social studies education, educational foundations, and secondary pedagogy. Her research interests include critical, constructivist, and community-based approaches to social studies education, teaching and learning in culturally and linguistically diverse contexts, and educational equity and social justice. She also works with local high schools to develop and support teacher pipeline programs in an effort to increase teacher diversity and address persistent teacher shortages in Nevada. She is a founding executive member of Nevada chapters of both TESOL International and the National Association of Bilingual Education. She has several years of teaching experience at both elementary and secondary levels in urban public schools.

Terry-Lee Beaudry has Métis/Cree ancestry and is the deputy superintendent of schools for the Central Okanagan Public Schools. Terry-Lee has assumed District responsibility for the Indigenous Education Program since September 2001. She also serves as an adjunct professor–Indigenous education for the Okanagan School of Education and is an education strategist for the BC Ministry of Education.

Jane McIntosh Cooper, EdD, is a clinical assistant professor of teacher education, specializing in social justice, diversity, and teacher education at the University of Houston. After a decade of teaching in urban public schools in Texas, she focuses on coaching preservice teachers to teach in those same environments. By applying postcolonial theory to educational practices, her research elucidates effects of standardizing practices on P–16 educational experiences. Her practice focuses on helping novice teachers connect to all learners, through differentiating practices, unpacking biases and creating relationships. She is the author of *Theory and Practice: Exploring the Boundaries of Critical Pedagogy through Self-Study*. She recently worked to pilot the restructuring of field experiences in a teacher education program resulting in national recognition.

Gayle A. Curtis, EdD, is a postdoctoral research associate at Texas A&M University and the University of Houston. After a career as a bilingual teacher and school administrator/principal in urban schools serving students from diverse—racial, ethnic, cultural, linguistic, socioeconomic—backgrounds, Dr. Curtis turned to teacher education and research. Expertise includes administration/leadership, teacher development/collaboration, bilingual/science education, reflective practice, and school-community-university collaborations. She received the 2014 AERA Narrative Research SIG Outstanding Dissertation Award for her dissertation entitled *Harmonic Convergence: Parallel Stories of a Novice Teacher and a Novice Researcher*. Current research focuses on STEM student recruitment and retention, teacher retention and attrition, and reflective practices. Upcoming publications include an invited chapter in *2nd International Handbook of Self-Study of Teaching and Teacher Education Practices*.

Benedicta Egbo is a professor emeritus of education at the University of Windsor. Her research interests are interdisciplinary, and include teacher education and education policy, minority education, social justice and equity issues, multiculturalism and multicultural education. She has published extensively in these areas. Her recent book, *Teaching for Diversity in Canadian Schools* (2nd Edition, 2019), explores the trajectories of transformative pedagogical practices and student success in demographically diverse teaching and learning contexts.

Leslie M. Gauna, EdD, is an assistant professor of bilingual/ESL education and cultural studies in the Department of Counseling, Special Education, and Diversity at the University of Houston–Clear Lake. She conducts qualitative research that has used narrative inquiry, self-study of teacher education, and an applied linguistics language program evaluation approach. She focuses on the preparation and retention of ESL/bilingual teacher candidates and novice teachers. She is the author of *"In Between" English and Spanish Teaching: Stories of a Linguistically Diverse Student becoming a Teacher* (2016). Leslie M. Gauna has worked with migrant populations in urban schools on projects related to multicultural and bilingual education, violence prevention, gender equality, and community participation issues, both in the United States and in Argentina.

Kevin Kaiser, a Dakelh member of the Caribou clan, has worked as the Central Okanagan Public Schools' Indigenous resource teacher/consultant since 2012. Kevin has been instrumental in the development of Indigenous curriculum and the school district's nationally recognized Academy of Indigenous Studies. Kevin is also an instructor of Indigenous studies for the Okanagan School of Education.

Julian Kitchen, PhD, is a professor in the faculty of education at Brock University. His work in education extends to studying and supporting teachers and teacher educators. Dr. Kitchen is lead editor of the *International Handbook of Self-Study of Teaching and Teacher Education Practices, Second Edition*. He is also lead editor of *Narrative Inquiries into Curriculum-making in Teacher Education, Self-Study and Diversity II: Inclusive Teacher Education for a Changing World* and *Canadian Perspectives on the Self-Study of Teacher Education Practices*. In addition, he is the author of *Relational Teacher Education* and lead author of Professionalism, Law and the Ontario Educator. Professor Kitchen is coeditor of *Studying Teacher Education* journal and past chair of the Self-Study of Teacher Education Practices Special Interest Group of the American Educational Research Association.

Yumei Li has taught social education courses in the United States and English as a foreign language in China. Her research centers on international education and multicultural education, social justice and equity, teacher education, and teaching English as a foreign language. She has published in both English and Chinese in these areas.

Barbara McNeil works chiefly in the areas of language and literacies. Her primary research interests include literacy teaching and learning (PreK–12—reading, writing, listening, speaking, viewing, and responding), critical literacies, critical pedagogies, writing pedagogies, children's literature, linguistic diversity, teacher education, arts education, multicultural education, children and war, and inclusive museums. Her research interests lend themselves to interdisciplinarity as well as multidisciplinarity in local as well as global contexts.

Karen Ragoonaden is a professor of teaching in the Okanagan School of Education of the University of British Columbia, Canada. Her pedagogy, research, and service reflect a strong commitment to culturally responsive approaches to teaching and learning. Her academic intersections span the breadth of Diversity Education, Indigenous Education, and Mindfulness in Education. She is recognized for the innovative stress management and resiliency techniques (smartEducation) curriculum integrating holistic well-being initiatives into professional and community contexts.

Awneet Sivia is an associate professor in the Teacher Education Department at the University of the Fraser Valley. She teaches courses in social justice, science and technology education, classroom research, school reform, and educational leadership. Awneet has developed programs that support the diverse needs of students, including international practicums, paraprofessional upgrading, foreign-credentialed teacher education, and master of education degrees. Her research and scholarship focus on science teacher education, social justice education, diversity leadership, self-study in teacher education, teacher learning, and school innovations. Awneet's PhD was completed as a self-study of teacher education practices and she is the founding member of a regional network of self-study scholars.

www.ingramcontent.com/pod-product-compliance
Lightning Source LLC
Chambersburg PA
CBHW021850300426
44115CB00005B/103